SEEDS OF POWER

AMALIA LEGUIZAMÓN

SEEDS OF

POWER

Environmental Injustice and
Genetically Modified Soybeans in Argentina

Duke University Press   Durham and London   2020

Designed by Courtney Leigh Richardson
Typeset in Whitman and Helvetica Neue by Westchester Publishing Services

Library of Congress Cataloging-in-Publication Data
Names: Leguizamón, Amalia, [date] author.
Title: Seeds of power : environmental injustice and genetically modified soybeans in Argentina / Amalia Leguizamón.
Description: Durham : Duke University Press, 2020. | Includes bibliographical references and index.
Identifiers: LCCN 2019054743 (print)
LCCN 2019054744 (ebook)
ISBN 9781478009788 (hardcover)
ISBN 9781478010852 (paperback)
ISBN 9781478012375 (ebook)
Subjects: LCSH: Soybean—Genetic engineering—Environmental aspects—Argentina. | Transgenic plants—Economic aspects—Argentina. | Agricultural biotechnology—Environmental aspects—Argentina. | Agricultural biotechnology—Social aspects—Argentina. | Genetically modified foods—Social aspects—Argentina. | Environmental policy—Argentina.
Classification: LCC HD9235.S62 A744 2020 (print) | LCC HD9235.S62 (ebook) | DDC 338.1/73347—dc23
LC record available at https:// lccn.loc.gov/2019054743
LC ebook record available at https://lccn.loc.gov/2019054744

COVER ART: *Soybeans.* © Prani Teiyng Ketu / EyeEm. Courtesy Getty Images. Structural formula for glyphosate synthesis.

Duke University Press gratefully acknowledges Tulane University's School of Liberal Arts, which provided funds toward the publication of this book.

For my parents,
Mirta and Osvaldo

CONTENTS

ACRONYMS

AAPRESID	Asociación Argentina de Productores en Siembra Directa (Argentine Association of Direct Sowing Producers)
AMLV	Asamblea Malvinas Lucha por la Vida
CASAFE	Cámara de Sanidad Agropecuaria y Fertilizantes (Argentine Association of Agrochemical Companies)
CEPAL	Comisión Económica para Latinoamérica y el Caribe (Economic Commission for Latin America and the Caribbean [ECLAC])
CIARA	Cámara de la Industria Aceitera de la República Argentina (Argentine Oilseed Industry Chamber)
CNA	Censo Nacional Agropecuario (Argentina's National Rural Census)
CONICET	Consejo Nacional de Investigaciones Científicas y Técnicas (National Council for Scientific and Technological Research)
CREA	Consorcios Regionales de Experimentación Agrícola (Regional Consortiums of Agricultural Experimentation)
EJ	environmental justice
EPA	US Environmental Protection Agency
FAO	Food and Agriculture Organization of the United Nations
FDA	US Food and Drug Administration
GM/GMO	genetically modified / genetically modified organisms

IASCAV	Instituto Argentino de Sanidad y Calidad Vegetal (Argentine Institute for Plant Health and Quality)
INDEC	Instituto Nacional de Estadística y Censos de la República Argentina (National Institute of Statistics and Census)
INTA	Instituto Nacional de Tecnología Agropecuaria (National Agricultural Technology Institute)
ISAAA	International Service for the Acquisition of Agri-biotech Applications
MOCASE	Movimiento Campesino de Santiago del Estero (Peasant Movement from Santiago del Estero)
RR	Roundup Ready (Monsanto's herbicide-resistant crops)
SENASA	Servicio Nacional de Sanidad y Calidad Agroalimentaria (National Service for Sanitation and Food Quality)
UPOV 78	1978 Convention of the Union for the Protection of New Plant Varieties
USDA	US Department of Agriculture
WHO	World Health Organization

ACKNOWLEDGMENTS

The seeds for this book were planted in 2008, when I took my first graduate-level course in environmental sociology, in the midst of *el conflicto del campo*. In the process I met many like me, struggling with "how to write a dissertation," and later, if that wasn't enough, with "how to write a book." I've learned from each and every conversation and held close every book that I could tell had its origins in a dissertation. I can only say, if that's you too, keep going. *Sí se puede*. Yes, you can.

At the Graduate Center of the City University of New York, Ken Gould was the most generous and supportive mentor a student could ask for. Thank you, Ken, for holding a learning space for being intellectually curious with scholarly rigor, while never losing the urgency of the problems we study and the passion for engaged scholarship. I appreciate that I continue to learn and seek advice from you well after graduation, and from Tammy Lewis too! Thank you both. I am also deeply grateful to Jack Hammond and Bill Kornblum for advice during the long learning and writing process. Thanks to CUNY Graduate Center, the sociology department in particular, and to CUNY School of Professional Studies for funding my graduate school experience.

I feel fortunate and grateful to have found a job and a home at Tulane University in the magical city of New Orleans. Thanks to my colleagues in the sociology department for their guidance and support. David Smilde, Michele Adams, Mimi Schippers, Mariana Craciun, and Camilo Leslie bounced ideas with me and provided crucial feedback on this project. Thanks also to Laura McKinney, Chris Oliver, and, beyond the department, Virginia Oliveros, Eduardo Silva, and Maria Akchurin.

I'm deeply grateful for the support I have received from Tulane University to complete this project. Heartfelt thanks to Tom Reese and the Stone

Center for Latin American Studies and to Ludovico Feoli and the Center for Inter-American Policy and Research. Many thanks to the School of Liberal Arts, the Newcomb Institute, A Studio in the Woods, and the Provost's Office, especially to Ana López. I am also deeply grateful to my Tulane students who, a captive audience, heard me talk about my research and asked me all the difficult and important questions to fine-tune my arguments and my capacity for storytelling.

I want to thank the many brilliant scholars who through the years read ongoing parts of this project and gave me invaluable feedback: Phil McMichael, Rachel Schurman, Sam Cohn, Gerardo Otero, Matthew Schnurr, Brian Dowd-Uribe, Gustavo Oliveira, Susanna Hecht, Linda Farthing, and Nicole Fabricant, as well as the anonymous reviewers of the peer-reviewed articles I have published on this topic. Pablo Lapegna and Shannon Bell read the first full manuscript draft and gave me thorough and insightful feedback. Thank you both, for helping me figure out what I had to say and how to say it better. I'm humbled by your generosity and your kindness.

Thanks to Gisela Fosado, my editor at Duke University Press, for believing in this project and bringing it to fruition. Thank you always for your constant and enthusiastic support. Thanks to Alejandra Mejía for her attentive and thorough assistance in putting the manuscript together. Before I could even think of turning in this manuscript, Anitra Grisales gave me substantial, if not radical, editorial assistance. Anitra, your comments and edits helped move this book (and my voice) to a whole new level: I am forever grateful. Kate Hahn-Madole at Tulane and Kirsteen Anderson helped me fix the citations and bibliography, and Bill Nelson drew the map of Argentina. Thanks to Ellen Goldlust, Lisl Hampton, Courtney Richardson, and everyone at Duke's production and design departments, as well as the copyeditor Christine Dahlin, who made this manuscript look tight and pretty . . . and a physical book! This book is a thousand times better thanks to the comments I received from two no-longer-anonymous reviewers, Javier Auyero and Shannon Bell.

My immense gratitude goes to the people in the field who have opened their homes, farms, and offices and helped me understand what's going on with the technological package of genetically modified soybeans and large-scale agriculture in Argentina. Many of you have asked me to share what I write; I have struggled knowing that this might not be what you were expecting. My wish is that if you eventually read this book, we get to talk more so I can learn more and better. I have aimed to be truthful and, of course, my writing is my responsibility.

Finally, thanks to my friends and family, who have helped me stay sane, happy, and healthy through this journey, many of whom also volunteered their own friends and family for me to interview. In/from Argentina: Silvina Soria, Virginia Guerstein, Mariana Severini, Laura Lezcano, Adriana Llinares, and Daniela Olivera. In/since New York City: Pilar Ortiz, Amanda Riesman, Yolanda Martín, Laura Limonic, and Antonia Levy. In New Orleans: Virginia Medinilla, Eric Normand, Izabela Steflja, and Timothy and Joan Kimbell. To Luke McEvoy, for your tender and loving care, and the many meals when I had to write, and for reading and re-reading, and then reading and revising some more. To my siblings, nephews and nieces, and to my cousins and aunts. And especially to my parents, Mirta Quattrocchio and Osvaldo Leguizamón. This book is dedicated to them.

"We do the best agriculture in the world."

By "we," Leo meant Argentines. He is an agronomist and a high school teacher at the local agro-technical school. It was December 2009 when I met him in Flores, a small rural town 180 miles east of Buenos Aires. Leo and his wife had moved to the countryside after a lifetime in the capital, looking for a slower pace of life to raise their three little children. Flores is very small, a perfect grid of eight-by-five blocks in the heart of the Pampas, Argentina's famous prairie grasslands, the storied home of roaming *gauchos* and world-class steaks. Compared with Buenos Aires, which at over twelve million people is among the largest cities of the world, Flores may seem like the perfect picture of pastoral living. It is safe and quiet, and neighbors greet each other. Nature surrounds it. The green of the farms blends with people's backyards. Just outside their doors, a vast, unending vista of green stretches to the horizon to meet open blue skies.

This sea of green is soybean farms. In two decades, Argentina has undergone a swift agrarian transformation based on the early adoption and intensive implementation of genetically modified soybeans. These crops have been modified to tolerate spraying with glyphosate-based herbicides, a biotechnology developed and commercialized by Monsanto (now Bayer) as Roundup Ready. Argentina adopted herbicide-resistant soybeans in 1996 as a central part of its national development strategy based on natural resource extraction for exportation. Genetically modified soybeans cover half of Argentina's arable land and represent a third of total exports. After the United States and Brazil, Argentina is the third largest grower and exporter of genetically modified crops. The country's "soy boom" is celebrated at home and abroad for bringing about modernization and economic growth.[1]

Argentina touts the GM soy model as a well-rounded success. In mainstream newspapers, headlines announce record-breaking profits and exclaim, "Only biotechnology can save the world."[2] National development plans have GM biotechnology at their core. State and corporate actors present GM soy as the promised "manna" to solve global hunger and poverty as Argentina reclaims its role as the "granary of the world." In the rural soy towns of the Pampas, people proclaim, "We all live off the countryside," and praise soybean economics. Even urban sectors ally with the rural population when the government proposes to lift export taxes that may limit soybean production.

But while the soy boom has generated economic growth, it has also created tremendous social and ecological harm.[3] Small rural towns like Flores are disappearing as locals migrate to larger rural towns and cities for employment and the amenities of city life. Land has been concentrated in the hands of a few large agribusinesses that farm extensive areas with the help of cutting-edge technology and a comparatively small amount of highly specialized labor. Soybeans have replaced traditional crops, such as wheat and beef, leading to food insecurity. The expansion of the agrarian frontier into the northern Chaco region has prompted rapid and wide-scale deforestation that has devastated ecosystems and threatened livelihoods. Violence against peasant and indigenous families is escalating. The health hazards of agrochemical exposure are also on the rise. Across rural towns, Argentine doctors have documented increasing occurrences of leukemia, cancer, miscarriages, and malformations in newborns.

Throughout the world, GMOs have been met with strong resistance.[4] In Brazil, India, and South Africa, large coalitions of peasants, students, scientists, and consumers have organized to contest GM biotechnology, raising important questions over the impact of genetically modified crops and agrochemical use.[5] In Canada and Mexico, farmers have demanded lawsuits against Monsanto for cases of genetic contamination of their crops.[6] In India, farmers have burned Monsanto's seeds in pyres after escalating debt around seed purchases has driven many to suicide. In France, small farmers have organized to contest GM crops, free trade, and industrial agriculture.[7] Across the European Union, stricter laws to regulate genetically modified crops and agrochemicals have been passed under the principle of precaution. GMOs are banned in France and Germany and are strictly labeled in the United Kingdom.[8] In California, rural workers have organized to defend themselves against the health hazards of pesticide drift on large-scale industrial farms. Increasingly in the United States, concerned urban sectors have led the organic and food-justice movements' anti-biotech activism.[9]

In contrast, in Argentina there have been no nationally organized campaigns or coalitions against GMOs.[10] While some local movements have emerged to protest the health hazards of agrochemical drift, and peasant-indigenous organizations have been vocal against deforestation and violent dispossession, their urgent demands remain mostly unheard and they have had a difficult time gaining support from the very people who are negatively impacted. Most of the rural folks who live near soy farms have little to no decision-making power over agricultural production and do not profit from GM soy; in fact, they bear the burden of agrochemical exposure on their bodies and in their lives. So why is it that more of them have not mobilized to halt or at least slow down the pace of GM soy expansion? Why, in the face of environmental injustice, where the literature and common sense would lead us to expect it, do people not resist? And why, in striking opposition to the anti-GMO sentiment around the world, is Argentina complacent in the face of the large-scale expansion of GM soy? That is the puzzle this book sets out to solve.

Seeds of Power tells the story of Argentina's swift agrarian transformation based on the early adoption and intensive implementation of genetically modified, herbicide-tolerant soybeans. What this story reveals is how powerful actors are able to gain support for extractivism as a national model for socioeconomic development and promote inaction in the face of environmental injustice. I use the case of GM soy adoption in Argentina to break down what I call the *synergies of power* that create and legitimate human suffering, social inequality, and environmental degradation.

To grasp this critical process, we have to understand the history and shape of Argentina's political economy as well as its national culture. Argentina is a developing country that, since the late nineteenth century, has relied on agrarian exports for foreign income. Like many others on the continent, this Latin American country has been unable to break free of its colonial past as a "nature-exporting" society (as Fernando Coronil has said of Venezuela's oil dependence).[11] Critical to this enduring bind is a neoliberal restructuring program that, in the late twentieth century, loosened regulations to make large-scale GM soy production possible to begin with, and then to make it easier and more profitable. Finally, nontraditional commodities like soybeans have garnered higher international prices throughout the first decade of the twenty-first century, mostly driven by higher demand from China and India. In this most convenient context, powerful corporate and state actors have promoted GM soy production as a continuation of Argentina's homegrown model for socioeconomic development to the benefit of all, when in reality they are the ones reaping the majority of the political and financial gains.

Here I reveal how a powerful synergy of influential actors—from the state to national and transnational agribusiness to their allies in the media and sciences—have assigned uses and meanings to GM biotechnology that draw from deep-rooted structural and symbolic inequalities; in doing so, they have managed to create acquiescence and diminish the power of social movements that might otherwise have diverted Argentina's development trajectory away from extractivism. Contributing to perspectives on the political economy of the environment, I show how culture, discourse, and national identity are central to the material interests of people in power.[12] These powerful actors use culture to shape and legitimate a political economy that is highly unequal in terms of class, gender, and race. In focusing on this synergy, I expand on environmental justice scholarship to highlight how political and economic *as well as* cultural and symbolic means, mechanisms, and strategies specific (though not unique) to Argentina can generate consent and support for an extractivist model that knowingly reinforces human and ecological harm.[13]

I trace the cultural roots of this model to the very foundation of Argentina as a nation in the nineteenth century, when the liberal elite of the time initiated a "civilizing," nation-building project that led to dominant myths of national identity. Those myths established Argentina as a modern, European nation and as the "granary of the world" at the turn of the twentieth century, that belle époque when Argentina held close the same promise of development as did other settler states like Canada and Australia.[14] When we follow the structural and historic threads of these core values and beliefs about national identity, we can see the long-lasting impact on Argentines' perceptions of nature, rural life, agricultural production, and the nation's role in the global economy.

Seeds of Power makes visible the complex web of power hidden behind the promising discourse of technological innovation for development. Powerful actors operating from the male-dominated spheres of the state and corporations down to local agribusinesses, the farm, and the household use various strategies to create consent, including economic redistribution and references to myths of national identity and scientific expertise. The "subjects of power"—the regular people who run the everyday operations in the rural communities of the Pampas; those who live, work, and play on and near the soy farms—tend to highlight the benefits of GM soybeans. Like Leo, many who neither control nor profit from farming feel included in that "we" who can boast about having "the best agriculture in the world." In a way this makes sense, considering that in recent years soybean exports have brought affluence to the rural sector, a huge relief after decades of crisis. But it is a puzzling situation at the very least, considering that more and more people are getting sick while soybeans grow in their backyards. Despite the known environmental and health risks of pesticide drift, rural inhabitants in the Pampas region often disregard potential harm, minimize toxicity, and emphasize the cutting-edge qualities of biotechnology and the economic rewards of soybean production. I argue that they consent because they reap economic and cultural benefits and because they do not "see" harm, due to the strategic construction of a no-risk discourse around agrochemical spraying.

Environmental justice (EJ) theory and methodology highlight unequal power dynamics in society that result in an unequal distribution of the costs and benefits of production practices. Thanks to a vast EJ scholarship, we know, with near-mathematical certainty, that people at the end of the power spectrum, the communities of poor people and people of color, bear a disproportionate burden of the costs, while those who reap the benefits live upstream and upwind, mostly untouched by the environmental harm they create with their decisions.[15] We know, too, of the motivation that drives those with decision-making power: a general mandate to increase profit- ability and to pursue economic growth.[16] But we know much less about the strategies corporate and state actors mobilize to legitimate injustice—that is, how they create compliance in unjust situations.[17] How multiple dimen- sions of inequality (class, gender, race/ethnicity, rural/urban divides, a his- tory of colonialism) intersect to exacerbate environmental injustice is also vastly undertheorized.[18]

This book delves into an understudied aspect of environmental justice studies to look at the actors who are often absent in the analysis of EJ's uneven-burden equation: those who are "in between" the distribution of power and their role in creating and reinforcing environmental injustice. Those who wield power are the CEOs of the agribusinesses, the soybean producers, and the state officials; these individuals control and profit from agricultural production and are able to mobilize science, media, and the rule of law to their advantage. At the "bottom" are the poor and powerless, those who due to their class, gender, and/or race occupy the lower rungs of society: indigenous peasants and working-class women. Those "in between" fall along the race/class/gender spectrum. They are the rural folks of the Pampas who are of European descent and who indirectly reap some of the benefits of soybean production: they are the employees of agribusinesses, landowners who rent their land for others to farm, the wives of soybean producers, and other professionals and business owners who benefit from rural economic development but are not in the "farming business." What those who are "in between" have in common is that while they do not have control over the farm, they reap some benefits from soybean production (mostly in terms of rent or income), but, because they live near toxic facilities (the farms, in this case), they also bear the health and environmental costs of extractivism. As I show, they are, perhaps without knowing or wanting to be, strategic in reproducing the status quo. This book illustrates the complex, ambiguous situation those rural inhabitants of the Pampas occupy, while it also reveals the strategies that more powerful actors engage in to quell dissent when the poor and powerless do eventually mobilize against injustice.

This book may not end with the message of hope that other books on the struggles for environmental justice deliver. Yet understanding how powerful actors create acquiescence over the unequal distribution of the social and ecological costs of extractivism and why ordinary people re-create an unjust system is essential to a fuller understanding of the forces that create—but may also potentially challenge—environmental injustice in Argentina and around the world.

What Are Genetically Modified Crops?

Genetically modified crops are the result of a plant-breeding method known as recombinant DNA.[19] With the aid of a gene gun, scientists insert a gene from another living being, bacterium, or virus into the DNA of plant cells to express a desired trait. Proponents of the technology have made bold claims over its potential to engineer crops that express world-saving traits, like enhanced nutritional value. Vitamin A–enhanced Golden Rice is one of the classic examples of how GM biotechnology could save the hungry and the poor. Yet, despite billions of dollars invested over decades, Golden Rice has still not been released commercially for cultivation. Plus, critics argue, it would be a woefully inadequate answer for addressing social and environmental problems in the Philippines, the country where the technology is targeted.[20] The range of available GM crops is actually quite narrow. The two most common transgenic traits, herbicide tolerance and insect resistance, are modified into four major commercial crops: soybeans, corn, cotton, and canola. These four products account for 99 percent of all transgenic crops planted globally. Soybeans alone make up 50 percent of that number.[21]

Transgenic soybeans have been modified to resist glyphosate-based herbicides—a technological development branded by Monsanto as Roundup Ready (abbreviated as RR) because the soybeans can tolerate spraying with Roundup, the company's best-selling weed killer. A new variety of transgenic soybean seeds "stacks" both herbicide-tolerant and insect-resistant traits (a technology developed and sold by Monsanto as Intacta Roundup Ready 2 Pro, first released in Brazil in 2010 and in Argentina in 2012). Insect-resistant crops (primarily corn and cotton, sold under the brand Intacta) have been modified to express Bt toxins, a pesticide, so that when insects feed on the crop, they die through poisoning.[22] This technological development reduces farmers' need to spray chemical insecticides to control insect pests (corn borers, rootworms, and bollworms, in particular). Herbicide-resistant seeds work in a different manner. In conventional farming, farmers till the soil before sowing to remove weeds. Soil tilling, however, breaks the soil structure, which causes nutrients and moisture to wash away; this was a major problem across the Pampas before the adoption of GM crops. Now, because RR soy plants are resistant to the chemical herbicide, farmers can sow without tilling and spray the weed killer later. This "technological package," the combination of the no-till farming method, RR soybean seeds, and glyphosate-based herbicide, thus came to solve important sustainability problems for producers in the Pampas. It also, most substantially, simplified production practices, lowered the costs of labor and input, and increased profitability (as I will detail in chapter 2). Throughout my fieldwork, producers and agronomists often sang the praises of the revolutionary qualities of "the technological package of RR soy."

The GM industry presents transgenic crops as a boon for farmers and the environment, as these crops would reduce applications of agrochemicals and enable farmers to transition to less toxic ones. In particular, glyphosate-based Roundup is advertised and sold as safe for humans and the environment.[23] Glyphosate is classified as having a low toxicity by the US Environmental Protection Agency and by its counterpart in Argentina, the Servicio Nacional de Sanidad y Calidad Agroalimentaria (SENASA). In the Pampas, before the introduction of RR soy, farmers were spraying more toxic and more expensive agrochemicals. Glyphosate substituted for those, thus simplifying farming practices; reducing per-hectare herbicide spraying, labor, and fossil-fuel expenditures; and minimizing environmental impact.[24] Over the years, however, farmers have encountered problems with resistance as weeds and insects have adapted to transgenic terrains. As early as 2002, farmers in Argentina and the United States began reporting the emergence of glyphosate-resistant "superweeds" in fields planted with herbicide-resistant soy and corn. In the summer of 2013, Brazilian farmers suffered a major pest outbreak of bollworms, causing them billions of dollars in losses from soybean and cotton harvests supposedly controlled by insect-resistant Intacta seeds. Such events force farmers to spray more and more agrochemicals to control pests.[25]

Glyphosate use in Argentina, the United States, and Brazil has risen sharply since the adoption of RR seeds.[26] Its toxicity has been under close scrutiny increasingly since 2015, when the International Agency for Research on Cancer of the World Health Organization reclassified the herbicide as "probably carcinogenic to humans."[27] Farmers have also fallen back into applying complementary herbicides of higher toxicity, like paraquat, 2,4-D, and atrazine.[28] Farmers resort to increasing agrochemical use and to adopting newer varieties of GM crops to maintain high productivity.[29] Thus, while the industry proposes GM crops as a sustainable technological solution, in practice the logic of capitalism pushes farmers into adopting the newly available technologies to sustain accumulation even if they increase social and ecological risk.

GM crops were first grown commercially on a significant scale in 1996. The United States and Argentina, alongside Canada, China, and Mexico, were pioneers in adopting the new GM biotechnology. Twenty short years later, GM crop acreage has expanded over a hundredfold—an astonishing fact that leads some to argue that GM crops are the fastest-adopted agricultural technology in human history since the invention of the plow ten thousand years ago.[30] In 2017, GM crops covered 190 million hectares mostly across three countries: the United States, Brazil, and Argentina. (For reference, this amount of land represents a fifth of the total land area of the United States and five times that of Germany.) These three countries alone account for 78 percent of global GM crop production. The top seven largest growers (including Canada, India, Paraguay, and Pakistan) plant 95 percent of the global GM crops.[31]

As these numbers suggest, while transgenic crops have spread fast, they have done so unevenly. GM crops have met with mixed reactions across the globe.[32] Farmers in the United States, Canada, and Argentina have embraced them, and they are increasingly predominant in South American agricultural lands (as they expanded from Argentina into Brazil, Paraguay, and Bolivia). But they face widespread resistance across the European Union, in particular in France, the United Kingdom, and Germany. GM crops have expanded over a fraction of the agricultural area of India and Pakistan but are almost nonexistent across the rest of Asia.[33] There is no commercial cultivation of GM crops in Japan or in most of Africa, though currently a second generation of GM crops (engineered using CRISPR technologies) is being forcefully promoted by philanthropic organizations like the Gates Foundation, particularly in Burkina Faso and Uganda.[34]

GM crops are framed as a technology that is "pro-poor" and environmentally sustainable.[35] The promise of GM crops is that they would allow poor smallholder farmers from developing countries to grow more food using fewer resources. According to the United Nations, 821 million people were hungry in 2017: that is one in every nine people in the world. Global food insecurity is exacerbated by civil conflict and the environmental challenges that threaten food production, such as droughts, flooding, and hurricanes.[36] Increasing food productivity via GM biotech adoption is proposed as a solution to address global hunger, poverty, and environmental degradation. It is a "daunting task," reads the first paragraph of the International Service for the Acquisition of Agri-biotech Applications' (ISAAA's) annual report, the pro-biotech think tank, "feeding the world which is continuously increasing and predicted to be 9.8 billion in 2050 and 11.2 billion in 2100."[37]

"How the world will feed itself," writes economist and sustainability advocate Jeffrey Sachs, "is one of the most complicated unsolved problems of sustainable development."[38] The humanitarian goal of "feeding the world" and the technological optimism that sustains the promising discourse of GM crops are not reserved for the industry and its think tanks but are also disseminated by public intellectuals like Sachs, Thomas Friedman, and Steven Pinker.[39] This type of discourse has taken a hold in Argentina. The root of the problem of global hunger, the narrative goes, lies in a combination of population growth and insufficient technologies, a problem that worsens with climate change. Thomas Malthus first warned us about the seriousness of this problem, writes Sachs. In 1798, Malthus theorized that population growth tends to overrun food supply.[40] Starting with the Green Revolution in the 1940s, the Malthusian narrative has buttressed arguments for the promotion and proliferation of agrarian technological innovation in the Global South, of which GM crops are its latest iteration, as I will detail in chapter 1.

Cutting-edge agrarian technologies like GM crops are the proposed tools for sustainable development. The goal of sustainable development, according to Sachs, is to achieve economic growth that is socially inclusive and environmentally sustainable.[41] Authors like Sachs, Friedman, and Pinker have revitalized modernization theory in the era of climate change. Their ideas matter because they influence development theory and policy at the global level, as exemplified by the United Nations 2030 Agenda for Sustainable Development. As I show throughout the book, their ideas have also been adopted by political and agribusiness leaders in Argentina.

In this paradigm, technological innovation is key to achieving the goal of sustainable development. In the tradition of modernization theory, these authors celebrate industrialization and mechanization as enabling economic growth through the harnessing of natural resources, particularly coal. But while the burning of fossil fuels on a massive scale gave humanity "modern civilization," Sachs argues, it has "such dire side effects, that it endangers civilization itself."[42] We *are* close to reaching the tipping point that would make this planet uninhabitable.[43] How then to further economic growth while minimizing ecological impact? According to these authors, and to ecological modernization theorists in general, the solution lies in the *knowledge* to innovate and to transition to "green" technologies. GMO promoters also emphasize this point: knowledge is key to farming and therefore to feeding the world. As I show in chapter 2, this narrative builds on the promise of ecological modernization to delink the logic of capitalism from its toxic, industrial material practices.[44] This narrative also relies on a traditional definition of development that quantitatively equates economic growth with social well-being and that qualitatively defines development as a linear evolution toward progress, civilization, and Western modernity via constant industrialization and mechanization.[45] These ideas and beliefs are deeply rooted in Argentina's national origins and have been appropriated and mobilized by political and economic elites to create consent over GM soy extractivism as a development tool for the country.

Why Do Soybeans Matter?

Soybeans are the most ubiquitous crop most people never think about. In 2017, they covered 125 million hectares across the world, growing mostly in the United States, Argentina, and Brazil.[46] (For reference, that is twice the size of Texas, the largest of the continental US states.) A soy plant grows as high as three feet tall in a bright green leafy bush, and each of its furry pods holds three precious light-brown beans (figures I.1 and I.2).

If you question whether you have ever eaten genetically modified soybeans, the answer is likely yes. Ninety-four percent of all soybeans planted in the United States are from herbicide-resistant seed varieties. In Argentina, that figure escalates to almost 100 percent.[47] While soybeans are used to make the usual tofu, tempeh, and soy milk, most of the soy we eat is unrecognizable as such. GM soybeans enter the food system in processed foods and animal-derived products. Soybean oil is the edible oil most widely used by the food industry. It is in crackers, chocolate, cereal bars, margarine, mayonnaise, salad dressings, dairy and meat substitutes, and more. Non–cow milk infant formula is also soy based.[48] However, while about 15 percent of US soybeans go toward the production of foods for human consumption, the primary market for soybeans is animal feed. More than 70 percent of US soybeans is used to feed poultry, hogs, cattle, and even fish.[49] The rest is used for industrial purposes, from personal care products (like cosmetics and skin and hair conditioning) to biodiesel and construction material.

Soybeans are a profitable business. In 2016, soybeans and their derivatives (soybean meal and oil) accounted for $86 billion in global exports. The United States, Argentina, and Brazil are the top global soybean exporters. Together these three countries hold 82 percent of the export market for soy and its derivatives. (Argentina is the largest exporter of soybean oil and soybean meal in the world.) China is the top buyer of global soybeans. Asian countries (with India at the top, followed by Bangladesh, China, and South Korea) import almost half of all global soybean oil exports. Almost 40 percent of global soybean meal exports is destined for animal feedlots across the European Union.[50]

The promise of GM crops to alleviate world hunger and to address climate change falls apart with the fact that most soybeans are not grown for

Fig. I.1. Rows of young GM soybean plants in the central Pampas region. Photo by the author.

Fig. I.2. Soybean seeds ready to be planted. Photo by the author.

human consumption. The high demand for soybeans in Asia is a response to the emerging middle class; as people grow more affluent, they tend to consume more meat. This rapid demand for animal protein, however, puts substantial pressure on the environment.[51] Meat production is resource intensive and thus not an efficient or sustainable way to feed more people. As Richard York and Marcia Hill Gossard note, "Up to 10 times the quantity of resources (land, energy, and water) is needed to produce meat relative to equivalent amounts of vegetarian food."[52] Intensive animal farming is also a major source of methane emissions, a greenhouse gas contributing to global warming.[53] As Gustavo Oliveira and Susanna Hecht argue, the expansion of soy to address Asian demand needs to give way to "a more truthful stance" about soybeans—that they are being produced less to address humanitarian concerns based on a Malthusian narrative than for their high profitability in the international market.[54]

The global soybean chain is controlled by a handful of transnational corporations that reap most of the benefits of the global soy trade. Three giant multinational agribusinesses (ChemChina-Syngenta, Corteva Agriscience, and Bayer-Monsanto) control more than 60 percent of the global commercial seed market and 70 percent of the agrochemical industry. Four grain-trading companies (ADM, Bunge, Cargill, and Louis Dreyfus—collectively known as the ABCDs) control 90 percent of the export market.[55] The agrifood sector is increasingly more concentrated as a result of recent mergers and acquisitions. In 2017, ChemChina acquired Syngenta, and Dow and DuPont became Corteva Agriscience. In 2018, Bayer merged with Monsanto. Altogether, the combined assets of these three giant agribusinesses amount to $352 billion, and their combined total annual revenue is $190 billion. The ABCDs are dominant exporters in South America as they have acquired local companies and invested in soybean storage, processing, logistics, and trade.[56] Financial capital is also pervasive in the global food system as financial actors and institutions (banks, hedge funds, and mutual funds) can trade—and increasingly speculate on—soybeans as commodities in the global financial market and also purchase and lease farmland for agricultural production.[57] The soybean chain in Argentina reflects the global trend of increased concentration and integration.[58]

In two short decades Argentina has positioned itself in the global food system as a strategic provider of soybeans for the livestock complex.[59] As I will explain in chapter 1, this came about as the result of a process of neoliberal agrarian restructuring that took place in the 1990s and accelerated drastically with the introduction of herbicide-tolerant seeds in 1996. This agrarian transformation resulted in a soy boom. Between 1996 and 2015 production has expanded yearly. By 2015, about 21 million hectares were sown with GM soybeans, over half of all Argentine land under cultivation.[60] Every year, farmers hit a new record harvest. A record-breaking sixty million tons of soybeans were harvested in 2015, 96 percent of which was destined for the export market. The share of soybeans in Argentina's total exports is highly significant. Between 1996 and 2015, soybean exports accounted for between a quarter and a third of total exports.[61] In addition to soybeans, Argentina is a large exporter of corn, wheat, and other crops. In fact, cereals, vegetable oils, and other agricultural and animal products and byproducts made up more than 60 percent of all Argentine exports for 2015.

The soybean chain is consolidated across just a handful of large agribusinesses that guide agrarian production from afar, distanced from the social and environmental realities where soybeans are grown. Large private companies have the power to guide technological development as they provide much of the funding for research and development.[62] Thanks to their adoption of the technological package of GM soy, farmers can grow a highly uniform and standard product, essential for meeting the needs of what Philip McMichael calls the "corporate food regime." Soybeans are a preferred "flex crop" because they can be sourced indistinctively from Argentine, Brazilian, or Paraguayan farms and given multiple and flexible uses by being processed into food, fuel, animal feed, or building material.[63] This is convenient and profitable for the national and transnational corporate actors that control agricultural production and guide technological innovation. Political elites benefit too because they manage to contain political conflict by accelerating economic growth.[64] Corporate and state actors are allies in the promotion of GM biotechnology as they reap the political and economic benefits of increasing economic growth.[65]

But what happens on the ground? So far, the literature on the political economy of soybeans has studied sky-high macro processes, thus missing the human dimension of the issue. The narrative on GM crops promoted by the industry and by modernization scholars also tends to high levels of abstraction by disembedding agricultural production from its social and ecological contexts, as they present GM crops as a one-size-fits-all solution for sustainable development. What we need are studies on GM biotechnology that go beyond broad generalizations about the benefits of GM crops to an abstract "poor" population in order to focus on the specific contexts in which specific crops are adopted.[66] Building from macro-level work by political economists of development and the environment, including my own, here I dive into the meso- and micro-levels of soybean production in Argentina, zooming in on the rural communities of the Pampas, Argentina's historic agro-export sector. I thus embed GM soybeans in context, tying allegedly immaterial knowledge-based agriculture to the material bodies, resources, and practices that make resource extractivism possible. In doing so, I trace the workings of power across the spectrum of social life, from the large-scale institutions of politics and the economy to everyday face-to-face interactions. I thus show how genetically modified soybeans matter not only as a profitable agro-industrial crop but as a site to study power dynamics that create and legitimate environmental injustice.

Synergies of Power

Various forces have played a role in making Argentina acquiescent in the face of a massive agrarian transformation based on the expansion of genetically modified soybeans. I propose "synergies of power" as a conceptual shortcut to refer to the intersecting structural and symbolic dimensions of domination that operate simultaneously and across time to create, compound, and legitimate environmental injustice.[67]

Much effort in environmental justice scholarship has been devoted to studying one or two dimensions of social inequality; most often, the focus has been on how race and class inequalities relate to exposure to environmental hazards.[68] But this strict focus misses the broad picture. Social inequalities in lived experience (of race, ethnicity, gender, or class) are not based on strictly separate categories, but as David Pellow argues, they are "mutually reinforcing in that they tend to act together to produce and maintain systems of individual and collective power, privilege, and subordination."[69] Traditional EJ studies also focus almost exclusively on the United States, so their conclusions about the place of race in socioenvironmental relations are often not applicable to Latin American countries, which have different systems of racial hierarchies and classification.[70] Moreover, by focusing mostly on the collective struggles for environmental justice, they miss the much larger picture: acquiescence is often the norm.[71] I address these limitations by studying how multiple historical forms of power and inequality intersect to exacerbate environmental injustice. I do this by considering racial and gendered hierarchies that result from settler colonialism, by focusing on the absence of mobilization, and by analyzing the efforts of political and economic elites to quell dissent.

Power underlies the social and environmental dynamics that create environmental injustice.[72] Yet most EJ scholarship often does not engage directly with the question of how power operates.[73] Rather, in the study of environmental injustice, the workings of power are assumed. As I have already noted, it is a trope in this literature to argue that powerful actors live upwind and upstream from the toxic facilities they command and benefit from, while communities of poor and people of color bear the burden of the toxic impact of the extraction and production processes and must ultimately mobilize for redress.[74] This scholarship often documents the distribution of environmental damage.[75] But the strategies, mechanisms, and dimensions of power that create and sustain these unequal dynamics are rarely explored. By bringing the study of power front and center to EJ scholarship, I want to emphasize the "often neglected, yet fundamental, legitimation and discursive processes" that underpin injustice.[76] Because, as Steven Lukes argues, the "most invasive and insidious form of power" is exercised when subjects come to comply with their situation of domination and thus remain acquiescent in the face of injustice.[77]

The Roots of Power

The book begins by tracing the historical and cultural roots of the political economy of soybean extractivism in Argentina. It is important to establish that dependence on agricultural exports for foreign income is not a recent development for Argentina, and neither is large-scale capitalist agrarian production in the Pampas. As early as the 1940s, Latin American structuralists and dependency theorists, such as Raúl Prebisch, Osvaldo Sunkel, Fernando H. Cardoso, and Enzo Faletto, were writing about the intrinsic disadvantages of the region's dependency on commodity exports.[78] Following Karl Marx, they took a historical approach to studying Latin America's political economy. The origins of extractivism, they argued, should be traced back to the colonial period. I also take a historical approach to studying structural formations and, thus, power and injustice. I attend to the temporal dimensions of inequality because power and privilege compound over time, while I also consider the cultural dimensions of inequality. Since Max Weber's and Antonio Gramsci's critiques of Marx, sociologists have paid attention to how history and culture are threaded into the social structure.[79]

By considering how culture interweaves with history structurally and in terms of interaction, I show how culture serves to shape and legitimate the political economy of extractivism—and thus promotes acquiescence and consent.

Chapter 1, then, is a cultural history of soybean extractivism, from the beginning of the nation to the present. I trace how agro-industrial production for export has been at the core of Argentina's development project since its independence from Spain in the early nineteenth century. I show how members of the intellectual elite of the time, known as the Generation of 1837, used their economic, political, military, and discursive power to shape Argentina's social structure and, most importantly, to legitimate it. In charge of building the nation, the Generation of 1837 crafted a model for Argentina on the ideals of European Enlightenment, modernization, and comparative advantage. With essays and novels, these intellectuals crafted the future of the nation. Domingo Sarmiento's *Facundo* established a foundational dichotomy of "civilization or barbarism" that set the tone of the nation-building project and was to become a guiding myth of Argentine national identity, in which savage nature must be tamed to make it productive.[80]

The use of violence, inflicted upon indigenous peoples and ecologies through military operations and the introduction of industrial agrarian technologies, was another main mechanism of social control. Thus, I also show how nineteenth-century elites put forward a plan to dispossess indigenous peoples from their territory and to populate it with European migrants. The conquest of the so-called desert implied the killing and displacement of indigenous populations.[81] This nation-building project shaped Argentina's agrarian structure.

During the late nineteenth and early twentieth centuries, European migrants settled in the Pampas and established a type of capitalist agriculture based on large-scale production for export. These migrants are known as *chacareros*, *gringos*, and *colonos*—closer to American farmers than to Latin American *campesinos* (peasants). By the turn of the twentieth century, with their novel farming arrangements and technologies, chacareros had turned the Pampas into the motor of Argentina's economy through agricultural exports like wheat and beef. This is the origin of a second guiding myth of national identity, that of Argentina as the "granary of the world."[82] As I show in chapters 1 and 2, by the turn of the twenty-first century, political and economic elites had mobilized the promising discourse of GM crops to feed the world sustainably, a discourse that taps into ecological moderniza-tion but moreover finds its cultural roots in these guiding myths of national identity.

An important way in which power operates to shape and contain con-flict is through the mobilization of bias.[83] Those in power draw from dis-courses that center on shared cultural values to enact and legitimate power and inequality. As Marisol de la Cadena argues, this form of power is also exercised through the exclusion of certain actors and issues from the po-litical arena altogether.[84] The nation-building project of the liberal elite of the nineteenth century created a racialized political economy built on an assimilationist ideology. It created a dominant myth of a "white" Argentina of European descent, where there are no races or racism. This, in turn, rendered indigenous peoples invisible and marginalized.[85] A less studied consequence of this ideology, one that I want to bring attention to, is that it also created a gendered political economy.

The newly arrived European migrants in the Pampas organized labor across traditional European gender lines, with men (husbands, fathers, and adult sons) responsible for the commercial farming and women charged with managing the home. Gender roles at the production level of GM soy have intensified historical patterns of gender inequity and inequality in the region; to this day, men of European descent still control large-scale soybean production.[86] In the political economy of soybean extractivism, racialized subjects (indigenous peoples, smallholder peasants) and femi-nized subjects (women who identify primarily as mothers and caregivers) are lower in the social hierarchy and thus excluded from decision-making power over large-scale farming.

Selling Revolution in the Pampas

Another important piece of the puzzle that explains acquiescence is eco-nomic redistribution. There is acquiescence and consent because in the short and medium term, some of the profits of GM soybean production trickle down through rural towns. The material abundance brought by the soy boom into the larger towns of the Pampas stands in stark contrast with the long period of crisis that preceded it. "We all live off the countryside" was a common refrain I heard from residents of the Pampas. Economic dependence, the literature shows, stifles mobilization.[87] When people are economically dependent on a single industry, they are less likely to protest against it. That is the case for rural soy towns in Argentina too.

But that is not the whole story. The workings of power are not always observable.[88] As I mentioned above, along with the distribution of material resources, powerful actors mobilize cultural values and beliefs to shape grievance framing and to secure consent. In Argentina, corporate and state actors have used their discursive power to present GM biotechnology as a positive and necessary development, a key strategy to create hegemonic consensus over soybean extractivism as a key accumulation strategy.[89] The media, in particular, is one of the most effective and widely used strategies to foster acquiescence and consent.[90] In chapter 2, I show how powerful corporate and state actors mobilize a pro–GM soy discourse that strategically and very effectively links the ecological modernization/sustainable development discourse of GM crops "feeding the world" to the guiding myths of Argentine national identity. Because this framing of GM biotech resonates with deeply held beliefs of national identity, rural inhabitants of the Pampas are, using Rachel Schurman and William Munro's words, "culturally predisposed" to perceive the biotechnology in a positive light and without much questioning.[91] That is because it is the familiar way in which they perceive the world. Therefore, the economic dependence and cultural identity created around agrarian technological innovation in larger rural towns have created consent around the benefits of the agro-industry.

Less spoken of are the costs of the soy boom: abandoned towns, rapid deforestation, violent land grabs, peasant displacement, corporate concentration of farmland, loss of food security, and the accumulating environmental and health hazards of agrochemical spraying. A well-established body of literature on the political economy of the environment situates the origin of social and environmental problems in the logic of capitalism.[92] The treadmill of production theory counters the ecological modernization theory espoused by promoters of GM biotechnology. As treadmill scholars Allan Schnaiberg and Kenneth Gould argue, powerful social actors (in this case, political and economic elites) promote technological innovation to speed up production and natural resource extraction.[93] This eventually leads to decreased social benefits, as machines replace workers, and to increased ecological harm due to pollution and depletion of natural resources.

Thus, in chapter 2, I juxtapose the positive framing of GM soy production—the economic growth, modernity-bringing discourse—with the social and environmental debt that results from GM soy expansion. From the perspective of traditional EJ studies, we would expect rural communities in the

Pampas, faced with mounting socioecological degradation, to organize in opposition. But this is not the case. I argue that another piece of the puzzle of acquiescence—alongside economic dependence and cultural identity—is that rural inhabitants do not "see" the negative consequences that could be framed as a grievance worth mobilizing for. On the contrary, when soybean producers and rural neighbors look out over the farms surrounding their homes, they do not perceive the potential toxicity and harmful health risks of agrochemical exposure. Instead, wearing their "modernizing" glasses (as the guiding myths that make up their worldview), they see productivity and technological advantage (a "civilized" nature) as well as "nature" itself (green and quiet as opposed to the polluted, busy life of the city).

The literature in social movements is clear: Why mobilize if there is not a grievance worth mobilizing for? While potential grievances are ubiquitous, not all injustices lead to collective action.[94] Framing theorists argue that the way people interpret their grievances is critical to participation.[95] *Frames* capture the cultural and emotional dimensions of movements, and they serve both as "persuasive devices" to capture adherents as well as "interpretive frameworks."[96] A problem often needs to be visible for "consciousness transformation" to occur, so that people may interpret/ frame the problem as a grievance that requires remediation.[97] In her study of acquiescence in Appalachia, Shannon Bell shows how the worst aspects of coal mining are out of sight and thus "out of mind." Similarly, Kari Norgaard argues that a reason for inaction vis-à-vis climate change is because the worst consequences of a warming planet are yet to be fully visible and experienced.[98]

However, as these and other authors argue, the visibility/awareness of environmental hazards is not an objective experience; it is socially constructed.[99] Powerful actors can influence perceptions, cognitions, and preferences in situations of latent conflict. The health and environmental impacts of agrochemical exposure, in particular, are often not even directly visible; they require medical and environmental scientists to determine and translate risk.[100] The negative consequences of pesticide drift unfold slowly over time, as agrochemicals accumulate in soil, water, air, and bodies over years and years of relentless toxic spraying. Chronic exposure to environmental hazards is a "silent" problem, as Thomas Beamish argues, and an invisible one, as I argue, which obscures the visibility necessary for the transformation of consciousness required for collective action.[101]

As corporate and state authorities, aided by their expert advocates, minimize risk to legitimate production technologies, they create acquiescence among laypeople, who trust the experts to keep them safe. Rural folks who make a living out of soybean production, in particular agribusinesses' employees and landowners who rent out their land, are caught "in between," and they help perpetuate injustice by invoking scientific expertise and cultural myths of national identity to support soybean production.

The Elephant in the Field

Power is most effective when subjects accept the order of things (the status quo) and willingly comply with their position of subordination. In such times, grievances may remain latent. A very necessary, though difficult, analysis of power requires that we broaden its scope to include latent grievances and the potential for conflict to fully understand how subjects accept and reproduce their structurally disempowered position.[102] How to recognize latent grievances, which are clear cases of not-observable non-events, poses an important challenge to researchers. In my case, however, latent grievances were hiding in plain sight. They were "the elephant in the room."[103] The real and potential health risks of agrochemical exposure are a gigantic presence in the rural communities of the Pampas, though most residents I encountered were actively pretending not to notice.

In chapter 3, I delve deeper into the households in rural Pampas communities, to the level of interactions and emotions, to show how grievances are kept latent among the public. I tell the stories of a group of women from a soy town I call Santa María to show that latent grievances exist and, therefore, to underscore how successful the mechanisms of power have been in creating acquiescence. These women are mothers who benefit from soybean production, mostly through their husbands in the agribusiness. In public, all the women celebrated soybean production and reiterated "we all live off the countryside." Yet in private, in murmurs and whispers, they shared with me their worries and fears over toxic agrochemical spraying in their surroundings. In their community, these women notice rising cancer rates among their neighbors, miscarriages among healthy women, and malformations in newborns. In contrast to the shared narrative I will describe in chapter 2 (all benefits, no costs), these mothers "see"—they perceive—the negative impact of soybean extractivism. But while they share latent grievances, they do not act on them. While individually they worry, in public, they silence and deny. This leads us to interrogate the factors that *impede* individual resistance from transforming into collective action.[104]

In chapter 3, I show how the women of Santa María socially construct denial through doubt, silence, and policing themselves and others.[105] I also show how perceptions of environmental harm have an emotional, gendered component. Feminized subjects responsible for children prioritize care and precaution—a way of knowing that is opposed to what is presented by the (male and masculinized) producers and experts who emphasize no risk and prioritize profits and growth. But while these women's gendered selves allow them to "see," their structurally disempowered social positions force them into silence. Following Vincent Roscigno, I highlight the dynamic and relational features of power.[106] As noted, there are hierarchies within rural folks. While these wives and mothers enjoy the wealth and privilege granted by their husbands' position, they themselves hold no control over farming. Caught "in between," they trade power for patronage and actively create their acquiescence.

Against the Grain

Conflict makes power explicit. Overt conflict reveals the actual existence of grievances, as a contradiction between the interests of power elites and their subjects and their (the subjects') willful resistance to domination.[107] In chapter 4, I shine a light on those who bear the brunt of the costs of the GM soy model and who have organized to protest against the resulting environmental injustice. They are women-led citizen assemblies in defense of health and life, triggered by the spread of agrochemically induced illnesses in the Pampas region. They are also peasant-indigenous peoples defending life and livelihood against the forced evictions and habitat devastation that result from the northern expansion of the agrarian frontier. These movements are doing very important, timely work, but they have not gained the traction one might expect given the urgency of their demands.

To scale up, activists face structural barriers that result from two centuries of agro-exporting: their own economic need (activists are poor or from working-class backgrounds); their gender (movements are led by women who identify as mothers who are concerned over the impact of agrochemical drift on children's health); their ethnicity/race (peasant-indigenous); and the economic well-being/dependence of the farms that surround them and of the country as a whole. They also face deeply ingrained cultural barriers erected by the guiding myths of Argentine national identity. Their mobilizing frames, which directly oppose large-scale agrarian production, do not resonate with mainstream values and beliefs. As Schurman and Munro argue, culture shapes opportunities for anti-biotech activism.[108] But here I show how the "cultural economy" also *constrains and suffocates* activism by creating acquiescence in the general population. Critical to this, I argue, are the overt and covert strategies power elites deploy to stall, silence, and demobilize activists and their demands. I thus reveal how corporate and state actors, aided by their expert advocates, use their structural and symbolic power to diminish the power of social movements that might otherwise move Argentina's development trajectory away from extractivism.

In the Fields and in the Kitchens

Seeds of Power is a case study of Argentina's agrarian transformation based on the early adoption and intensive implementation of herbicide-resistant genetically modified soybeans. Case studies allow us to capture the complex, rich texture of social life by focusing on the detailed study of a single case.[109] This is key to studying the explicit and hidden manifestations of power.[110]

I define my case in terms of the type of agricultural system: my unit of analysis is the agricultural export sector.[111] For Argentina, this refers mostly to the Pampas region (see map I.1). The Pampas extend across the provinces of Buenos Aires, Entre Ríos, Santa Fe, Córdoba, and La Pampa. The region is characterized by its vast plains of fertile land, temperate climate, and adequate rainfall, making it ideally suited for large-scale grain production and cattle ranching. As I show in the following chapters, the rural population in the Pampas is characteristically of European descent, and the population density in rural areas is very low. Historically, the Pampas have been the core of Argentina's agro-export model, reliant on capitalist agriculture, and where farmers first adopted the technological package of GM soy. Eighty-seven percent of the country's herbicide-resistant soybeans is grown in this region.[112] Since the early 2000s, the agrarian frontier has expanded past the Pampas into the northern Chaco region, over the provinces of Chaco, Formosa, Salta, and Santiago del Estero. The northern Chaco forest is the largest forest ecosystem and the largest biomass reservoir in Argentina and extra-tropical South America.[113] The Chaco region relies on forestry and cotton production. In terms of population, it hosts a mix of people of

Map I.1. Map of Argentina, showing the Pampas region and the area of soybean production. Created by the author with data from Argentina's Secretary of Agroindustry. Map drawn by Bill Nelson.

European descent and the majority of indigenous peoples who live in Argentina. The region has historically been poor and marginalized.

I take a multilevel, multimethod approach to capture the synergies of power. I used a variety of qualitative methods, including interviews, participant observation, and content analysis, to gather data on the micro- and meso-levels of interactions, culture, and community. I relied on quantitative data from online databases to grasp the macro-level of the political economy and the meso-level of farms and rural towns. I relied on statistical information on economic and social development from the Observatory of Economic Complexity, the Economic Commission for Latin America and the Caribbean, and the Argentine government, particularly the Ministry of Agriculture, Livestock, and Fisheries (Secretary of Agroindustry since 2016) and the INDEC.

My fieldwork took place mostly in the Pampas region during four different visits from 2009 to 2015, though I made one visit to the Chaco region in July and August of 2011 (to the provinces of Chaco and Santiago del Estero, in particular). In the Pampas, I visited small and larger rural towns in the center, northwest, and southeast of Buenos Aires province and the center and south of Córdoba province in December 2009 to January 2010, June and August 2011, January to April 2012, and August 2015. I conducted forty-five formal interviews with soybean producers; agribusiness employees, investors, and consultants; rural inhabitants; indigenous-peasant and anti-fumigation activists; and Argentine academic experts. I use pseudonyms for interviewees and places of residence when I tell their stories, except when I refer to public figures.

While this is a case study of agrarian transformation, not all my interviews took place in rural areas. I interviewed activists and academics in the cities of Córdoba, Buenos Aires, Bahía Blanca, Rosario, and Santiago del Estero. I interviewed agribusiness leaders, investors, and employees in these cities and even in a summer resort on the coast of Buenos Aires province (during the summer of 2012). Soybean production, as I show, can be managed from afar, and that is a key to acquiescence. While there are soybean producers and employees living in rural towns, the technological package allows a highly qualified labor force to manage very large areas of farmland from a distance—aided by technologies like computers, cell phones, and satellites. Many people with decision-making power over agrarian production do not live in rural areas (and, thus, they do not have to bear a critical cost of soybean production: exposure to agrochemical spraying). I interviewed soybean producers, investors, and employees in the least likely of places to be considered part of the rural sector, from the wealthy Recoleta neighborhood in downtown Buenos Aires to the beach.

Most of my formal interviews were with men. That was not because I purposely decided to do so, but because I decided I would study Argentina's agrarian transformation based on the adoption of GM biotechnology. The agribusiness model is male-dominated; men of European descent are mostly in charge of organizing and performing production. I realized later that I took this fact so much for granted that I did not see it as special, as something that needed to be problematized. It took me a long time to realize I was spending most of my "downtime" during fieldwork in rural towns with women, but by the time the formal interviews would start or when I was to visit the farms, the women would leave me "to do my work" and men would lead me into "what I have to know."

However, in one town in particular, which I call Santa María, my main informant, Nidia, was close to my own family, and she took me in, I felt, like her own daughter. Thanks to this, I gained insider status among a tight-knit group of women/mothers quite quickly. We cooked together, washed dishes, and sipped *mates* while watching over children who refused to take their siesta in the hot summer of February 2012. I believe I gained the confidence of these women thanks to Nidia, of course, but also because they saw me as their equal: a cisgender woman of childbearing age who, like them, is a middle-class woman of European descent born and raised in the Pampas. They assumed that marriage (undoubtedly heterosexual) and raising children were in my near future. Thus, I believe that in their minds I shared their potential worries over children's health. The unspoken subtext was always, "You understand because you are a woman and thus a future mother." As I write in chapter 3, these interactions puzzled me. I am not a mother, and I do not believe that women have, by nature, a mother's sixth sense. As a sociologist, I explain the so-called mother's intuition to care about children's health (the women activists I write about in chapter 4 also emphasized that) as a gendered way of knowing that is a result of gendered structures (as I detail in chapter 3). Yet these interactions were so powerful that they gave me new insight.

While in the field, across rural towns in the Pampas, people like Leo told me repeatedly, "We do the best agriculture in the world" and "We all live off the countryside." Who am I, as an outsider, to doubt my interviewees? To claim that they live in an unjust situation, that there are potential or latent grievances that should lead to mobilization? It was this group of women who, in close connection among equals, shared their worries and fears with me and exposed the contradiction between what people were saying and what they were worrying about. That is, they exposed the latent grievances I was looking for—latent grievances that I was able to notice later as being unspoken in other conversations, even with the men. For a moment, they unveiled the elephant for me. In this book, I explain why they have to veil it again and again, why they keep silent in the face of the health hazards of agrochemical exposure. My hope is that this book voices what for them, in the Pampas, remains unspeakable.

1. The Roots of the Soy Model

Germán is an agronomist and a part-time professor of agricultural engineering at the National University, where I met him in his office on a cold winter day in July 2011. "Outside of the university," he told me, he is "also a producer and a son of producers, a consultant for sowing-pool agribusinesses, and a member of the Argentine Association of Direct Sowing Producers" (known as AAPRESID).

"So many hats!" I said. "How do you define yourself primarily?"

"As a *productor-asesor* [producer-consultant]," he said. "I have a pragmatic view of production. That is the difference I have with the other professors. Apart from a concern over technical evaluations, I look at the economic viability, among other things, as it relates to every productive system in a business [empresa]. It is part of my vision, to think beyond technical and scientific matters."

Germán is a tall, blond, blue-eyed man in his early forties. That day he was dressed in a light blue shirt, a fleece vest, jeans, and leather sneakers: informal for a professor but far too formal for farming. His was a common look among many Pampas producers I interviewed. It is common on TV too, on the programs of *Canal Rural*, the Rural Channel on cable. I came to call this style "chacarero chic," a variation of typical clothing worn by chacareros but adapted to farming from the city. (When outdoors, some complete the style by wearing a *boina*, the typical chacarero beret, and a handkerchief tied around the neck.) The people in charge of farming in the Pampas are no longer chacareros but producers, as Germán described himself, and entrepreneurs overseeing the farm as a business. Their clothing links back to the rural tradition in the Pampas but is updated for living in the city, where much of the large-scale farming is managed remotely.

Germán runs a 650-hectare family farm in southeastern Buenos Aires province; 430 of those hectares are planted with commercial crops—wheat, barley, sunflowers, soybeans, and corn—and the remaining 220 hectares are dedicated to livestock production. The southeast of the province is cut through by the Sierra de la Ventana, creating a fragmented topography and rolling hills that are uncharacteristic of the flat landscape of the Pampas. It also has a colder and drier climate than the rest of the Pampas region, known as the "humid Pampas." Environmental conditions make the southeast less suited for soybeans, which require a mild wet climate, deeper soils, and flat terrain to accommodate the no-till/direct-seeding machinery.

By any other measure, a 650-hectare farm is large (it is slightly over 1,600 acres and about twice the area of Central Park in New York City). But in Argentina's agriculture industry, Germán is considered a medium-size producer. The median farm in Argentina, according to the latest rural census of 2008, has 620 hectares. This criterion has increased over the years, up from 469 hectares in 1988 and 588 in 2002.[1] This shift to relatively larger farms is trending across the United States as well, but even the median US farm is smaller than that in Argentina. (The median farm size in the United States is 1,234 acres or slightly less than 500 hectares.)[2] Very large farms have also increased alongside medium-size ones in Argentina, though there has been a reduction in the total number of farms, thus showing a trend for increasing concentration and growing inequality. In Argentina in 2008, 10.2 percent of very large farms (of more than 1,000 hectares) occupied a staggering 79 percent of the farmland. Of those, only 2.2 percent of megafarms (of more than 5,000 hectares) held over 50 percent of the land.[3]

Germán's family inherited the farm from his great-grandparents, who emigrated from Germany during the early 1900s at the peak of European migration to Argentina. Germán is the only one still in the farming business; his siblings have professional jobs and live in the city. Germán lives in the city too, but he commutes often to the farm, which is about two hours away. Though he is in charge of organizing production, he neither operates nor owns any machinery, relying completely on contractors to do the agricultural tasks of sowing, agrochemical spraying, and harvesting. He has only one permanent employee, who lives on the farm and is in charge of the livestock. That, however, is "not very efficient," according to Germán, because the ideal would be one person for every five hundred cows. "The problem," he said, "is that I, with only 150 cows, have one employee. . . .

I cannot cut him in half!" and burst out laughing. The other most important task for *el encargado de la chacra*, his rural worker who lives on-site, is to guard the *estancia*, the ranch or manor typical of large farms in the Pampas. Surrounded by a well-groomed garden with large trees, the estancia now houses the family only on long weekends and summer vacations.

Germán and I spent most of our time talking about how to make agricultural production in the Pampas profitable, "the main goal" of farming in his words. To achieve this, technological innovation is key. In Argentina, he said, the "level of technology is very high; we are at the cutting edge." I was told this repeatedly throughout my fieldwork. Technological innovation is ingrained in the history of the Argentine Pampas, a history that Germán seemed very proud to be a part of.

He described how "we" Argentines "were at a time world leaders" in agrarian technologies: "The first combine harvester [cosechadora autopropulsada] in the world was Argentine, from the 1930s! My grandparents went on a honeymoon to Europe, and when they told people there that we had combine harvesters in Argentina, no one believed them; they were accused of lying!" He continued, "At that time, we were more advanced than the Europeans."

"What happened afterwards, then?" I asked.

"Well . . . after that, came decadence [la decadencia]. In the 1930s, we were the granary of the world. We were on a par in everything, in GDP, with Australia, with Canada. And then we went downhill [nos vinimos abajo], while Australia and Canada became what they are today," he explained.

The stark contrast with what Argentina *was*, that moment in time in the early twentieth century when the country was on a similar path to development as other settler countries, is practically a folktale in Argentina. This guiding myth is particularly strong when contrasted with contemporary Argentina. Germán called it "la decadencia," Argentina's downhill slope, the reverse of development. It is the despair that follows a promise and potential unfulfilled, as Argentina is today not part of the rich Global North, like Australia and Canada, but subject to recurrent economic crises like many nations of the Global South.

However. In a twist I heard often, despair and crises were countered by the country's agricultural progress. Germán continued: "As far as I understand it, the reality of the agricultural sector is different from that of the rest of the country. While the country is not at the top in global terms [el país no es punta a nivel mundial], the agricultural sector is." Germán was unequivocal in his affirmation. "Today," he said, "in terms of the technologies employed and the level of [agrarian] technological innovation, we are world-class."

What explains the early and vast adoption of herbicide-resistant soybeans in the Argentine Pampas? The basic explanation is that growing commercial crops with cutting-edge technology makes the farm an economically viable business. That is the main goal of farming in the Pampas, as Germán said, to make it profitable, and GM soy meets that goal. But, besides providing important economic benefits, Germán's story highlights other important reasons why Argentine farmers have embraced GM biotechnology. First, the swift adoption of herbicide-resistant soybeans needs to be understood within the historical context of capitalist agriculture in the Pampas. Germán, calling himself "a producer and a son of producers," with his clothing and his stories about immigrant great-grandparents and the mechanized family farm, situates himself in this proud history. Two centuries of Argentine history resulted in people like him—middle- and upper-class men of European descent who are professionals, technicians, and entrepreneurs—holding decision-making power over large commercial farms and working hundreds of hectares with the sole help of cutting-edge technology and contracted labor. In tracing the synergies of power that have made the agricultural industry in the Pampas the unequal yet unchallenged territory that it is today, we have to look at it from a historical perspective. Because time accumulates unequal and unjust effects, temporality is key to the synergies of power. By the turn of the twenty-first century, feminized and racialized subjects had been occupying the lowest rung of the social ladder for a century and thus hold no decision-making power over farming in the Pampas.

Germán's story also highlights how supporters attach cultural and social benefits to GM biotechnology that cannot be fully disentangled from the profit motive. Economic growth achieved with increased mechanization and technification of the farm is associated with development, modernization, and progress—not just for the individual or private business but for the country as a whole. The adoption of GM biotechnology and the commodity export boom represent a glimmer of hope for a return to prominence, Argentina's rightful claim to its role as the "granary of the world."

A key explanation for the swift adoption of herbicide-resistant soybeans lies in the historic shape of Argentina's political economy. Agro-industrial production for export has been at the core of Argentina's development project since its birth as a nation-state in the nineteenth century. In this chapter, I trace the historical and cultural roots of the political economy of soybean extractivism to expose how structural and symbolic inequalities were seeded and emerged. I show how members of the nineteenth-century elite used their material and discursive power to shape and legitimate Argentina's unequal structure. They set the stage for the first agro-export boom in the early twentieth century, when Argentina became known as the granary of the world and was, effectively, as rich as Canada and Australia. I go on to connect that to the political economy of soybean extractivism today. Ultimately, I conclude that powerful state and corporate actors build on structural inequalities and symbolic myths of national identity to promote acquiescence and consent over a model of development based on large-scale agriculture for export.

Building the Argentine Nation

Argentina won independence from Spain in 1816. Under Spanish colonial rule, Buenos Aires was the capital of the Viceroyalty of the Río de la Plata, the latest of the Spanish viceroyalties to be established (in 1776) and the shortest in duration. Across more than three centuries and from New Orleans to Buenos Aires, the Spanish Empire had established a system based on the extraction and exportation of the region's abundant natural resources for the benefit of European economies at high human and ecological cost.[4] Potosí, Bolivia, is one example of a city that has suffered from what Alberto Acosta calls Latin America's "curse of wealth." Once the "jugular vein" of the empire and "America's fountain of silver," as Eduardo Galeano describes it, Potosí was one of the world's richest and largest cities.[5] By the end of Spanish rule, 40,000 tons of silver ore had been extracted from its Rich Hill and siphoned abroad.[6] Today, Bolivia is one of the poorest countries in the world. As for Argentina, the Spanish Empire devastated the human and ecological wealth of the northwest and northeast of the country, but it spared the central Pampas, mostly because it found the area lacking.[7] The natural landscape did not provide gold or silver, and it did not have the tropical climate necessary to grow cotton or sugar, precious commodities to the empire. As the capital of the Viceroyalty of the Río de la Plata, Buenos Aires was significant not for its own natural riches but as a commodity trading port. It was the closest to Potosí and, other than Montevideo, was one of the only Spanish ports on the southern Atlantic Ocean, the most direct route to European markets.[8]

Soon after Argentina's independence, the criollo elite set to the task of creating a nation-state where there was none. Argentina was constructed by uniting multiple scattered pieces.[9] There was the main city, Buenos Aires, home of the elite, former capital of the viceroyalty, linked to Europe through its port. There were a handful of smaller cities, like Tucumán, Salta, Jujuy, Santiago del Estero, and Córdoba, which had been important inland trading hubs during colonial times. There were the Pampas, the vast grasslands controlled by big landowners known as *hacendados*, scarcely populated with cattle, sheep, and mestizo and indigenous peoples. And there were some smaller, scattered rural towns and villages producing for domestic consumption. What remained was a huge landmass, ostensibly unlimited, unknown, and unexplored in the view of the Buenos Aires–based elite. Nothing united these scattered pieces: there was no sense of shared history or future, no shared myths of peoplehood. Defining *nation-ness*, creating a national identity, became a project that the intellectual elite in Buenos Aires set out to do almost from scratch. Similar efforts were taking place continentwide, throughout the newly independent nations of Latin America.[10]

In Argentina, a group of young intellectuals referred to as the Generation of 1837 began creating the myths of national identity that were essential for uniting the country.[11] In *The Invention of Argentina*, Nicolas Shumway calls these myths "guiding fictions." They are the stories that make up national identities. In the United States, for example, there are the myths of America as "a melting pot" and of the "American Dream." These stories, most significantly, do not have to be real to be believed and acted on. As Shumway notes, the "guiding fictions of nations cannot be proven, and indeed are often fabrications as artificial as literary fictions. Yet they are necessary to give individuals a sense of nation, peoplehood, collective identity, and national purpose."[12]

The Generation of 1837 was deeply embedded in the spirit of the time. Latin American intellectuals from the 1830s to the 1870s were often men who held many simultaneous positions across government, academia, the arts, science, and commerce.[13] Many of them were the children of Europeans and had been educated in Europe, and they turned north to understand the Southern Cone. They admired the revolutionary feats of France and the United States. Their values and ideals were modeled after

French positivism and British liberalism. Jean-Jacques Rousseau, Alexis de Tocqueville, Auguste Comte, Adam Smith, and David Ricardo were the authors they read and admired. Progress, industrialization, and free trade were their cherished beliefs. Modernity was their ultimate goal.[14]

The "modernization is progress" ideology that these intellectuals espoused and their alignment with positivist ideals were not unique to Argentina; they were shared among the intellectual elites in many newly independent countries in Latin America, such as Mexico, Chile, and Colombia.[15] While these intellectuals learned from European philosophy, science, and history, their modernity project was not an exact copy of European modernity. These lettered men were of European descent but, unlike their predecessors, did not live under colonial rule. Thus, they learned from Europe, but they also aimed to develop and test their own ideas. In other words, their project for modernity was neither autochthonous nor imposed from abroad but rather was a mixture or a hybrid, adapted to the realities of these nations as peripherals, as countries dependent on the exploitation of their natural resources for foreign income.[16]

The Argentine nation-building project took shape from these values and ideals, and as such, Argentine national identity and modernity became inextricably linked. Of the Generation of 1837, Domingo F. Sarmiento (1811–88), Juan Bautista Alberdi (1810–84), and Esteban Echeverría (1805–51) were the ones who contributed the most to the task of defining *la argentinidad* (Argentineness).[17] Skillful writers, they used novels and essays to craft a national identity after independence. Sarmiento's *Facundo: Civilization and Barbarism* (published in 1845) and Alberdi's *Bases and Starting Points for the Political Organization of the Argentine Republic* (1852) are considered the seminal texts of Argentine national identity.[18] These books established the guiding myths that conceived of the Pampas as fertile ground for agricultural modernization and of Argentina as an agro-exporting nation.

Civilization or Barbarism

The disease from which the Argentine Republic suffers is its own expanse: the desert wilderness surrounds it on all sides and insinuates into its bowels; solitude, a barren land with no human habitation, in general are the unquestionable borders between one province and another. There, immensity is everywhere: immense plains, immense forests, immense rivers, the horizon always unclear, always confused with the earth amid swift-moving clouds and tenuous mists,

which do not allow the point where the world ends and the sky begins to be marked in a far-off perspective.
—Sarmiento, *Facundo*

The famous opening lines to Sarmiento's *Facundo* summarize how the intellectual elite assessed the Argentine situation in the wake of independence. The goal of the nation-building project was to make Argentina modern, but from the elites' perspective, many obstacles were impeding Argentina's path to join the civilized nations of the world.[19] The men of the Generation of 1837 called these obstacles to development *males*, "ills." As Sarmiento wrote, in a classic functionalist analysis of society, Argentina suffered from disease.[20] What problems needed to be addressed in order to "cure" the Argentine Republic? The intellectual elite of the nineteenth century identified three. First, there was *la tierra*, "the land," the wild rural territory, or what Sarmiento called "the desert"; second, the Catholic Spanish tradition, the religion of the masses and of conservatives; and, third, *la raza* (the race), the nonwhites who populated the rural territory: gauchos (ethnically mixed rural men) and *indios* (the original and derogatory term to refer to indigenous peoples).[21]

Sarmiento's book, in title and content, simplified the ideas of his generation into a formula: "civilization or barbarism." The "civilization" of the metropolis was opposed to the "barbarism" of rural living. It was a dichotomous view of Argentine society whereby the countryside and its rural, mixed-race, and indigenous populations represented the source of disease in Argentina, while the city, such as Buenos Aires, Paris, or London, was the prescription, the model of what Argentina should become.[22] Racism was imbued in the character of the epoch; neither Sarmiento nor his peer intellectuals across the region challenged or questioned racist hierarchies as social problems. On the contrary, "racial theories were central to many positivists' prescriptions for social and political reform," including those of Sarmiento in Argentina, Justo Sierra in Mexico, and José María Samper and Mariano Ospina in Colombia.[23]

Sarmiento was influenced by positivist ideas and the feats of the Industrial Revolution. In his writing, "barbarism" is the wild nature, the unexplored rural territories, and indigenous peoples. His examples of "civilization" are in northern Europe and the United States: the factories of Britain, the high culture of Parisians, and the work ethic of Protestant farmers in the United States. In *Facundo*, the Pampas are a dangerous place. Sarmiento warns the reader of the possibilities of getting bitten by a snake, savaged by a tiger, or attacked by the "wild indians." He also dreads the vagaries of the weather, telling menacing stories of thunderstorms in the open fields. For every story he tells of the ugliness and dangers of rural life, Sarmiento poses the beauty of theaters and literary societies in Buenos Aires.

Sarmiento blamed the land for the Argentine disease. Nature, from his perspective, conditioned (negatively) Argentine political and social life.[24] As a man of modernity, he believed that natural landscapes were problematic: they were still unseen by the European scientific gaze and untouched by capitalism. It was the *unproductive* land that is the source of the so-called ills, the land that is not yet subdued to human and machine power. Sarmiento points to the potential productive capacity of the countryside, how the Pampas region was meant for agricultural production:

> In the center, parallel zone, the Pampas and the jungle dispute the land for a long while; the forest dominates in places, then breaks down into sickly, spiny bushes; the jungle appears again thanks to some river that favors it, until in the south the Pampas finally triumph and display their smooth, downy brow, infinite, with no known limit, no noteworthy break. It is an image of the sea on land, the land as it looks on the map, the land still waiting for a command to produce plants and all kinds of seeds.[25]

In the mid-nineteenth century, when Sarmiento wrote these lines, the ecology of the Pampas region had long been transformed by Spanish colonization. When the Spanish arrived, they, too, probably found it deserted, especially in comparison to the lush tropics and the massive Aztec and Inca Empires. The Pampas region was then a vast flat landscape of tall grasses and not many trees. It comprised 52 million hectares spotted infrequently by *ombú* (the native evergreen tree of the Pampas), small forests (*montes*) of *chañar* (a yellowish small spiny tree, probably the sickly bushes Sarmiento wrote about), and patches of trees (native willows, *ceibos*, *sarandíes*, and spiny *acacias negras*) abundant only at the margins of a handful of rivers, because, as Sarmiento noted, the river favors them. Indigenous tribes were hunters, but big animals were scarce due to scant fresh water or vegetation, limiting how large tribes could become. The guanaco, an animal close to the llama, was the basis of the natives' diet, and thus tribes spread over the region to hunt it.[26]

The Spanish radically transformed the society-ecosystem relations of the Pampas region by introducing cows, sheep, and horses as well as commercial crops such as wheat, barley, and alfalfa.[27] They also brought the plow, an agrarian technology previously unknown to the region. When Sarmiento wrote *Facundo*, the Pampas were sheep- and cattle-ranching territory. After independence, Buenos Aires had lost its most precious export commodity: the silver from Potosí. The port city then survived almost exclusively from livestock-derived exports: leather from cows and feral horses (known in Argentina as *cuero bagual*), dry salted beef (known as *tasajo*), and wool.[28]

Yet while livestock-derived commodity exports were the source of most of Buenos Aires's foreign income, Sarmiento still perceived the Pampas as an unproductive region. Why? Because of his modernization mindset. From this perspective, efficiency is measured in quantitative terms and relates to the ability to control production to keep a homogeneous and, most important, *predictable* flow.[29] Nature, without human or machine intervention, does not comply with the efficiency standards of capitalism. Livestock, free to roam among the vast grasslands, graze at will and become fat unevenly depending on the quality of the grass—grass that depends on the quality of the soil, which depends on variable weather across four different seasons. Compared to the British factories that Sarmiento so admired, the Pampas are a terribly unreliable place to do business. The British Industrial Revolution stood on the scientific discovery of coal-based energy: a source of energy that, unlike rivers and wind that were previously used to pump mills, can be controlled, shipped, and stored. It also stood on the development of a very special machine: the clock.[30] Thanks to the artifice of the clock and steady energy to move machines and provide artificial lighting, every working day at the factory could begin at 6 a.m., rain or shine, summer or winter. Thus, to civilize the Pampas, Sarmiento and his fellow intellectuals proposed industrializing them to make them as efficient and productive as a British factory.

Sarmiento's civilization/barbarism dichotomy became the motto of Argentina's young intellectual elite and, with time, has become the most basic way in which Argentines still understand their country.[31] It is one of Argentina's most enduring guiding fictions. Pampas producers, like Germán, celebrate the technological package of herbicide-resistant soybeans in the light of this guiding myth: GM biotechnology is a cutting-edge technology that produces a homogeneous, reliable, and profitable product in an efficient manner. If Sarmiento were to see the Pampas now, its unending neat rows of soybeans, he would be proud. Except for a handful of protected natural areas, the Pampas region is either farmed or built.[32] Nature has been duly conquered and subdued. The region is a factory of commercial crops.

Poblar el Desierto (To Populate the Desert)

Juan Bautista Alberdi, another member of the Generation of 1837, was responsible for developing the main program to "civilize" Argentina. Alberdi's program put forth promoting emigration from Europe and, second, freeing up trade.[33] Following economic liberal theory advanced by Adam Smith and David Ricardo, Alberdi believed that countries should specialize in producing and exporting what they produce more efficiently (in terms of cost benefit). When all countries do so and trade their goods and services, they are all better off, and therefore trade is to every country's advantage. Argentina's comparative advantage, like that of other Latin American nations, is its wealth of natural resources. Alberdi's perception of nature was less dramatic than Sarmiento's. He saw the Pampas as a bountiful resource demanding exploitation.[34] His vision for Argentina was a hybrid of European modernization adapted to the Pampas landscape. Thus, his plan focused on how to make the rural territory productive in industrial terms.

Alberdi recommended a move away from livestock exports to specialize in agriculture, which is both capital and labor intensive. If the Argentine government did not have enough funds to invest in adequate technology, then, he suggested, "let others do it." Alberdi recommended abolishing all protective tariffs and opening up the country to foreign investments, loans, and partnerships to jump-start the process of technological transformation. For Alberdi, the solution to Argentine development problems would then involve "some sort of appeal to Europe and the United States, through imitation, immigration, investment or imported technology."[35]

The projects and ideals envisioned by the Generation of 1837 became a reality in a relatively short time. In the 1880s, the political and intellectual elite known as Generación del '80 consolidated the modern nation-state and the agro-export model. Under the presidency of Julio Roca (1880–86), the Generation of 1880 sponsored European immigration into Argentina and created a national system of free, secular, and mandatory primary education, a strategy for the socialization and assimilation of the newly arrived immigrants.[36] (This project was led by Sarmiento himself, first as president [1868–74] and then, under Roca, as superintendent general of schools for the education ministry.) They, too, set up a model of economic development based on Alberdi's program.[37] Thus began, in the late nineteenth century, the process of modernizing the Pampas through the promotion of European immigration and foreign direct investment for technology transfers and infrastructure development. This process reached its peak at the turn of the twentieth century with the agro-export boom of 1870 to 1914, when Argentina became known as the granary of the world.

Populating the vast territory and expanding industrial agriculture in the Pampas came about through massive emigration from Europe. In 1840, before massive migration began, the country's population was fewer than 700,000 inhabitants and was mostly concentrated in the northwest. The Pampas had, at the time, a population density of one person per 100 hectares.[38] Most criollos lived in the city, in Buenos Aires. Rural areas were mainly populated by gauchos. At that time, these men were mostly mestizos, ethnically mixed, the sons of indigenous mothers and conquistador fathers. They were landless and usually vagrant, living off small rural jobs. They primarily worked in sheep and cattle ranching on the big estates (estancias) owned by the hacendados, who were often of Spanish descent.[39]

Anything outside the humid Pampas was beyond the control of the Buenos Aires–based government and, except for the former colonial towns in the northwest, was in fact under the control of indigenous groups. The goal, then, became to populate what, from the elites' perspective, was "the desert" and "the land of barbarism." In order to do so, the government engaged in a colonization program quite similar to that in the United States. With the help of private colonization companies, Europeans were recruited to migrate to Argentina, often with transportation costs covered. They were promised land to cultivate at arrival (in a tenancy system, unlike direct ownership as in the United States), a home, and agricultural tools and seeds.[40]

Starting in the 1850s, the port of Buenos Aires became to Argentina what Staten Island was to the United States: the port of entry for millions of Europeans who landed on shore to make a new home in the New World. Between 1870 and 1914, the peak of European migration to Argentina, 5.9 million people got off the boat; 3.2 million of them remained, making Argentina their permanent home.[41] Most were from Italy, Spain, France, Germany, Switzerland, Wales, and the Netherlands. Many Russian Jews migrated to Argentina during this time too; escaping the violence of the Russian pogroms, they were brought over by the Jewish Colonization Association, led by the German Jewish financier and philanthropist Baron Hirsch. While many European immigrants stayed in the city, many others, as planned by the government, settled in the countryside in settlements known as *colonias*.[42] They thus became known as colonos and gringos. The farm came to be called *chacra*, and the gringos who farmed it, chacareros.

But there was no such "desert," in either geographic or demographic terms.[43] The Pampas and beyond, the Gran Chaco region in the north and Patagonia in the south, were occupied by indigenous peoples. Spanish colonial power had decimated native peoples and landscapes by establishing a model based on natural resource extraction for exportation. The Argentine northwest was the southern frontier of the Inca Empire, which the Spanish destroyed.[44] The northeast was populated by seminomadic tribes of Guaraníes, many of whom, like Incas and so many other natives, were forcefully removed to work as slaves in mines and plantations across the region.[45] Yet, despite the rabid violence and widespread pillage of the Spanish conquest, Buenos Aires–based elites still had a "barbarian" problem.

By the late nineteenth century, the frontier to settle the contour of the nation-state was weak as a result of decades of civil war post-independence. Moreover, indigenous peoples stormed it often in looting raids. To complete the nation-building project, then, it would be necessary to wage war against the "barbarians" beyond the control of Buenos Aires. Here we can see parallels with US history and its guiding myths of "manifest destiny" and making the Western "wasteland" productive by clearing it of native peoples and large animals. The darker side of the modernization project was the near-extermination of the indigenous populations blocking the path to "progress."

"The constitution of Argentina as a nation-state in the late 19th century," Gastón Gordillo and Silvia Hirsch argue, "was based on the systematic attempt to eliminate, silence, or assimilate its indigenous population." Between 1874 and 1880, the national government launched a series of large military campaigns to conquer the territory for "civilizing" purposes.[46] The aim was to subdue indigenous peoples and to settle the geopolitical borders with neighboring Brazil and Paraguay in the north and with Chile over southern Patagonia. In 1878, then-General Julio Roca led the campaign known as the "conquest of the desert" to tame the territory from Buenos Aires down to the Río Negro, the known frontier of Patagonia. It was a military campaign over the Pampas region, land of Puelches, Pehuenches, and Ranqueles, and over the Patagonia region, land of Tehuelches and Mapuches. These groups were helpless against an armed military that greatly outnumbered them. In total, there were no more than 12,000 indigenous peoples in groups no larger than 4,000, scattered over millions of hectares across the Pampas and the Patagonia regions. They had only lances, bows and arrows, and *boleadoras* with which to fight back.[47] General Roca's men used Remington rifles, the latest of technological innovations, to subjugate indigenous groups. Similar military campaigns were also sent north into the Chaco region, where they defeated Toba (Qom) and Mocoví (Moqoit) groups.[48]

The killing and displacement of indigenous peoples and the expropriation of their land made agrarian capitalism possible in Argentina, in a process David Harvey terms "accumulation by dispossession."[49] The success of General Roca's military venture gave the national government control over millions of hectares. These public lands, writes Felipe Pigna, had been intended for the settlement of colonos under immigration law; instead, they were distributed among a small number of wealthy families who had financed the military campaign through prior land sales. In the aftermath of the "conquest of the desert," over 8.5 million hectares passed into the hands of only 391 individuals.[50] The Pampas, tamed and under the control of the elite, became the cleared ground on which to settle the foundational stones of the Argentine Republic.

The consequences of the civilizing project are lasting. The process of colonizing and "whitening" Argentina continued throughout the twentieth century.[51] Most indigenous and peasant families were marginalized to smaller and smaller territories in the Argentine north in the provinces of Salta, Jujuy, Tucumán, Chaco, Santiago del Estero, Formosa, and Misiones.[52] In a 2004–5 national survey on indigenous peoples in Argentina, fewer than 460,000 people self-identified as indigenous. The survey accounted for thirty-one different groups, some large, such as the Mapuches, Kolla, Toba, and Wichí (accounting for 60 percent of all indigenous peoples), and many smaller ones with fewer than one thousand people. In the 2010 census, almost a million people identified as indigenous, accounting for 2.4 percent of the total population.[53] As I explain in chapter 4, this higher number is the consequence of a new wave of indigenous activism across Latin America and in Argentina starting in the 1990s and the inclusion of indigenous rights in the new Argentine Constitution of 1994. Yet, despite their higher numbers and the diversity of cultures, languages, and traditions, indigenous peoples in Argentina are still at a disadvantage to the rest of the population. Generally, they lack access to formal education, and their literacy levels are much lower than those of the average population. Too often they lack access to health care, particularly those who live in rural areas. In general, indigenous peoples in Argentina face situations of great social and economic vulnerability.[54]

"By and large, public policies and research 'invisibilized' peasant populations," Pablo Lapegna argues, "subsuming the regional economics of the Argentine North into the Pampas, while conceptualizing peasants in negative terms—as an actor lacking capitalization or having a marginal participation in the creation of value."[55] Unlike other Latin American nations such as Brazil, Mexico, and Peru, Argentina successfully aimed to erase its indigenous and mestizo heritage. Contemporary Argentina claims to be urban, white, and European.[56] Discussions about race and racism are foreign to everyday life. But while most Argentines would claim that racism is not a social problem, race-based discrimination and verbal abuse against poor, mestizo, and indigenous people persist. As I show in chapter 4, the use of violence and racism against indigenous peasants who fight in defense of what remains of their territory continues today.

The Granary of the World

The project envisioned by the elite of the nineteenth century quickly bore fruit. The countryside, pacified and cleared of unruly populations and unpredictable natural patterns, gave way to a wave of European immigrants as well as foreign loans, infrastructure, and technologies. The Pampas began to have the industrial farms envisioned by Sarmiento, Alberdi, and the like. From 1880 to 1914, Argentina saw the consolidation and success of a model of development based on the production and exportation of grains and livestock-derived products. The Pampas became the motor of the first agro-export boom, and with it another myth of national identity was created—that of Argentina, "el granero del mundo," responsible for feeding the hungry mouths of the world.[57]

Argentina entered what Harriet Friedmann and Philip McMichael term the "first food regime" as a provider of grains and livestock to Great Britain.[58] British intervention through loans, credits, and direct investment was essential for the development of the agro-export model of the late nineteenth century. Railroads and ports built and financed by the British, as well as new technological developments, including the transoceanic refrigerated ship (essential for transporting beef), linked production in the Pampas to European markets. New planting and harvesting machinery were introduced from the United States, Great Britain, and France. New breeding techniques and breeds of cattle were introduced at the time as well.[59] In exchange for technology transfers and infrastructure development, Argentina's temperate food exports (alongside tropical foods from its former colonies) fed the growing British working class, upholding British hegemony and "underwriting the British 'workshop of the world.'"[60]

The boom was real. Income growth per capita at the time was among the highest in the world.[61] Argentina was on par with Canada and Australia—countries that had recently gained independence and were exporting their temperate foodstuffs to Great Britain—and shared their potential to join the rich nations of the world. By 1914, Argentina had become the third largest grain exporter in the world, exporting more than 50 percent of its wheat production, almost two-thirds of its corn, and more than 80 percent of its flaxseed.[62] Argentina's production accounted for two-thirds of global corn exports, 20 percent of wheat, 80 percent of all flaxseed, and 60 percent of global beef exports. By 1929, GDP per-capita levels were 86 percent of that of Australia and 90 percent of that of Canada.[63] The Argentine countryside was producing vast amounts of food and foreign income. These "golden years" of the Pampas settled on a mixed model of agriculture and cattle production.[64] Huge waves of Europeans arrived to populate Argentine territory. Their children became Sarmiento's version of Argentine citizens, thanks to the newly developed public education system. The model became a success, and from it, the myth was created. It was Argentina's belle époque.

The industrious colonos who settled across the Pampas made the grain-export boom possible. While the success of cattle ranching is attributed to wealthy landowners, the labor of millions of chacareros made large-scale agricultural production possible.[65] Yet they were not reaping its benefits. The rewards of the agro-export model were not spilling over to those who sustained it. By the turn of the twentieth century, the Pampas had become the land of mechanized, large-scale monocultures, not the welcoming pastures the immigrant colonos had dreamed of. The vast distance between farms, hundreds and hundreds of hectares, had a negative impact on social life. These enormous distances, Haim Avni explains, "separated the colonos from their friends, children from their schools, and to most farmers, from the town and the train station, and thus were a formidable obstacle to the development of an articulated agrarian society."[66]

The structure of landownership continued to be highly unequal and was another obstacle for agrarian development. When American sociologist Carl C. Taylor studied Argentine rural life in the 1940s, he celebrated the mechanized progress of the Pampas. But he also highlighted its very high levels of inequality. "The major portion of the land in the corn belt of the Pampas," Taylor explains, "is owned in large holdings but operated in moderately small farms." These "operating units were at one time parts of estancias" but were "converted partly or wholly into tenant-operated farms when cereal culture began to develop within the cattle belt." How large were the holdings? Huge. Taylor describes one of 45,000 acres, which is 18,000 hectares and larger than Washington, DC. Of this huge farm, Taylor continues: "15,000 acres are operated by a farm manager, his assistant and twenty-eight hired men; the other 30,000 acres are operated by 105 tenants (*colonos*). Each tenant is an entrepreneur living in his own home and operating his own farm enterprise."[67] The colonos whom Taylor described were crop farmers and operated between 120 and 300 acres each (around 50 to 120 hectares); thus, at the time, they were working at a larger scale than most corn-belt farmers in the United States. Land tenancy contracts were for three- to five-year periods depending on the farm, and rent was an amount equal to a set percentage of grain harvested, typically between 30 to 40 percent depending on the fertility of the land.

Unequal landholding patterns immediately resulted in highly unequal living conditions. Compare Taylor's account of the tenants who work on this large farm to those who own and manage it:

> The writer visited three tenants on this large farm. Two of them lived in mud houses with thatched roofs, the other house had adobe-brick walls with zinc roof, all had hard dirt floors. Two of them had cooking ranges, the other used an open fire. All the homes were lighted by kerosene lamps and candles, two had radios, one a bathroom. None of them had any heating equipment except that of the cookstove. All had chickens, vegetable and flower gardens.
>
> The 15,000-acre portion of the farm operated by *administración* (i.e., by a salaried farm manager) is managed by an Englishman, assisted by an English-speaking Argentine of Italian stock. They live

in a substantial, entirely modern house which sits in the beautifully landscaped estancia park. This park occupies about 160 acres of land, in the center of which is located the great estancia mansion—a house of not less than thirty rooms. In the park are great flower gardens, a tile swimming pool, a six-hole golf course, tennis courts, a polo field, and a chapel. The landscaping was done by an artist who planned some of the most beautiful parks in Buenos Aires. Members of the estanciero family occupy the mansion a few months each summer at the most.[68]

Most tenants could never afford to buy the farmland they were promised before boarding those boats that brought them from Europe into Argentina, so they slowly but steadily abandoned the farm and moved to the city.[69] Some were able to purchase land during periods of high grain prices; Germán's family is one of these success stories. But even they chose to send their children off to the city. "We have planted wheat and cultivated doctors," a popular saying, describes the rural exodus and the decrease in the number of farmers in the Pampas.[70]

European migrants were drawn to the city in Argentina. Migrating to the New World, Kristi Stølen argues, did not mean breaking with European culture and lifestyle.[71] Most people who landed in the city stayed there, leading Argentina to experience an early and rapid urban transition that was exceptional for Latin America. By 1914, the urban population outnumbered the rural population.[72] Most immigrant chacareros aspired to leave the farm after a few years of work. The goal of many European farmers in the Argentine Pampas was to make enough to send their children to the city to get an education and, for their daughters, to get married.[73]

These characteristics of early rural life in the Pampas left a long-lasting imprint in Argentine life and agriculture. Pampas farmers—gringos of European descent—populated the land and provided the labor for large-scale crop production, growing the wheat, corn, and flaxseed that, alongside beef exports at the turn of the twentieth century, made Argentina the granary of the world. They adapted to tenancy patterns of land leasing; instead of purchasing their own land, they prioritized reinvesting their profits in agrarian technologies to increase productivity.[74] They organized life and labor following traditional European gender roles and hierarchies, with women in charge of the household and men running the farm, and the women in the family (wives and daughters) were not expected to work on or manage the farm.[75] Indigenous peoples were displaced when not killed, pushed out of the agrarian frontier, and denied the benefits of the agro-export boom; they were invisibilized in the dominant narrative of a white, modern Argentina. And even the farmers preferred urban living. These characteristics were all but naturalized by the time I met Germán.

While not all colonos reaped the benefits of the agro-export boom, for some, their hard work paid off extremely well. That was the case for Abraham Grobocopatel, one of the Russian Jews who arrived on the boats of the Jewish Colonization Association.[76] In 1912, Abraham became a *gaucho judío*, a Jewish colono in Carlos Casares, a rural town in the center of Buenos Aires province. Abraham could not afford to buy land, but his son Bernardo could; in 1961, he bought 200 hectares. When Bernardo passed, he left 700 hectares to his sons, Adolfo and Jorge, who had worked on the family farm as tractor drivers. They continued to work and invest in the family business, which by the 1970s had grown to 3,000 hectares. Adolfo's son, Gustavo, moved to Buenos Aires to study at the National University. When Gustavo graduated as an agrarian engineer in 1984, he proposed that his father modernize the farm by incorporating computers and planting soy. The rest is history. Adolfo and Jorge divided the family farm, and then Adolfo and Gustavo Grobocopatel founded Los Grobo, one of the largest agribusinesses in the world.

Soybeans in the Pampas

Soybeans entered the Pampas in the late 1960s alongside the technologies of the Green Revolution. The first agro-export boom of the early twentieth century had busted by midcentury with the decline of global demand during the Great Depression and the Second World War. In the 1940s and 1950s, agricultural production in the Pampas declined as the government promoted an inward-looking model of development based on domestic industrialization.[77] During this time, populist leaders in Argentina and across the larger Latin American countries—Peru, Mexico, and Brazil—put forward a model known as import substitution industrialization (ISI) to break free of the colonial legacy of dependency on commodity exports.[78]

Juan Domingo Perón was most responsible for promoting the ISI model in Argentina. As he aimed to transcend the agro-export model and uproot the power of agrarian elites through state-promoted industrialization, he also developed a discourse that confronted the dominant myth of

Argentine identity as a modern nation. As Shumway argues, what emerged was a "competing" myth of nationhood in which the elements of "barbarism" were aggrandized and placed at the core of national identity.[79] Argentine identity is not one but two, dichotomous and opposed. It was Perón and his Peronista party who best articulated a nationalist and populist discourse that directly opposed the guiding myth of Argentina as a modern European nation. Under Peronismo, those who supported the agro-export model, particularly the large Pampas ranchers and landowners, were targeted as *imperialistas, oligarcas, vendepatrias*, "imperialists, oligarchs, traitors to the homeland." This discourse is still alive in contemporary Argentina and, as I show later, has continued to be strategically wielded by political elites of the Peronista party in the early twenty-first century. Yet, while the government stood in opposition to the agro-elites, there also was continuity. The push toward industrialization further promoted a dominant myth of Argentina as an urban nation that turned its back on its agrarian roots. Perón's populism was primarily an urban and industrial movement.[80] Under his administration, the state promoted industrial development mostly in the greater Buenos Aires area, encouraging internal migration from the provinces to the capital, further emptying the countryside.[81] Industrialization (mechanization and technification), though not in the name of nineteenth-century modernity, was still considered the path to development and progress via increased economic growth.

The late 1950s and the 1960s saw a renewal for agriculture in the Pampas with the adoption of the technologies of the Green Revolution.[82] The Green Revolution was the result of a public-private initiative aimed at addressing food security in the Global South via the transfer and exportation of agrarian technologies from the Global North, most significantly, hybrid seeds, machinery, and chemical pesticides and fertilizers.[83] From the 1940s to the late 1960s, the US government, the Rockefeller and Ford Foundations, and the World Bank funded agricultural programs in places like Mexico, South Korea, and India; their aim was to address what they argued was a looming Malthusian crisis. As part of this program, Norman Borlaug developed new varieties of hybrid crops, including wheat, corn, and rice. Eventually, Borlaug would receive a Nobel Prize for his scientific achievements and be celebrated worldwide as the father of the Green Revolution and genetically modified crops. He is particularly lauded in Argentina; for example, a 2011 institutional video for the Argentine Seed Association celebrates Borlaug's scientific developments for increasing yields and productivity, which allowed Argentina, as a pioneer innovator, to "produce food for a growing world population."[84] In chapter 2, I provide more examples to show how local corporate elites mobilize rhetoric about GM crops that naturally link the global Malthusian narrative distributed across the developed and developing world to the specific historical development and narrative of Argentina as a food producer, as the granary of the world.

The Green Revolution's results in terms of increasing food production are astonishing. Between 1960 and 1985, total food production more than doubled in the developing world. Yields increased dramatically and farmers could grow more food on less land.[85] The Argentine Pampas region was part of this explosion of productivity. Starting in the 1960s, the Pampas began to reclaim its role as the motor of the Argentine economy through its increased production of agricultural crops for export. New varieties of wheat, corn, sorghum, sunflower, and soybeans—"improved seeds" adopted in conjunction with a "complex technological package," Osvaldo Barsky and Jorge Gelman argue—resulted in "the productive and technological transformation of the Pampas."[86] Argentine scholars use the term *agriculturización* (agriculturization) to refer to the expansion of commercial crops by replacing cattle ranching across the Pampas.[87] The pace of this growth would only increase, and one crop would win the race. In the 1970s, soybeans accounted for less than 1 percent of the region's total agricultural production; by 2013, they were almost half. Since the early 2000s, agriculturización has given way to *sojización* (soyification): the massive expansion of soybean production due to crop substitution (the replacement of other commercial crops by soybeans) and its expansion over nonagricultural lands.[88]

The key to the swift expansion of soybeans across the Pampas was the 1996 approval of genetically modified herbicide-resistant seeds for commercialization and use.[89] As I will explain, neoliberal restructuring during the 1990s provided the most conducive institutional framework to pass these laws and for the consequent expansion of GM soybeans. Yet, as I have been illustrating, GM crops were not introduced to Argentina in a vacuum. Historical context is critical to understanding the current situation. The structural and symbolic characteristics of agriculture in the Pampas that emerged in the nineteenth and twentieth centuries have shaped what it is today: a large-scale capitalist industry generating commercial crops and led by men of European descent, to the exclusion of feminized and racialized subjects as actors with knowledge and decision-making power. During this time too, an urban nation was created—a country that depended on agricultural exports, but where the majority of its population lived in the city, and where the countryside had lost much of its natural environment, having been tamed and made productive by cutting-edge technologies.

Soybean Extractivism at the Turn of the Twenty-First Century

"Two key events mark the beginning of neoliberalism in the countryside," Norma Giarracca and Miguel Teubal told me in an interview in December 2009. Before her passing in 2016, Giarracca was a pioneering scholar of rural Latin America and a professor of rural sociology at the University of Buenos Aires (UBA). Teubal is a professor of economics at UBA and a researcher at CONICET. "The first was the coup d'état in 1976. Then, in 1991, there was the deregulation decree." In 1976 in Argentina, a coup d'état installed a bloody military dictatorship that would last until 1983. The 1976 dictatorship welcomed neoliberalism in Argentina by opening up the Argentine economy to transnational corporations and foreign banks.[90] By violent means, instilling fear, and kidnapping and killing leaders of social-movement organizations, the dictatorship also served "to silence farmers and the rural sector," Giarracca said. "Once the population was disciplined," she concluded, "the technologies came in."

The 1960s and 1970s in Latin America and across the developing world were a particularly restless time. Starting with Cuba in 1959, across Central America, and up to the murder of Salvador Allende in Chile in 1973, the region was the ground for multiple communist guerrilla movements and socialist experiments.[91] China, Vietnam, Algeria, and Iran also experienced these uprisings. What these so-called Third World revolutions had in common was that they drew from rural masses.[92] Peasants, historically marginalized, fought for agrarian reform. In Latin America, inequality in land distribution was—and continues to be—among the highest in the world.[93] The struggles for land reform radically challenged power and the status quo. As Vandana Shiva and Raj Patel argue, the Green Revolution was strategically deployed in these revolution-prone countries. The *green* in "Green Revolution," Patel writes, refers to the color of plants and also to the desire to fend off the red communist revolutions of the time.[94] Beset by food shortages and surrounded by peasant and guerrilla movements fighting for land reform, those who pushed the new agrarian technologies aimed to pacify a rebellious population.

In an urban country like Argentina, the wave of leftist guerrilla movements adapted to an urban setting.[95] But while most Argentines resided in the city, landholding patterns were as highly unequal as in the rest of the region.[96] Interestingly, while agrarian reform was needed and often called for, Argentina became the Latin American exception: land reform never took place.[97] As Ray Hora argues, land inequality in the Pampas had historically been at the heart of Argentina's political debate. From the early days of the republic, elites across the political spectrum had criticized large ranchers and landowners as obstacles to the country's social, political, and economic development. But the reforms they proposed were meek, and their goal was mild. Argentina's "agrarian utopia," Hora says, was far from a communist proposal: the shared ideal was a countryside populated with capitalist farmers with small- and medium-size landholdings.[98]

By the 1970s, the agrarian question had faded away. By increasing yields and profits, and by displacing rural workers, the new technologies of the Green Revolution settled the debate on agrarian reform in the Pampas. And as Giarracca and Teubal told me, state violence further pacified what remained of a mobilized rural population.[99] By the early 1990s, with society duly disciplined, unpopular neoliberal reform (and genetically modified crops) could be introduced without massive social protest.

In 1991, President Carlos Menem, advised by his minister of economy, Domingo Cavallo, signed an executive order called the Deregulation Decree. During the 1980s, like most countries in Latin America, Argentina was drowning in a deep economic crisis; the period was so hard on people that development scholars call it Latin America's "Lost Decade."[100] Hyperinflation in Argentina peaked in 1989 at over 3000 percent.[101] To rein in inflation and promote economic growth, Menem's administration, at the recommendation of the International Monetary Fund, told Argentines that drastic measures were necessary.[102] The government then implemented an all-encompassing neoliberal restructuring: with the stroke of a pen, the Deregulation Decree, under the Convertibility Plan, ended most regulations that protected domestic economic activity, including the import and export sectors of goods, services, capital, and direct foreign investment. It set a new currency scheme that pegged the Argentine peso to the US dollar at a fixed exchange rate of one-to-one, making foreign imports such as seeds, machinery, and agrochemicals cheaper. It also wiped out all the boards that had regulated agricultural activities since the 1930s.[103]

The core of the neoliberal program for Argentina, as for many other Latin American countries during this period, was based on the specialization in a few nontraditional commodities for the export market.[104] As Argentina, like Brazil, specialized in the production of soybeans, Chile, for example, focused on salmon and fruits, and Colombia provided fresh flowers for the American market.[105] Neoliberal extractivism meant a return to a model of development based on natural resource extraction for exportation under the logic of comparative advantage.[106] Transnational corporations and international financial institutions like the World Bank and the International Monetary Fund were strategic in encouraging the modernization of agriculture to promote export-led growth.[107]

As Gerardo Otero argues, governments were instrumental too.[108] The Argentine state actively helped to permit and promote soybean extractivism by developing a favorable institutional and regulatory framework for the commercialization and use of herbicide-resistant seeds and glyphosate-based herbicides. On March 25, 1996, Felipe Solá, then the secretary of the Ministry of Agriculture, Livestock, and Fisheries, signed Resolution 167 approving glyphosate-tolerant transgenic soybeans and their derivatives for production and commercial use in Argentina. This decision was highly controversial.[109] Earlier that year, experts from the IASCAV had asked Solá to delay his decision, demanding further testing on this novel technology. In 1996, the biotechnology of GM crops had yet to be released commercially anywhere else; Argentine scientists, echoing concerns from scientists across the world, raised their own over the potential negative impact of GM biotechnology on health and the environment.[110] Moreover, Argentine scientists cautioned that the scientific reports used to justify the safety, quality, and efficacy of GM biotechnology were provided by Monsanto, the company responsible for developing and commercializing the technology. Solá signed the approval anyway.[111]

In a similarly contested process, the SENASA classified glyphosate-based Roundup herbicide as class 4, representing minimum risk and toxicity.[112] According to the SENASA-approved label, Roundup poses no risk to living beings or the environment if used under phytosanitary guidelines and expert agronomist advice.[113] Critics question the approval on several grounds.[114] Like IASCAV scientists with Roundup Ready seeds, they note that SENASA did not run its own risk-assessment tests but rather relied on international standards, which are themselves highly scrutinized. Critics point to scientific evidence that shows links between illnesses and glyphosate spraying and claim that these studies have been systematically ignored and denied by regulators because of lobbying pressures, among other reasons.[115] Critics also question SENASA's trade-secret clause, which prevents disclosure of the composition of agrochemical products or the test reports presented for approval.[116] As I show in chapter 4, laypeople have allied with scientists to continue to raise concerns over the potential health and environmental risks of agrochemical spraying.

Supporters and critics alike highlight a weak system for the protection of intellectual property rights as one of the main institutional factors in the fast diffusion of herbicide-resistant soybeans in Argentina.[117] Genetically engineered seeds, owned and patented by corporations, are typically a matter of contention for farmers.[118] Patented seeds are expensive and, under contract, cannot be saved for replanting. The Argentine government, however, upholds UPOV 78, an international agreement that protects farmers who legitimately replant saved seeds. Moreover, Argentine farmers who plant RR soybean seeds are not compelled to sign a contract with Monsanto, as is customary in other countries, such as the United States.[119]

Argentine farmers benefited from a legal loophole that allows them to sow RR soy without paying patent fees.[120] There is also a large black market in RR seeds, commercialized in unlabeled white sacks that farmers refer to as *bolsa blanca*.[121] Due to cheaper prices for foreign inputs, a consequence of the Convertibility Law that pegged the peso to the dollar, and no added patent costs, the transition to GM soybeans made good economic sense. The adoption of the technological package promised dramatic cost reductions, for it required fewer and relatively cheaper inputs and less labor than conventional crop growing.[122] For farmers, the result was that GM seeds were an inexpensive component of the technological package. In 1996, Argentine farmers paid $9 for a fifty-pound bag of RR soybeans, whereas US farmers were paying $21.50.[123] Glyphosate prices also went down, from $28 per liter to $3—again, cheaper than in the United States.[124] Therefore, altogether, the adoption of the package represented a dramatic cost reduction, as imported glyphosate was cheaper than other agrochemicals in use, seeds could be saved for replanting, and the no-till method reduced the price of labor and fossil fuels. Roberto Bisang estimates the switch to the technological package of GM soy represented a 15 percent profit increase compared to the use of conventional techniques in soy-corn rotation.[125] For many farmers, growing GM soy became the cheapest and most profitable of options.

A New Extractivism? The KircÚer Administrations (2003–2015)

The neoliberal model implemented in the 1990s collapsed by the end of 2001, leaving behind a shattered country. A decade of neoliberal adjustments had left half of Argentines living in poverty and having among the highest rates of inequality in history.[126] The twentieth century ended with immense despair in a context of institutional, political, and economic crisis.[127] People protested for months all across the country, picketing in the streets and on national highways, banging pots and pans. On December 20, 2001, it all came to a head with two days of protests and riots. Argentines cried, *¡Que se vayan todos!* (Everyone out!) By the end of the day on December 21, President Fernando de la Rúa resigned and was forced to flee the presidential palace, surrounded by protestors, in a helicopter.

A transition government followed. In 2003, Eduardo Duhalde, the last of five appointed presidents during this transition time, called for elections. Néstor Kirchner, at the time an unknown figure in the political establishment running on a Peronista platform with a strong anti-neoliberal discourse, won. The Kirchners, Néstor and his wife, Cristina, would be in power for the next twelve years. After four years as president of Argentina (2003–7), Néstor was succeeded by Cristina. The presidential couple worked in tandem until Néstor's passing in 2010. The following year, Cristina was reelected for a second term, which ended in December 2015.

The Kirchners were elected in the "pink tide" that spread across Latin America at the turn of the twenty-first century.[128] Néstor Kirchner, alongside Hugo Chávez in Venezuela, Luiz Inácio Lula da Silva in Brazil, Evo Morales in Bolivia, and Rafael Correa in Ecuador, among others, swung Latin America's political pendulum to the left. These post-neoliberal governments were elected across the 2000s on a social justice platform, promising social inclusion and economic redistribution to address poverty and inequality. They proposed—and delivered—strong state intervention and increased social spending to address the needs of the most marginalized. Venezuela, for example, implemented an extensive welfare program called Misiones (Missions) that delivered universal education and health care to the urban poor.[129] Brazil developed an innovative campaign called Fome Zero (Zero Hunger), in conjunction with the cash-transfer program Bolsa Família (Family Allowance), to alleviate poverty, hunger, and malnutrition.[130] In Argentina, the Kirchners introduced a noncontributory pension program known as Moratoria Previsional (Pension Moratorium) and expanded direct cash-transfer programs, such as the Asignación Universal por Hijo (Universal Child Allowance) and the Programa de Jefas y Jefes de Hogar Desempleados, a program targeting unemployed heads of households.[131]

These programs and policies have had remarkable results. From the late 1990s to the late 2000s, income inequality in Latin America declined steadily and significantly. Poverty rates also dropped, from 41.5 percent of total population down to 29.6 percent, as government transfers lifted roughly 49 million Latin Americans out of poverty.[132] In Argentina, the increase in social spending resulted in a rapid fall in poverty and inequality rates, at a proportionally higher rate than the rest of the region. Between 2003 and 2009, poverty rates dropped from 38.2 percent to 14.4 percent while Gini coefficients (which measure income inequality) fell from 0.52 to 0.45.[133]

How to fund increased social spending in the aftermath of the neoliberal economic crisis? Behind the success of the pink-tide governments lies the fact that extractivism picked up the bill.[134] Across the region, progressive governments boosted the economic model based on natural resource extraction for export: from hydrocarbons and mining to large-scale agriculture. Eduardo Gudynas terms this development model a "new extractivism" because, unlike extractivism's historical/traditional form, here the state controls a larger share of the revenues from commodity exports—either through the nationalization of resources, such as with crude oil in Venezuela and Ecuador, and with natural gas in Bolivia; or via export taxation, as in the case of soybeans in Argentina.[135] Moreover, by redistributing the profits of extractivism, the model has gained substantial legitimacy among a general population historically excluded from its benefits (thereby, as I show in the following chapters, redistribution mollifies potential grievances and buys acquiescence). But while much has changed under neo-extractivism, the pattern of resource dependency and resource depletion continues. And thus, as Tammy Lewis reflects on the case of Ecuador, profits fueled by environmental damage ultimately limit the long-term sustainability of neo-extractivism as a development model.[136]

The Kirchner administrations heavily promoted soybean extractivism in Argentina. In 2004, Néstor Kirchner signed off on a ten-year development plan (2005–15) that promoted agricultural biotechnology as a core element of Argentina's development strategy. "The future of agricultural production faces multiple challenges," the report about the plan states in its executive summary, such as "limited resources, increasing demand in quantity and quality, sustainability, etc. In this scenario, biotechnology is proposed as the main technological solution to confront these challenges." The plan's discourse repeats the corporate rhetoric on the promise of biotechnology for sustainable development. It also taps into the liberal modernizing discourse rooted in the agro-export model of the nineteenth century: "The natural conditions [that make Argentina] prone to agricultural production constitute a comparative advantage that, powered by a strong science-and-technology arm dedicated to the development of new bioengineered products, will necessarily provide a competitive advantage for the development of national production."[137] GM biotechnology is presented as the key to development, as it promises to exploit Argentina's potential for agro-industrial production. Cristina Kirchner followed up on this development plan with the Agricultural Strategic Plan for 2010–16 (known as PEA2). This second plan is another example of the continuity of the model, as it focuses on increased agricultural production through technological innovation. And, yet again, the plan also distinguishes Argentina's unique capacity to produce enough food to respond to increasing global demand.[138]

Furthermore, the global context at the time was particularly beneficial to Argentina's GM soy-based agro-export model. In 2008, an increase in global food demand based primarily in China and India, increasing financial speculation, and crops diverted to agrofuels created the "perfect storm": food scarcity, hunger riots, and a spike in commodity prices.[139] Soybean prices escalated to over USD $600 a ton. The Argentine government and producers were poised to profit from this crisis: soy production was a gold mine. The government decided that these extraordinary conditions necessitated extraordinary measures. On March 11, 2008, Cristina Kirchner signed an executive order—known as Resolution 125—to increase soy export taxes from 35 to 44 percent; this was a floating-rate tax tied to export prices, meaning that the higher the prices, the higher the tax.

The announcement of this tax hike was the catalyst for the most important agrarian conflict in Argentine history.[140] In response, soy producers, big and small, hit the streets. This protest came to be popularly known as *el conflicto del campo*, or "the conflict with the countryside," and was led by the four major national associations of rural producers: Sociedad Rural Argentina, Federación Agraria Argentina, Confederaciones Rurales Argentinas, and the Confederación Intercooperativa Agropecuaria Limitada. Despite their different allegiances and memberships, these four organizations assembled under the same umbrella organization, the Mesa de Enlace.

Fig. 1.1. Protest in Buenos Aires, with 300,000 people. Many are waving Argentine flags to support el campo against the Kirchners.
Photo from the cover of *Diario Clarín*, July 16, 2008.

The protests sparked major chaos across the country. The Mesa de Enlace's tactics included blockading major national routes, which interrupted the circulation of goods and people and led to massive shortages. Several mass rallies were held in the cities of Buenos Aires, Rosario, and Córdoba, the capitals of the largest soybean-producing provinces. Urban sectors supported the protest, filling up the plazas in the hundreds of thousands (as figure 1.1 shows), banging pots and pans, and carrying signs declaring "Yo estoy con el campo" (I am with the countryside). This sign became a motto for urban sectors disgruntled with the government and was displayed on car bumper stickers and window signs in shops and homes. The magnitude of the protest was so unprecedented that it made the world news, with the *New York Times*, CNN, and the BBC all running stories on it.[141] The conflict lasted more than four months, finally ending on July 18, 2008, with the repeal of Resolution 125 in a dramatic last-minute veto by Julio Cobos, president of the senate and Kirchner's own vice president.[142]

Most significant, the most important agrarian conflict in Argentine history was over a tax hike. During the time the conflict lasted, there was little to no discussion about Argentina's massive agrarian transformation that had occurred in the countryside with the swift takeover of GM soybeans. The debate was not about agribusiness extractivism as a model of development (much less on its potential negative consequences) but about who got to reap most of its benefits. It was a struggle between the state and agribusiness over a larger share of the profits of the soy boom.[143]

Yet the break in the corporate-state alliance had unintended consequences. The Kirchners turned their discourse against soybean producers, calling the blockades "the pickets of abundance."[144] In an intense verbal provocation, Cristina Kirchner referred to soy as *yuyo* (weed), stripping the genetically engineered crop from its modernizing qualities and likening it to "savage" nature.[145] Soybean producers were quick to spin the message, assigning patriotic qualities to soybeans as the motor of Argentina's economy. "Al gran yuyo argentino, ¡salud!" (All hail the great Argentine weed!) read the headlines in *Clarín*, paraphrasing the lyrics of the Argentine national anthem ("Al gran pueblo argentino, ¡salud!").[146]

The 2008 agrarian conflict over soy taxes created a cleavage between the corporate and state sectors that would only intensify through the rest of Cristina Kirchner's administration. As Gabriel Vommaro and Mariana Gené argue, it was a turning point in the Kirchners' politics and discourse about soybean producers that led to increasing social polarization and the eventual demise of the party.[147] In this post-2008 context, I conducted my fieldwork in the rural communities of the Pampas. The antagonism between the rural sector and the state was palpable within the conversations I had with rural inhabitants, who claimed the Kirchners' policies hindered the progress of the countryside. Yet, despite the dispute over taxes, as I show in chapter 2, agribusiness leaders and state authorities continued to ally in mobilizing mainstream media to encourage support for GM biotech.

Chapter 2 turns to the meso- and micro-levels of soybean production, focusing on how consensus and acquiescence over GM soybean extractivism are encouraged and enacted in the rural communities of the Pampas.

2. Revolution in the Pampas

The Los Cardones headquarters is in downtown Santa María, a booming rural town in the northwest of the Buenos Aires province, the *zona núcleo* (core area) of soybean production. With its slightly faded brick facade, Los Cardones looks on the outside like a fancy vintage shop. Inside, past the front desk, the decoration is modern, with a dozen computers on individual desks arranged in a U shape. The room is bright white, freshly painted, air-conditioned. Young men are at work, chatting in small groups or sitting attentively behind their monitors. Like a law firm or an IT department, this area is dedicated to the junior employees. The pictures on the wall, colorful country motifs of grassland prairies and gaucho caricatures, give the office its "rural touch" and reveal the true purpose of this business. Los Cardones is an agribusiness dedicated to grain and livestock production for the beef and dairy industries. The business spans 12,500 hectares of owned and rented land across Buenos Aires, Córdoba, and Santa Fe, growing mostly soybeans, corn, wheat, barley, and sunflowers.

It was February 2012, and I was there to interview the CEO. At the front desk, the secretary greeted me kindly; overhearing our short conversation (she, of course, had to ask me who I was and why I was there), two young men, clearly employees, enthusiastically volunteered to tell me about the business while I waited for my meeting. Curious about my visit, they jumped into asking me about my graduate studies and my research topic ("the adoption of new agrarian technologies," my noncontroversial answer). Lucas, the one with the glasses, was the more talkative of the two. He started telling me "all about it" before I even finished setting up my recorder. "First things first!" I said. "First tell me about you! What do you do?"

"I work in an agribusiness firm [empresa agropecuaria]," Lucas said. "I work in the area of agriculture. I am in charge of crop management." He had been an employee for the last five years. Tomás, the other young man, had been in the office roughly the same amount of time. Neither could have been over thirty.

Like most of the other young men working in this office, Lucas and Tomás had graduated from the university as agrarian engineers before coming to work at Los Cardones. "We are in charge of the farm [encargados de campo]," Lucas said while Tomás nodded. "We go to the farm, do the rounds, and come back here." The office where we were talking was in the administrative and production-planning headquarters of Los Cardones. Six people work in the administration office and another fifteen in the office of agriculture and livestock where the computers are. From their explanation, I understood that "the rounds" referred to taking crop and soil samples that would then be analyzed in this office.

"Are you in charge of doing any agricultural tasks? Or is it done by contract?" I asked them, wanting to know if Los Cardones had its own employees to plant, spray, and harvest, or if, as is most common, both the labor and machinery were contracted out.

"The *contratista* who does most of the acreage is right there!" said Lucas, pointing to the administration office. "Yes! I can hear his voice," confirmed Tomás, adding, "He's often here; he lives in town." The contratista, they explained, is in charge of Los Cardones's production. "He has his own business where he hires people to work for him [El tiene su empresa que contrata gente y le da a realizar las tareas]."

The figure of the contratista in Pampas agriculture emerged during the first agro-export boom in the early twentieth century. Their numbers and relevance, however, have grown significantly with the soy boom of the early twenty-first.[1] Because machinery is expensive and used for only a few days at a time per farm, producers find it more efficient to contract these services. Contractors typically have no control over the farm. They own the machinery (or sometimes rent it) and perform (or hire other people to carry out) the main agricultural tasks of large-scale agriculture: sowing, agrochemical spraying for weed and pest control, and harvesting.

I knew how rural contracting worked already. What was not fully clear to me was what Lucas and Tomás's work as crop managers entailed on a day-to-day basis.

"So, what exactly do you do?" I asked.

Lucas went straight into presentation mode: "My role in the company is this: I am given a certain amount of inputs to use, they tell me what acreage is ready for planting, and what I have to do is turn out the product [sacar el producto]."

If I did not fully understand before, now I was mystified. "But then, what is your *job*?"

"My job is to produce!" Lucas said, enthusiastically. "I'm given all the factors and I. . . . We are a team, and each team has a work plan—part of the annual work plan—which lists the acreage we have to produce, the farms available, et cetera." His team, composed of six people, meets weekly "to discuss the situation regarding the crops and other possible issues. Weekly communications are essential for doing coordinated work." Each team is in charge of a specific area in production, management, or logistics. Lucas was in charge of the crop management for more than 2,400 hectares, which he visited by himself, once a week.

Most of his colleagues also live in town and come to work in eight-hour shifts, either at the office or in the field. "It's amazing," Lucas said of the work at the dairy farm, "because the technology has completely changed, compared to the old ways [el tambo antiguo]." Los Cardones's dairy farm has one thousand cows and thirty-five employees, "all coming and going. What changed was the need for someone to be there constantly. Now it is managed like an industry," Lucas explained. "Most jobs consist of an eight-hour day. There's a rotation of people who have a specific function and who are specialized in those tasks."

With his explanation, Lucas gave voice and body to the goals envisioned by the intellectual elite of the nineteenth century and to modernization theory. According to modernization theorists, the replacement of workers by machines is a necessary and positive development, as machines relieve us from hard physical labor, and by standardizing production, machines also produce larger quantities of higher-quality goods. In the modern mindset, the role of the new worker is to oversee the performance of the machine, to become technicians and engineers in charge of organizing production, rather than performing the work themselves.[2] The agro-industry is the farm converted into a factory. The goal of agro-industrial production is the mechanization and automation of the farm in order to increase yields and profits and to reduce variability and costs (the definition of *efficiency*). It is the civilizing project of the intellectual elite of the nineteenth century come true: nature tamed, the Pampas a factory of crops.

After the rounds at the farm and back at the office, computers are essential to analyzing the data, keeping records, and tracking and formalizing procedures. In the office, one of the trash cans oddly caught my eye. It was a regular trash can, full of balled-up sheets of paper. But, there, popping out, was a huge sunflower. It was totally out of place in this IT-like environment. I asked about it. "Data," they answered.

I asked them what agriculture would be like without the spreadsheets, without information technologies or specialized knowledge. Their puzzled faces gave away the clearest of responses. "Well, maybe in the past . . . ?" Tomás fumbled an answer. Lucas did not even entertain the possibility. "Not if you want to stay in business."

My exchange with Lucas and Tomás is another example of a repeated theme: technological innovation is at the core of farming genetically modified soybeans in the Pampas, the main goal of which is to increase profitability. As treadmill scholars argue, technologies are not neutral or objective but have orchestrated social trajectories. Corporate actors adopt and promote new technologies to increase their economic benefit.[3]

To understand how power operates to create inaction and consent, however, it is critical to also consider the cultural and symbolic dimensions of the political economy of the environment. As Max Weber taught sociologists long ago, a structural analysis should not be split from the culture that creates and sustains it.[4] Material interests and practices are "always structured and laden with ideas," writes Lisa Wedeen, proposing a dialectical rethinking of the material-discursive split to study power and domination.[5] In this chapter I show how the positive framing of GM soy production relies not just on its potential for profitability but also on its promise for ecological modernization—that is, as I explained in the introduction, on the promise that technological innovation will lead to sustainable development and that GM crops will "feed the world." This discourse holds fast to the guiding myths of Argentine history and identity described in chapter 1, as the proud return of Argentina to the concert of nations as the "granary of the world." As I show in this chapter, powerful actors mobilize this discourse through the strategic use of corporate media to create acquiescence and consent.

The adoption of "the technological package" (the combined use of herbicide-resistant soybeans with no-till machinery and glyphosate-based herbicide) has radically altered social relations and socioenvironmental dynamics in the Pampas and beyond. New actors have emerged: producers, entrepreneurs, and businessmen in control of agricultural production, like Germán in chapter 1 and others whom I will introduce in this chapter. There are also new actors in charge of managing and organizing the agricultural tasks, mostly young men like Lucas and Tomás, recent university graduates who farm at a distance within IT-like environments and who are engineers, technicians, and business administrators.

This is a "revolution" in farming, soybean producers and journalists claim, one that builds on the history of technological innovation and European immigration into the Pampas. In this chapter, I illustrate how the adoption of the technological package has seen a shift toward what agribusiness leaders call the "new agricultural paradigm." In a remarkable spin on what agriculture is and means—a life-sustaining, food-producing activity built on the very material foundation of land and labor—the corporate discourse around this new agricultural paradigm emphasizes *knowledge* as the most important means of agricultural production. Know-how is presented as more valuable than the material value of the land and the labor that sustains agriculture itself. As such, agribusiness aims to disconnect and to disembed agriculture—in its discourse, but also as I explore here, in practice—from the social and ecological contexts that make it possible.[6]

Countering this popular positive discourse, I show there are hidden and not-so-hidden costs to the expansion of transgenic monocultures. As critical environmental sociologists argue, technological innovation for capital accumulation creates a rift between society and the environment.[7] Automatization and mechanization displace workers and increase ecological risk. As with the example of Lucas and Tomás, large-scale soybean production does not require much labor. With the help of the right technology, just one employee can manage very large acreages of farmland. Rural workers need specialized skills that are provided and certified by higher-education institutions, creating further barriers for entry into the rural labor market.[8] On the positive side, the technical jobs are potentially better paid and definitely more comfortable, as they allow workers to keep their families in urban environments with their important amenities: electricity, paved roads, hospitals, and schools.

While soybean farms do not require much direct labor, they nonetheless require large amounts of agrochemicals. Scientists and activists warn that these agrochemicals might potentially endanger the health of those who live and work in and near the soy farms. Yet the inhabitants of "soy towns" like Santa María, as I show in this chapter and in chapter 3, often do not raise concerns over potential risks of agrochemical spraying. Instead, most of them insist on the economic benefits of large-scale farming, which they claim trickle down through town. "*Todos vivimos del campo*"(we all live off the countryside), they often said, referring to the increasing material abundance in larger rural towns.

In this chapter I highlight how agribusiness executives and government officials are able to manipulate community perception and the visibility of the externalities of production. To encourage acquiescence and consent, they mobilize a rhetoric of bias—particularly through the use of mainstream media. They also mobilize material resources, of which the trickledown redistribution economics of the soy boom is key. The economic dependence on large-scale agricultural production and the cultural identity created around agrarian technological innovation obscure the social and ecological costs as well as create consent by touting the benefits of the agro-industry. I show how actors "in between" the power spectrum (those who reap some benefits but bear the impact of agrochemical exposure) stand in a complex situation vis-à-vis GM soy production, as many perceive/receive significant cultural and economic benefits while negative costs are invisibilized.

In particular, actors who are higher in the hierarchy of power *within the "in-between" category* help perpetuate the status quo by reinforcing dependence (reproducing the rural motto "We all live off the countryside") while downplaying the negative costs. I refer to agribusinesses' employees, landowners who rent land to soybean producers, and other rural inhabitants who do not participate in farming but benefit from the increased consumption of the agro-related class. Last, I show the extent of the invisibilization of the toxic hazards of agrochemical spraying, as soybean producers, who do wield power over their farms, willingly decide to farm herbicide-tolerant soybeans in their own backyards.

The New Agricultural Paradigm

Federico recalled the summer of 1996 when they first adopted the technological package. "It meant a change of mentality. It was a paradigm shift," the CEO of Los Cardones told me. While we talked, two phones were constantly ringing and pinging.

"Was it like some kind of a shock, adopting the new technology?" I asked, thinking about the language of the Green Revolution that promoters of the technology use to describe GM biotechnology.

"No, it was totally natural," he said. "We had always tested new varieties of hybrids and other seeds. Then this one that was resistant to glyphosate appeared. So, we tried it, and it worked. We started [sowing] a small [area] one year, a little more the next one, and now we sow all [the land] with it." It was, he continued, "a productive explosion. It was a huge change for the care and conservation of the soil. The use of no-till methods associated with RR soybeans means there is no erosion by the wind, or at least minimal. This results in huge [environmental] benefits. In addition to the economic benefits, for producers and for the country. We produce much more and at a lower cost."

To him, the adoption of the technological package of genetically modified crops implied continuity in the history of agrarian technological innovation in the Pampas. Federico's words echoed a theme I heard often among producers in the Pampas: genetically engineered seeds are, at their simplest, an input just like chemical pesticides and fertilizers. "They are just another tool," I was told by many agronomists and producers. This position toward GM biotechnology stands in stark contrast to claims raised by anti-biotech activists, who argue that the introduction of GM crops represents a violent threat to traditional cultures and knowledges.[9] However, for Pampas producers who were already so accustomed to constant technological innovation, the "natural" thing to do, as Federico said, was to adopt the new variety of herbicide-resistant seeds as soon as they became available.

It is the combined use of the herbicide-tolerant seeds with the no-till technology, or *siembra directa* (also known as the direct-seeding farming method), that agronomists and producers highlight as the truly revolutionary technology. It became a solution to the problems of soil erosion and nutrient depletion associated with conventional farming methods, which required tilling the soil for weed removal, breaking the soil structure and the protective layer of fallow crops from past harvests. Glyphosate-based Roundup also replaced a gamut of more toxic and more expensive chemical herbicides.[10] Based on those justifications, supporters of GM biotechnology argue that the package promotes environmental sustainability. When proponents talked about the technological package, interestingly, the discourse of GM seeds as simple "tools" often morphed into calling them *mejores semillas* and *semillas mejoradas* ("better" and "improved" seeds). The technological package creates a "virtuous cycle," an example of how Argentina is on the technological cutting edge of agricultural production.

Importantly, in this context the language of sustainability is deployed most often in relationship to economic sustainability. The profit motive of the entrepreneurial mindset is at the heart of decision making around which crops to grow and which technologies to incorporate. The benefits are defined by an increase in yields and profitability through a reduction of costs. Yet these benefits are often presented as shared, not just for the enjoyment of the corporate elite—thus projecting soybean extractivism as beneficial and desirable for society as a whole. As Federico said, "We produce much more and at a lower cost," resulting in "benefits for producers *and for the country.*"

Although the adoption of GM biotechnology implied continuity in terms of technological innovation, it also implied radical change. Los Cardones is just one agribusiness that has followed larger companies like Los Grobo, El Tejar, and Cresud in revolutionizing Argentine agriculture. Their conception of this new "paradigm" of agricultural production is based on novel arrangements of land and labor as well as constant technological innovation.[11] It is, indeed, a "paradigm" in the sense that it is a comprehensive worldview consisting of social, structural, technological, cultural, and symbolic dimensions. The discourse of paradigm shift, as Carla Gras and Valeria Hernández argue, draws from the discourse of the Green Revolution of the 1960s, showing continuity with a process in which "the productive and ideological functions of technology converge."[12]

Gustavo Grobocopatel, CEO of Los Grobo, is acknowledged as one of the main drivers of the new agricultural paradigm, a model adopted abroad and considered by prestigious universities like Harvard to be the "future of farming."[13] This is known as a "knowledge-based network model" centered on building a network of input and service providers, including land-owners, agronomists, contractors, and branch managers, so that instead of directly hiring employees or owning land or machinery, the company operates through land leases and third-party contracting. Los Grobo's associative network model thus represents a shift away from the materiality of farming (i.e., direct ownership and control of resources) and toward leasing, contracting, and specialization in the managerial/organizational aspects of production. It is due to this reliance on land leasing for farming that Grobocopatel controversially said of himself, "I am landless [Soy un sin tierra]."[14] His was a direct verbal reference that minimizes the struggles of the Movimento dos Trabalhadores Rurais Sem Terra, the peasant-indigenous landless movement in Brazil.

In the new agribusiness model, knowledge is at the core of farming. From this perspective, the value of agriculture lies not in the natural conditions that make it possible (land, labor, climate) but in the expert know-how to manage and organize production and in the scientific knowledge to develop new agrarian technologies (e.g., no-till machinery and GM biotechnology). Agribusiness elevates knowledge as a means of production more valuable than land itself. Whereas the demands of neoliberal globalization push for efficiency and flexibility, land, being fixed, means immobility. Therefore, in the new agribusiness paradigm, land becomes a drag, a hindrance to the mobility of capital.[15]

Large producers thus aim to accomplish a fabulous feat: making land disappear from the farming equation. How is it possible to overcome land as a fixed factor of agricultural production? How do "landless" farmers become the largest agrarian producers?[16] Large agribusinesses accomplish this by leasing land (and machinery and labor) instead of owning it. Land leases, generally on one- to three-year contracts, afford flexibility: once the contract ends, producers are free to move elsewhere. Small landowners benefit as well, because it is more profitable to rent their land than to farm it themselves, and risk losing it altogether when they are unable to compete with larger producers.[17] Leasing land also allows agribusinesses to become bigger, expanding production over greater areas. Landownership thus has become less relevant, though control over land is still crucial. Large-scale farming then becomes, in some cases, akin to land grabbing.[18]

In another strategy to achieve flexibility, large agribusinesses extend production into other countries. Farming in different climates, environmental and political, accomplishes another main objective of soy producers: to reduce variability and uncertainty. Whether the challenge is variable weather and rainfall cycles or government-imposed export quotas and taxation, expanding production across several countries diversifies risk and stabilizes production output. Planting soybeans also helps reach these objectives, as soybeans are "flex crops" with multiple and flexible uses, as food, fuel, animal feed, and building material. A regionally integrated South American soybean chain, where soybeans can be interchangeably produced in Paraguay or Brazil and then processed in and shipped from Argentina, closes the cycle.[19] Flexibility, efficiency, and predictability—required characteristics of just-in-time global capitalism—are thereby achieved. Farming, once constrained within the limits of the natural environment, now expands over a "virtual territory."[20]

This approach to agriculture and nature responds to, and is part of, the growing financialization of land and food crops around the world.[21] The financialization of farmland is the latest frontier in this global wave, a process that accelerated after the rise of food prices in 2008. As Madeleine Fairbairn notes, the farmland investment boom is not merely speculative, meaning speculating on financial returns from land appreciation. Investors' interest also relies on a farmland's productive capacity: that is, investors engage in agricultural production for a potential return in commodities. Those consortiums solely interested in the land's productive capacity engage in a strategy Fairbairn identifies as "lease-operate," which they prefer over landownership. Compared to "own-lease out" and "own-operate" investment strategies, lease-operate gives the highest risk return. Under a lease-operate strategy, agribusinesses speculate not on the value of land but on the value of crops, explaining the preference for flex crops. However profitable lease-operate agricultural production might be, there are important implications to short-term contracts. As Fairbairn notes, "Aside from the obvious impact this has on the structure of agriculture, it also reduces the farmer's incentive to use sustainable practices by removing his or her stake in future productivity."[22]

The agribusiness emphasis on knowledge is attractive: potentially, knowledge does not decrease as a result of being shared, unlike limited resources necessary for agricultural production such as land and water. As Federico said of the benefits of knowledge-exchange networks, "It is like the founder of the CREA [Regional Consortiums of Agricultural Experimentation] movement says, 'If I go to a meeting and I bring an apple and you bring an apple, we exchange the apples and each one leaves with one apple. But if I bring an idea and you bring an idea, we set the ideas in motion and we both leave with two ideas.'" The promise of knowledge-based farming is to transcend the physical boundaries of the planet: to overcome the limitations of resource scarcity and climate change with cutting-edge technologies. Most significant, knowledge-based development aims to transcend traditional development dichotomies (rural/urban; agrarian/industrial) in an alleged win-win scenario. In theory, knowledge can be shared without personal or environmental loss and, most enticingly, without conflict, which is otherwise intrinsic to the control over scarce natural resources.

This new agricultural paradigm is disseminated across the country via trade groups like the AAPRESID, agricultural fairs like Expoagro, the media, and government-funded academic and scientific institutions. Expoagro, for example, is hosted by *Diario Clarín* and *La Nación*, the two newspapers with the largest circulations in Argentina. It is one of the most important and largest annual agricultural fairs in the country; it is a place to see, according to the Expoagro website, "the latest developments, innovations and trends for agricultural machinery and productive systems."[23] Expoagro is one of the main venues for the dissemination of new agricultural technologies and practices in Argentina. Exhibiting alongside the leading research companies for biotechnology and agrochemistry are financial institutions, insurance companies, communication groups, commercial and industrial chambers, and academic institutions. During the year, smaller versions of Expoagro take place around the country. Groups like AAPRESID and CREA, which Federico referenced earlier, take the lead in organizing training and learning networks, environments in which to learn and share experiences around new agrarian technologies and methods. These meetings have the support of think tanks like ArgenBio (which calls itself the Argentine Council for Information and Development of Biotechnology), as well as of government-funded research institutions, like the INTA and the CONICET. These institutions cooperate to create and promote the new agribusiness paradigm that is commonly taught across the curriculum of farming-related majors in the public university system.[24]

Soybeans in the Public Eye

The use of discursive means to present GM biotechnology as a positive and necessary development is a key strategy to create support for the new agrarian technologies. Powerful corporate and state actors are allies in the creation and dissemination of the hegemonic pro–GM soy discourse.[25] This corporate-state alliance is critical to spreading the discourse for GM biotech and the new agrarian paradigm to laypeople and the wider Argentine society.

When Monsanto presented its newest variety of Roundup Ready seeds (branded as Intacta Roundup Ready 2 Pro) in Buenos Aires in 2012, Minister of Agriculture Norberto Yauhar said, "Today is a very special day for Argentina, because we are moving toward the next generation of soybeans. Today we approved [the latest variety of GM seeds], and biotechnology is a tool for sustainable growth."[26] Yauhar praised Monsanto's biotechnology and argued that it will benefit Argentina and the world. He celebrated GM biotech as key to increasing food security in an increasingly challenging world struck by climate change, droughts, energy scarcity, and a growing population. His words mirror Monsanto's corporate language.[27] They demonstrate the alignment of pro-GM corporate and state discourse. Prominent Argentine newspapers also celebrated the presentation of Monsanto's newest seed variety, calling Roundup Ready 2 soybeans "super soy" and the crop "of the future."[28]

Media dissemination is one of the most effective and widely used corporate strategies to create consent.[29] What is said to the public and, just as important, what is hidden from public view promote a particular opinion within civil society. In other words, these messages influence the public and build a hegemonic discourse. In Argentina, decisions over which events are reported to the public are concentrated in the hands of a small number of media corporations. Grupo Clarín leads the pack as the largest media conglomerate in Argentina and one of the largest in the Spanish-speaking world.[30] Established in 1999, Grupo Clarín publishes print news (most prominent of which is *Diario Clarín*, with the highest circulation of all newspapers in Argentina) and oversees internet access, cable TV, radio, and television. Grupo Clarín owns one of the two leading television channels in Argentina, ARTEAR/Canal Trece, as well as the country's leading twenty-four-hour news channel, Todo Noticias, popularly known as TN. Viewers commonly see commercials and sponsorships from Monsanto, Dow AgroSciences, seed sellers like Nidera, and organizations that represent agro-export-related interests, like the CIARA, on TN.

The mainstream news media has been a strategic actor in creating support for the GM soy model among the wider (urban) Argentine public. In *Clarín* and *La Nación*, the two most widely read Argentine newspapers, GM soy production is usually depicted as a well-rounded success. "Soybeans, a phenomenon that amazes the world," ran a headline in a *Clarín* special issue on soybeans in 2005. News stories on soy production and its share of exports run often and prominently, on front covers and typically in the regular economy and politics sections. News reports generally use the laudatory language of breaking records: "Soybeans boosted export records," "Soybeans [prices] have no limit," "Better [yields]? Impossible."[31] The editorial section also serves to spread and celebrate the soy model. Héctor Huergo, a weekly columnist for *Clarín* and director of *Clarín Rural* (the paper's rural magazine) is a prominent promoter of GM crops in Argentina. Among his editorials are "Only Biotechnology Can Save the World" and

"Soybeans, 21st-Century Manna."[32] With evangelical zeal, Huergo has used the pages of *Clarín Rural* to create and disseminate the discourse on the "second revolution of the Pampas" to promote GM biotechnology.[33]

The media amplifies and legitimates the discourse on the development potential of GM crops, tapping into the guiding myths I highlighted in chapter 1. For example, an article entitled "The Granary of the World," published in the economy section of *Clarín* in 2002, begins with the following claim: "One permanent tribulation afflicting Argentines is that 'we were The Granary of the World and now we have disappeared.'" The story echoes Germán's narrative in chapter 1, in which he lamented Argentina's "decadence" after the first agro-export boom. Just like Germán, the *Clarín* journalist emphasizes the role of GM biotechnology in reversing the turn of events. "Nothing could be more wrong," he writes. "Over the last ten years, Argentina's agricultural sector has had the highest growth rate in the world. As a result, national participation in the global food basket is increasing." This is thanks to, he continues, the "Second Revolution of the Pampas. The first one occurred in the late nineteenth century, when gringos and pioneers populated the territory and transformed, plow in hand, the fertility of the Pampas into wheat, corn, flax, and beef. Now we are in the era of technological conquest. [There are] new forms of production that are both more efficient and more environmentally friendly." The journalist's words repeated those I heard throughout my fieldwork: "Argentina is leading technological change worldwide," at the cutting edge of technological innovation, and doing the best agriculture in the world.[34]

The media has also promoted soybeans as a "miracle" food. During the post-2001 economic and political crisis, hunger became a public issue for the first time in Argentine history. In November 2002, four children died of malnutrition in the province of Tucumán, a story that shocked Argentina and made global news. "Shame and Controversy in Argentina over the Deaths of Four Malnourished Children," wrote *El País*, the Spanish newspaper.[35] How is hunger possible in the granary of the world? As farmland is diverted from food crops to feed crops, soybean expansion threatens Argentina's food security.[36] Yet the papers run stories on the potential of the second revolution of the Pampas to feed Argentina and the world, touting soybeans as *porotos maravillosos* (miracle beans), a "weapon loaded with future" that could solve the problem of hunger because of its higher yields, cheaper prices, and higher protein value.[37] Soy-based recipes and ads for free cooking workshops aimed at training Argentines on how to include soy and soy-based products in their diets appeared in the media during the post-2001 crisis. Soy-promoting articles sprouted up, portraying the crop as the best replacement for meat consumption. As one *Clarín* article asserted, "In the Absence of Cheap Meat, Goodness Turns Out to Be Soy."[38] The stories appealed to nutritionist arguments based on scientific expertise: "It Is Confirmed: Soybeans Reduce Cholesterol and Protect the Heart," read one headline in *La Nación*.[39] Cultural values, however, collide with so-called expert knowledge and its medical advice. Beef is a main staple of the Argentine diet and culture. Argentines pride themselves on having the best beef in the world. Despite the media efforts to convince Argentines otherwise, soybeans continue to feed cattle, not people.

The Argentine mainstream news coverage of soybeans has been very positive in general. Yet just as important as analyzing how powerful actors and institutions publicly portray GM biotechnology is to question what is hidden from view, or what is *not* on the media's agenda. The decision over which issues and events will become "news" is in the hands of those who control information channels.[40] Keeping controversial events out of public view helps to suppress public participation. For more than a decade since the introduction of GM crops in 1996, stories reporting on actual or potential negative impacts of the GM soy model had been conspicuously absent from the media. But that changed with el conflicto del campo, the agrarian revolt over export taxes in 2008. That year, soybeans were all over the news.

Throughout the four months the conflict lasted, the mainstream media reported daily on the protests and devoted long sections to discussing soybean production. Pre-conflict, soybeans had received only scattered media attention. But the events brought sudden public attention—and thus high visibility—to a process that had been unfolding for more than a decade. The conflict created a "window of opportunity" to question publicly the GM soy model and its potential negative impact.[41] For the first time in the Argentine mainstream media, the health and environmental risks of toxic agrochemicals were reported.

On a cover for *Página/12*, the third-largest paper in national circulation, in bold capital letters, superimposed over the image of a crop duster flying over a soy farm, ran the headline, "POISON."[42] The striking full-color image occupied the entire front cover of the newspaper. This was the first in a series of articles published by the pro-Kirchner paper, starting in January 2009, on the ill effects of glyphosate, GM soy's herbicide companion.

These articles publicized breakthrough findings on glyphosate effects in lab tests run by a team of Argentine scientists at the Molecular Embryology Lab at the University of Buenos Aires, led by Dr. Andrés Carrasco.[43] Carrasco's study, the first of its kind at the local level, refuted Roundup's alleged claim to low toxicity. Its main finding reported glyphosate to be toxic to amphibian embryos at even lower doses than those used in agriculture, producing malformations and neural, intestinal, and heart disorders.[44] Investigative journalism TV graphically presented the effects of agrochemicals on health. Many of my interviewees recalled in particular an episode on *La Liga*, on the Telefé channel.[45] It showed heartbreaking images of the effects of long-term exposure to agrochemicals: toddlers with crippling malformations, pregnant women terrified by fumigation season, and the atrophied naked body of Fabián Tomasi, a former fumigation worker.[46]

The conflict of the countryside sparked a media battle between the government and agribusinesses. With the sudden media exposure of glyphosate as a health risk in the midst of the conflicto del campo, it was clear that the Kirchners were threatening the soy producers.[47] The pro-agribusiness press (*Clarín* and *La Nación*) retaliated with a campaign to defend glyphosate, calling on scientific expertise to assess risk. "According to SENASA, the herbicide [glyphosate] complies with all regulations," said the expert agronomist and head of agrochemicals for SENASA in an interview with *La Nación*, reminding the public of its low toxicity and accordance with the international standards of FAO and WHO.[48]

The government strategy to subdue the agribusiness sector and end the strike did not go unnoticed. On the contrary, it fueled a strong reaction from powerful international actors, most significantly Monsanto and the US government. "The pro-government press [referring to *Página/12*] is waging a campaign against the use of glyphosate . . . which appears to be driven more by local politics than health concerns," reads a confidential report from the US Department of Agriculture leaked by Wikileaks. The leaked USDA report claims that Carrasco's findings are "unverified," stating that "the alleged study does not have scientific credibility." Thus, the USDA proceeded to provide SENASA with "information on studies conducted on glyphosate" through the US Embassy in Buenos Aires. SENASA did not request this information. The studies provided, according to Wikileaks, were Monsanto's own, and they endorsed Roundup's claim to low toxicity.[49] As with the approval of herbicide-resistant seeds and glyphosate, as I showed in chapter 1, this is another example of how corporate lobbying is a powerful tool for creating acquiescence and consent over GM biotechnology.[50]

As I will detail in chapter 4, the change in the political climate during the conflicto del campo created a conducive context for social movements against agrochemical spraying to gain momentum, as more and more people learned about the impact of glyphosate on health and the environment. Yet those news stories were the exception, and they faded slowly after the conflict ended. During the Kirchner administrations, the potential negative impact of soybean expansion and the mobilization of anti-spraying activists were severely underreported. As one activist told me in 2012, "It does not appear on 6, 7, 8 or on TN," pointing out that there was little to no discussion of these issues either on the Kirchner administrations' propaganda TV news show, 6, 7, 8, which aired on public television, or on TN, Grupo Clarín's corporate news channel.[51]

In the following section, I show how this information (or lack thereof) impacts rural populations as well as how the paradigm shift in agricultural production has transformed everyday life and labor in the Pampas. Rural inhabitants claim "to live off the countryside." I disentangle the meanings of this shared phrase and how the actors "in between"—rural dwellers who do not wield power over large-scale farming yet enjoy cultural and economic benefits—often help perpetuate the rhetoric around GM biotech. Last, I present Bernetti, a soybean producer who proudly farms 1,000 hectares of GM crops in his very own backyard, to show the extent of the invisibilization of the risks of glyphosate-based herbicide exposure.

Todos Vivimos del Campo (We All Live Off the Countryside)

Antonio turned up the volume of his hearing aid in preparation for our conversation. Since he turned eighty and his wife passed, his eyes and his heart had also been giving him trouble. Yet when we talked, he would never turn his good ear to me or stop moving around, walking in and out of the kitchen to keep an eye on the grill outside. Antonio was clearly unaccustomed to the quiet domestic life of retirement. "Thirty-eight years of living off the countryside!" he said of his lifetime working as a field manager (encargado de campo). Antonio is a retired rural worker for very large producers. His parents had emigrated from Spain with his two oldest siblings. Antonio and the rest of the eight children in his family were born and raised in Argentina. He had raised his own family on and off the farm.

Antonio and his wife were first hired to live on-site "as a marriage." In a typical gendered arrangement of Pampas labor, her task was to look after the farmhouse and cook for farm employees while he was in charge of field tasks.[52] But as the children grew older, his wife moved the children to town with her so they could attend school. Antonio would stay the night at the farm some days, but most of the time he commuted. When talking about his life working on the farm, Antonio never tired of praising his employees and their farming methods. "*Son productores muy de punta.* They are at the cutting edge of technological change," he kept telling me. I interviewed him twice between June and July 2011. On this day we were at his home in General Artigas, a rural town of fifteen thousand inhabitants in the southeast of Buenos Aires province. The plan was to visit some of the farms where he had worked.

"How do people here make a living?" I asked Antonio and Rosa, a neighbor hired to help him with household chores. The three of us had been talking for a while, drinking mate and snacking on dried salami until lunch was ready.

Del campo. "Off the countryside," they replied almost in unison.

"We all live off the countryside" was the most common phrase I heard across my fieldwork in the Pampas. Some, like Rosa that morning, would sometimes say *en el campo* (on the farm). Yet, as I would find out across my fieldwork, as well as later that day when Antonio and I visited different farms, my impression was that no one was actually living on the farms. Rural displacement as a consequence of agrarian technological innovation—as automation, machines, and petrochemicals replaced human and animal labor—preceded the adoption of the technological package of GM crops. When Pampas farmers began adopting the technologies of the Green Revolution back in the 1970s, the Argentine rural population was already significantly smaller than in other Latin American countries, accounting for slightly more than 21 percent of the total population, compared to 43 percent for the rest of the region. With further adoption of innovations, this declining trend continued. By 1995, right before the adoption of GM biotechnology, the rural population had declined to less than 12 percent. In 2015, barely 8 percent of Argentines lived in rural areas.[53]

The family agribusiness that employed Antonio farms more than sixty thousand hectares of owned and leased land across the country (roughly ten times the land area of Manhattan). Rural depopulation has gone hand in hand with a decrease in the number of farms, as well as an increase in farm size and the concentration of landholdings. According to data from the rural census, close to eighty thousand farms in the Pampas vanished between 1988 and 2008. That is a 42 percent reduction in the number of farms in only two decades.[54] Almost half of that reduction occurred in six short years during the soy boom. Between 2002 and 2008, the census accounted for an 18 percent decrease in the number of farms in the Pampas. Farm sizes and the corresponding land inequality, as I indicated in the previous chapter, have also increased.

In July 2011, Antonio took me to visit three of the farms he used to work on before retirement. They were large farms, each between 1,000 and 1,500 hectares. The first two we visited were mixed use for agricultural crops and livestock. The cattle feedlots, like the dairy farm Lucas described in the opening of this chapter, hired specialized labor in eight-hour shifts. Animal enclosure, typical in the United States, was not common in Argentina, although it is rapidly being applied to all animals grown for human consumption—cows, chickens, and hogs—freeing land for agricultural use. Feedlot-raised animals carry their own socioecological consequences: increased use of hormones and antibiotics, health issues related to consumption of feedlot-raised beef, and degraded environmental quality, as feedlots pollute air, water, and soil.[55] I still remember the pungent stench in the air, the cramped cows wading in dung and mud up to their bellies.

The third farm we visited was exclusively dedicated to grains. That day, they were bagging the harvest—corn and soybeans—in *silobolsas* (silo bags). This is a recent technological development that allows producers to store grains on-site. They are white bags that look like gigantic sausages, 240 feet long and 9 feet wide (see figure 2.1). Producers prefer them because they can save their harvest for up to two years instead of having to sell it right away, which allows producers to speculate on higher prices (and to put pressure on the government by withholding tax payments and exports). That day, two middle-aged men with robust bellies completed the job of filling these bags in less than an hour with the sole aid of a tractor and a hopper. Each of the ten silobolsas was filled with 200 tons of grain in a matter of minutes. At more than USD $300 per ton for corn and more than $500 per ton for soybeans (in June 2011), there was a fortune in those bags.[56] "It's such an advancement!" Antonio said. "Before, it used to take so long, you even had to shovel [the grains] into the truck." Antonio joined the chorus of voices celebrating modernity and the advent of time- and back-saving machinery that provided relief from hard labor. None of the men I

Fig. 2.1. Silobolsas allow producers to store their harvest on their own farms. Each silo bag can store 200 tons of grain. Photo by the author.

met that day who worked at any of these three farms lived on-site. Rather, like Los Cardones employees, they resided in town and commuted to the farm as needed. There was one worker living on-site, I was told. His main task was to protect the silobolsas against potential thieves.[57]

The Argentine Pampas region is quite underpopulated, and its expanse is striking. One can travel for a hundred miles without seeing a soul, particularly once you turn off the main arteries of the national route system. The three farms I visited with Antonio, for example, are adjacent, and together they cover more than nine thousand acres; they were only three of many farms around. We drove for hours with only crops and cows on the horizon, and I hoped that my compact city car would not get stuck in the dirt roads. ("That's why you need a truck around here!" Antonio kept saying. "Not a horse anymore. They are a waste of time.")

The paradigm shift in agricultural production has radically transformed life, labor, and the environment in the Pampas. Not many people live and work in the countryside. Yet those who remain have received an economic boost from the soy boom, triggering support for GM soy production. The shared phrase "we all live off the countryside" captures how Pampas inhabitants positively perceive the economic redistribution of agricultural production.

The economic benefits of the soy boom trickle down through rural populations in multiple ways. One of them is through direct job creation. Like Los Cardones in Santa María, many agribusinesses have their headquarters in larger rural towns. For example, Los Grobo's is in Carlos Casares, Buenos Aires province. These agribusinesses create a number of technical and specialized jobs planning and supervising production, and many of their employees reside in town—like Lucas and Tomás explained. Los Cardones, for example, employs fifty people for its agronomic, livestock, and administrative positions. They also hire, through the contractor, another handful to perform the agricultural tasks of planting, fumigating, and harvesting. Thus, there is job creation: jobs that are comfortable and well paid. But one could argue that the number of jobs is not high enough to prompt phrases like "we all live off the countryside." In the case of Los Cardones, a maximum of sixty people are employed to cover a territory of twelve thousand hectares. That is a larger area than the entire city of Paris, in which 2.2 *million* people live and work.[58]

Job creation in the soy industry is mostly indirect. Soybean production creates a broad sector of input and service providers to attend to the agroindustry: seed and agrochemical developers, producers, and sellers; truck and train carriers to transport harvest to ports; machinery development and sales; and the branch offices of export grain traders, among others. Large rural towns typically have their offices on the main (and sometimes sole) artery leading into downtown. Thus, when you enter a town, you are greeted with a parade of banners and billboards: grain exporters Cargill and Louis Dreyfus Company; agrochemical sellers Syngenta, BASF, and DuPont; and Nidera, Don Mario, and Compañía Argentina de Granos selling seeds. Claas, John Deere, and Ford attract potential customers with their fleet of shiny tractors, combines, and trucks parked in their front lots. As agribusiness leaders argue, a wealth of jobs is also created in the oil-, fuel-, and food-processing factories fed by agricultural crops, yet these jobs are not included in the statistical counts of benefits to the rural sector because the workers typically live in cities and are counted there.[59]

A whole other set of jobs is created through the increased consumption associated with the higher incomes and profits of the agro-related class: domestic and commercial cleaners and maids, supermarket and retail jobs, and jobs in construction, among others. The construction sector in particular benefited from the soy boom, as property investments are considered one of the most reliable means of saving in Argentina—understandable in a country beset by sudden currency devaluations and bank system meltdowns. The state also adds to the soy-derived income that flows into rural towns through the monthly subsidies of cash-transfer programs I described in chapter 1.

Another important way in which economic benefits spill into rural towns is through landownership. Some rural residents are former chacareros who, unable to compete with larger producers, have chosen to exit agriculture and lease out their land, as it is potentially more profitable and less risky than engaging in farming themselves.[60] Others are landowners who have never been involved in agriculture themselves but have inherited a fraction of the family farm. Sergio is one of them. He is a lawyer who lives in Álvarez, a rural town of about nine thousand people in the south of Córdoba province. That is where I met him in March 2012.

The south of Córdoba and Santa Fe provinces used to be Argentina's powerhouse of dairy production. "Between 1920 and the late 1980s," Sergio said, "dairy farming [la tambería] was the primary activity in this area. But it all changed with soybeans. Now [the area] is agricultural, soy growing [sojera]." We spoke at a café downtown. Sergio is divorced, probably in his fifties. His son was visiting from Buenos Aires, where he studied graphic design at the university. His daughter majored in architecture at the University of Córdoba. Sergio would like them to take over the administration of the farm eventually, but they did not seem interested in doing so or in returning to Álvarez, where they grew up. Sergio is quite reserved and did not answer when I asked him how much land he owns or what the profit margins on his lease are. I respected his privacy and did not inquire further; he was not the first of my interviewees to give me a cautious look when I asked these private questions (many, before answering, would joke, "Are you from the AFIP [the Argentine tax-collection agency]?").

On the following day, Sergio, his son, and I drove less than half an hour away to Colonia Schoos to visit their farm. Sergio seemed happy to have an excuse for the drive. "I don't come here often," he said. They lease their land to a "sowing pool" based in the province of Corrientes, six hundred miles away. *Pools de siembra* (sowing pools) are collective investment funds for large-scale soy production. They combine technical, managerial, commercial, and financial expertise, and, more important, investment capacities.

Sowing pools are a relatively new actor in Argentine agriculture: they emerged after the 2001 crisis. An important characteristic of these sowing pools is that they bring urban inhabitants into farming purely as financial investors. As in other investment opportunities, the investors' main goal is to maximize returns in the short term.[61]

Sergio's lease contract is for four years with the option to extend. He receives a percentage on profits calculated over the average yield of each plot. His deal, he told me, is less profitable than the usual. "Most people do short term, two years, and set a fixed price," he said. "The problem [with this kind of contract] is that you only receive the money. You have no say over the [use of] the land."

"Why is it that people prefer this kind of contract?" I asked.

"There's a huge change in the way of thinking [el cambio de ideología es muy fuerte]. Now it's all about the money, without thinking what is it that yields that money. Then, in four, five, six years, the land is useless [el campo no sirve más]. Because monocultures bring consequences."

Sergio was emphatic that he prioritized the quality of the soil over the money he could receive for exploiting it. "We must maintain the sustainability of the soil," he told me repeatedly.

"How do they do that?" I asked, referring to the agricultural practices of the sowing pool.

"With no-tilling and high-quality fertilizers and herbicides," he replied. "For a top-quality management of stubble to protect against erosion." In this way, he said, "We can have profitability in the long term." His main concern, he told me repeatedly, is that el campo gives him "an income to live with ease [para vivir tranquilo]" and enables his children "to have a good life."

Sergio's words repeated verbatim the positive discourse of the technological package I heard often from agronomists and producers. Like the CEO of Los Cardones had told me earlier, Sergio also claimed that the combined use of no-tilling, agrochemicals, and herbicide-tolerant seeds were the key to both the environmental and economic sustainability of his farm. For all his emphasis on crop rotation to maintain healthy soils, I was surprised to find out, once at the farm, that the rotation involved was solely of soy and corn, both transgenic crops planted with the technological package.

Transgenic monocultures bring consequences, indeed. Despite all of Sergio's praise, his farm seemed abandoned: no one worked there permanently or lived on-site. In better days it used to be a dairy farm,

Fig. 2.2. Walking among rows of GM corn on Sergio's farm, south of Córdoba province. Note the lack of stubble that would protect against soil erosion. Photo by the author.

Fig. 2.3. Diseased GM corn stalk at Sergio's farm, south of Córdoba province. Photo by the author.

Fig. 2.4. Colonia Schoos, a small and poor rural town, in the south of Córdoba province, in the process of disappearing. Photo by the author.

like other farms in the area. Now everything that was needed to sustain roaming milk cows was left to rust: the fences to contain them, the water mill, the water tank. The crops, too, were poorly looked after, many affected by fungi and disease. In stark contrast to his emphasis on sustainability, even the soil showed clear signs of erosion (see figures 2.2 and 2.3).

Colonia Schoos, the town by the farm, seemed abandoned as well: another small Pampas town in the process of disappearing. The town is mainly one long dirt road flanked by a handful of homes, some more than a hundred years old (figure 2.4). This is the German colony where Sergio's emigrant grandfather arrived in the 1890s. We stopped because Sergio's son wanted to bargain on some antique metal chairs he saw by one of these houses; I figured these chairs sold for several times their rural price in hip parts of Buenos Aires. We got out of the car, and Sergio walked toward the old man who was standing outside, drinking mate. They greeted each other pleasantly, as they knew each other.

With his scrambled and scant white hair, José seemed to me in his seventies, but he might have been younger and just worn out by the rural lifestyle. He was wearing flip-flops, long pants, and his white shirt open, showing his big, round belly. It was a warm and sunny day. José had a calm attitude and a big smile: *un tipo muy simpático*, I wrote in my notes, "a very nice guy." His job, he told us, was to slaughter steers. "Before, up to sixty a day," he said. "But now it's only one or two a week," adding, "if we're lucky."

"There's nobody left in town," said José. "Only the old folks."

"Tapera," Sergio confirmed. *Tapera* is a word Argentines use to refer to poor, abandoned rural homes.[62] I heard it often across my fieldwork; rural residents used it to describe their own towns or other towns nearby undergoing this same process of outward migration.

"Kids go away, to study," said José. "They are sent to boarding school or to Álvarez. Then their mothers need to go too, to look after them. It makes no sense to commute to school. They would have to wake up at 3 a.m. . . . They would arrive so tired, they wouldn't learn anything."

"And the others?" I asked.

"They all leave," he said once more. "Why are they going to stay, if there are no jobs? Before, the dairy farms employed families by the dozen." José started listing the names of all the estancias and how many people each employed: a long list. "But now they are all closed," he said. "It's nothing but soybeans [Es pura soja]."

Definitely nothing but soybeans surrounded us. From his house I could see, at the end of the road, a soy farm. It was not farther than three hundred feet: barely one long block. I, too, had seen almost nothing but soybeans all along our drive from Álvarez to Colonia Schoos. Soybeans were even planted on the shoulder of the road, land that is technically publicly owned (Sergio said the town hall was behind it, that they use soy profits for town improvements).

Suddenly, without prompting, José said, "It's a problem with the fumigations."

I stood still, curious. Pampas dwellers had told me "we all live off the countryside" and shared the many ways in which the benefits of soybean production trickle down through their towns. Either in the shape of rent, income, or profit, people like Sergio, like Antonio, Lucas and Tomás, and Federico, reap the economic benefits of the soy boom. For all the benefits, however, I was often puzzled that they would repeatedly minimize, disregard, or plain ignore the costs that come with GM soy production.

In particular, they did not refer to the risks of glyphosate-based herbicide fumigations.

As I explained in the introduction, glyphosate use in Argentina has risen sharply with the expansion of herbicide-resistant crops, heightening ecological and health risks.[63] Glyphosate annual use rose from less than 1 million kilograms in 1996 to 88 million kilograms in 2014, sprayed on 20 million hectares of GM soy.[64] Lab studies show that glyphosate and Roundup formulations have endocrine-disrupting effects on rats and rat embryos, leading to chronic kidney and liver deficiencies and severe malformations.[65] Argentine physicians have documented increased rates of miscarriages and congenital birth defects among mothers who have a history of direct exposure to pesticides across the country.[66] As previously mentioned, the WHO reclassified glyphosate as "probably carcinogenic" in 2015.[67]

Yet, when I had asked Sergio earlier at his farm, "Do fumigations have any impact on you?" he replied with a resounding "no." Instead, he repeatedly told me about "the need to think long-term [pensar a futuro] and to maintain the sustainability of the soil." For this, as he said constantly, the technological package (of which a main component is glyphosate-based herbicide) is key. Antonio had nothing but praise for agrochemicals: "For the best weed control, mix glyphosate and 2,4-D. *Te queda todo limpito* [You'll have a sparkling clean field]," he said. Leo, whom I introduced earlier in this book and who is raising his children in a backyard of soybeans, reiterated glyphosate's low risk. "Yes, glyphosate has an impact," he told me when I questioned the sustainability of the technological package. "But it is low, and it leaves little residue," he said.

Leo, like other agronomists I interviewed, underscored the low toxicity of glyphosate-based herbicides by mobilizing the discourse of scientific expertise: a strategy to create acquiescence and quell dissent, which I expose in the following chapters. "GMOs have been more tested than medicines," Leo said when talking about their impact on health, and he dismissed laypeople's claims to toxicity as "supposed [supuesta] contamination." Germán, with whom I spoke in the aftermath of the conflicto del campo when glyphosate was all over the news, said, "There are specific studies, and not from today [but] from thirty years ago, saying than an organophosphorus insecticide is more polluting, carcinogenic, etc., than glyphosate, and yet everyone is talking about glyphosate and nothing is said about the other [agrochemicals applied]." He then proceeded to minimize its toxicity.

"Some say," said Germán, "that the glyphosate molecule unfolds into other molecules, and those have been found in groundwater. . . . Oh well!" he sighed, mockingly. "In groundwater, they even found aspirin! Molecules of aspirin! There are so many things," Germán said. "Anything we use ends up contaminating the groundwater."

As the economic benefits of the soy boom trickle down through the Pampas, those who enjoy them emphasize the positives and minimize the costs of GM soybean production. Those who are higher in the synergies of power—due to the compound effect of the privilege given by their class, race, and gender—are more likely to approve of agrochemicals and to minimize any potential negative impact. But many of them also reside in the countryside and are thus exposed to pesticide drift, which is the unintentional diffusion and potential negative effects of spraying agrochemicals. Despite bearing some costs, however, those "in between" (like Sergio, Leo, and Antonio) reproduce the positive discourse of GM crops and, in consequence, also the status quo. The exception is the women of Santa María, whose story I tell in chapter 3, who would at times speak of potential health hazards but kept their grievances latent through self-policing and denial.

Poor and powerless rural folks like José bear the brunt of the soy boom. As Jill Harrison argues, pesticide drift is a matter of environmental injustice because its costs are disproportionately borne by the poor, farmworkers, peasant and indigenous families, women, children, and the elderly.[68] In this unjust context, it is understandable that José would find fumigations to be "a problem." Yet this does not necessarily translate into collective action. My exchange with José continues below.

"Do they fumigate with planes?" I asked José when he brought up the fumigations.

"No, it's all terrestrial," he replied. "But it's still the same. . . . The other day they were fumigating, and the wind was blowing north," toward town, I understood from his hand gesture.

"Doesn't that harm you?" I asked.

"¡Ay!" said José. But to my surprise, he also minimized harm. "To those of us who are in good health, no. But to those who have asthma and such, yes," he said.

"And do you ever say anything about it?" I asked.

José shrugged in resignation and replied, "If you complain, you gain an enemy [Si uno rezonga, se gana un enemigo]."

While according to the literature on environmental justice we would expect the poor and powerless to rise against those responsible for contamination (and some do, as I explain in chapter 4), most do not. On the contrary, small rural towns in the Pampas are vanishing without a whimper. Like José alluded to, rural folks choose an individual solution (moving out for school and jobs) rather than collective action to address their grievances. José's example also illuminates the extent to which residents ignore (or, at least, are uncertain of) the health risks of pesticide drift, as he claimed that fumigations did not harm those "in good health" like him. As Javier Auyero and Débora Swistun expose in a case of environmental suffering in an Argentine shantytown, it is not uncommon for poor, unemployed, and underemployed residents to be so confused and mystified about their toxic surroundings that they profusely *support*, rather than condemn, the industry that is the source of their contamination. This same industry is the source of their scant material well-being as it provides some jobs and resources to the community.[69]

Rural towns in the Pampas are economically dependent on large-scale agricultural production. GM soy brings jobs and income to rural communities, which explains the widespread support of the agribusiness model in these towns. When communities are too closely tied to a single industry, scholars argue, it creates a political and economic context that is not conducive to mobilization.[70] If the business of GM soy were to shut down, whole towns could collapse—as has already happened in Colonia Schoos with the closing of the dairy farms. The threat of massive unemployment in areas with no alternative job sources forces compliance and acquiescence despite poor labor and environmental conditions.

Moreover, the objective experience of harm is complicated by the fact that the environment does not appear visibly polluted. In Colonia Schoos, as across the many soy towns I visited, I did not see landfills, open sewers, gutted mountains, or smoking stacks. I did not see rats or people scavenging on garbage. There was no foul smell in the air and neither violence nor crime. Contrary to the toxic environments in which the urban poor are forced to live in, or to classic extractivist sites like mining towns, the countryside, even in tapera towns, felt like "nature."[71] The Pampas are verdant with open, blue-sky horizons, and people lead a tranquil lifestyle. As such, it is difficult for locals to objectively "see" the harm that may come with GM soy.

Soybeans in My Backyard

Most illustrative of the state of the invisibilization of the potential health hazards of agrochemical spraying is how many producers proudly use soybeans to landscape the backyards of expensive homes (as shown in figures 2.5 and 2.6).

That was also the case with Bernetti and his wife (everyone called this Italian gringo by his last name). The couple lived atop the natural slope of their farm, which is about fifteen minutes away from Santa María. Bernetti ran his own 1,200-hectare farm with the help of contracted labor, planting half of it with GM soy and the other half with GM corn and sunflowers in rotation. He clearly loved his job and was very proud of it, working on the farm daily and taking care of even the smallest details. When I met him in February 2012, he was painting the gate and putting up a new sign with the name of the farm: La Enamorada.

"People ask me, 'Don't you get bored in the country?'" Bernetti told me as we talked about living in the countryside, far from urban amenities. "How am I going to get bored," he said, "if I've got no time for anything! Right now, the chicks are hatching. There's always something to do."

Bernetti, in his own words, is "not a typical farmer [un productor atípico]." To show me what he meant, he compared his farm entrance, with the freshly painted gate, the grass cut, and the Argentine flag waving, to the farm across the road: a ramshackle gate, rotten and rusty, toppled fences, weeds crawling and overgrown. Later in the day, his wife would make a similar comment, praising the time and attention Bernetti puts into his farm. "The master's eye makes the livestock fat [el ojo del patrón engorda el ganado]," she said, reciting a popular saying that means that people should take close care of their business if they want to make the most out of it. "The others," she added, in reference to the more typical producers, "want to farm by remote control," that is, at a distance aided by cutting-edge technology.

Bernetti took me on a tour of his farm in his Ford truck. We stopped at each plot growing the different crops. With tender care, he reached for a soy leaf here, a sunflower there, showing me how to tell the health of a crop and, thus, its yield and profit potential (figure 2.7). One of the soy fields we skipped because it was, in his words, "dirty [sucio]," meaning invaded by native grasses, or "weeds" from a producer's view. In the manner I explained earlier, Bernetti had a modern take on nature and farming: his

Fig. 2.5. Soybeans used to landscape the backyards of expensive homes, northwest of Buenos Aires province. Photo by the author.

Fig. 2.6. Soybeans used to landscape the backyards of expensive homes, south of Córdoba province. Photo by the author.

goal was for his farm to be proper and ordered, highly productive, tamed. The soy fields he showed me were stunningly neat: a broad extension of uniform, bright green bushes (figure 2.8). When the breeze blew, the field gradually changed colors, a soft swell, like a sea of soy.

On the elevated area of Bernetti's farm, surrounded by more than one thousand hectares of GM crops, sits their home, an orchard, and a garden that grows food for personal consumption. I saw lettuce, tomatoes, and ripe peaches. Chickens roamed freely with their little chicks pecking around behind them. They were proud that they grew everything they ate; they even made their own cheese.

"Do you eat the corn and the soy you grow too?" I asked.

"No. It's all for export." Bernetti made no grandiose claims like the other producers who championed their role of feeding the world. I could tell from his expression of disapproval and the passion with which he spoke of his food garden that he did not think of industrial crops as "food." He was also planning on going back to raising cattle for their own meat consumption. "The meat you buy in the supermarket is all from feedlots, it tastes like fish," he said curtly.

After showing me the crop fields and the orchard with the chickens, he invited me into the house for a cold drink and to introduce me to his wife. The house was beautiful. It was spacious, bright, and tastefully decorated in a rustic style: exposed brick, rawhide carpets, wooden furniture. Fresh-cut sunflowers were displayed in large vases. Glass doors like huge windows overlooked the horizon, providing a panoramic view of the GM soy fields growing no more than a hundred feet away. I was puzzled. The literature on US environmental movements had taught me that, at its origin, activists organized around NIMBY (not in my backyard) demands.[72] But there I was, looking at a 1,000-hectare backyard of genetically modified crops. While many rural inhabitants of the Pampas may not have the means to move away from toxic fields, many of those who do have the power to do so, still *choose* to site their homes there.

I did not ask Bernetti or his wife what they thought about the risks of agrochemical spraying. *I* was the one dumbfounded and confused. In my mind there was no doubt they were exposed to pesticide drift. All over my fieldnotes I had highlighted and underlined, "need to know with ethnographic detail how do people feel and think about fumigations," but, on the spot, I blanked and could not ask. It felt evident to me that they did not view agrochemicals as a harmful risk: otherwise they would not spray by their own home. Two other interactions had also led me to believe Bernetti

Fig. 2.7. Bernetti on his farm, demonstrating the health of a sunflower plant. Photo by the author.

Fig. 2.8. Field of GM soybeans on Bernetti's farm, northwest of Buenos Aires province. Photo by the author.

considered agrochemicals a benefit of modernity rather than a risk: first, when he had said that agrochemicals are "just a tool to improve nature" and later, when Bernetti's wife had asked him for advice on how to treat the bug-infested tomato plant growing on their doorstep. With the same tender care, Bernetti told her, "No worries, darling, I'll spray it later."

Standing in their living room, I imagined Bernetti and his wife hugging sweetly as they faced that glass window, proudly overlooking the bright green fields after a long day of work. It created an idyllic picture of pastoral living, away from the stressful, polluted city. Yet I could also picture the menacing threat of fumigations. I could see, graphically, that GM soy production is perceived by those who profit from it solely in terms of benefits, and that the potential health risks of agrochemical spraying are hugely underestimated.

Why are rural inhabitants acquiescent in the face of increasing social and environmental harm due to the expansion of GM soybeans? The economic dependence on soybean production and the cultural identity created around agrarian technological innovation create consent toward the benefits of the agro-industry even though they also create extensive social and ecological disorganization. Chapter 3 engages more deeply with the category of the in-betweens and how they perpetuate the status quo. In particular, how do women in Santa María present an alternative (gendered) way of knowing that emphasizes care for their children and thus leads them to question the risks of agrochemical spraying? Because of their structurally disempowered position, however, instead of mobilizing, they construct their acquiescence with silence and denial.

3. The Elephant in the Field

It was the late afternoon on a hot summer day in February 2012 in Santa María. I met Julia at her home. She was about my age, late twenties or early thirties, and everything about her life seemed to fit into the mold of a comfortable, white, middle-class family. The dining room where we chatted was spacious and the furniture was new. Glass doors connected the dining room to the courtyard through which we could see Julia's daughters playing with their friends. The four girls were going up and down a slide, in and out of the swimming pool. Julia's third and youngest was less than a year old, a baby boy sleeping pleasantly in his stroller by our side. Her husband was at work.

Julia handed me a mate as she gave me yet another example of how well the town and her family were doing with the soy boom. She and her husband run two stores downtown selling toys and school and office supplies. Their business was doing well because, as Julia said, "When el campo does well, we all do well." For the first hour or so, my conversation with Julia seemed to be yet another example of the "we all live off the countryside" theme I noted in chapter 2.

Santa María is visibly reaping the benefits of soybean production. The main plaza is one contrasting example of how affluent the town is compared to other rural towns I visited. It is very well taken care of, efforts that require resources. It has brand-new tiled paving, pruned trees, and well-groomed flowerbeds. In the center of town, the plaza is the heart of the community's social life. I strolled it often in the late evenings with Nidia when it cooled off, and everyone old and young seemed to come out to socialize, play, and enjoy ice cream. Surrounding the plaza, as most towns in the Buenos Aires province are laid out, are the main public buildings: the town hall, the church, the police station, and the Banco Nación.

All these buildings are recently renovated. Around town, there are plenty of paved streets (uncommon in rural areas), large, expensive homes, and brand-new cars. There is a vibrant construction sector too, the result of soybean farmers' reinvestment efforts as well as a response to increasing demand from new residents. According to INDEC census data, Santa María's population was about 12,000 inhabitants in 2010, a growth of 10 percent since 2001.

Like the rest of the Pampas, the fields surrounding Santa María, which have historically grown wheat and fed roaming cattle, have given room to soybeans. Herbicide-resistant transgenic crops grow almost exclusively up to the edge of town (figure 3.1). Soybean producers, as I have mentioned and saw often across the country, even plant on the shoulders of the roads (figure 3.2). Billboards advertising crop-dusting services line the roads into town. Bordering the town are multiple silos for grain storage, the offices of several grain traders and input providers, agribusinesses selling tractors and other agricultural machinery, and a sizable fertilizer plant. All these create jobs for locals but are also a potential source of agrochemical contamination.

Julia seemed proud of the soy boom. But as we spent more time talking, her story began to drift away from the all-benefits territory. Julia mentioned her neighbor, a rural contractor for terrestrial fumigations. She said she did not like how he often parked his fumigation tractor right across the street, too close to her home. Julia later mentioned the fumigations and how the farms extend to the entrance of town. Then, she brought up the fertilizer plant. I could sense something was not quite right. Julia seemed concerned and at times even afraid, but she was never too specific about what or why, as she would bring up a topic but then suddenly drop it from the conversation.

So, I prodded. "Are there any problems with all that?"

Julia brought up how the plants in her front garden were dying. Was it because of the neighbor's *mosquito* parked across the street? She mentioned this fumigation machinery in one sentence and "forgot" it in the next. Our conversation grew slowly but steadily from uneventful to terrifying. Connected to nothing in particular, Julia mentioned the growing number of people suffering from cancer in town. "Young people, of thirty-something, forty," she added, to clue me in to how unusual those cases were. A sense of unease and concern grew between us. Julia did not stop talking. She told me about young, healthy women she knew of having miscarriages and ba-

Fig. 3.1. Outskirts of Santa María, with the soy farm extending to the edge of town. Photo by the author.

Fig. 3.2. Soy growing on publicly owned shoulders of the road. The private farm ends at the fence at the tree line. Photo by the author.

bies with birth defects. I knew how unusual that must have felt for young women with resources and routine access to health care. Her own niece was among those babies. Julia told me how her sister's family had gone to Buenos Aires for treatment.

And then Julia went silent. Eerily silent.

I did not have to say a word before she asked, "Would *that* be the reason?"

That. We both knew what she was talking about. Glyphosate. Toxic agrochemicals. Is pesticide drift to blame for her dying plants, for young neighbors getting cancer, for the miscarriages and birth defects?

Julia had raised the thorniest of questions, and she did not wait for me to answer. She replied right away, seemingly talking to me, but not really. She was mostly talking to herself: "I don't know. No one knows."

Santa María is one of the many Pampas towns that have benefited from GM soy production in the ways I explained in chapter 2. These were towns where locals consistently told me, as Julia did, "We all live off the countryside," and praised the cultural and material benefits of large-scale agroindustrial production. Santa María is also a typical soy town because of the absolute absence of mass protest against soybean extractivism. But life is not all soy and roses in this boomtown. Julia's story highlights the existence of latent grievances arising from soybean production, in particular around the health hazards of agrochemical exposure. As Steven Lukes argues, latent grievances indicate a conflict of interest between the powerful and their subjects.[1] This situation of latent conflict reveals the workings of power, as subjects—that is, the ordinary folks who bear the toxic brunt of large-scale agriculture—comply and consent instead of rebelling against the unjust situation.

In this chapter, I tell the stories of a group of women who, like Julia, shared with me in murmurs and whispers their worries and fears around agrochemicals; they were alarmed by rising cancer rates among neighbors and concerned about children's health. Despite their fears, however, these women never attempted to dig deeper. Much to the contrary, by the time a doubt emerged, they or other women in the room automatically stifled it—as Julia did when she muttered, "I don't know. No one knows," to put an end to our conversation. Having shown how power operates to create acquiescence and consent, in this chapter I delve into the micro-level of social interactions and emotions to show how acquiescence is enacted in everyday life. The stories I share in this chapter illustrate that even when there are grievances worth mobilizing for, they are actively kept latent. These stories prove how successful and efficient the workings of power have been to create acquiescence and consent around GM soybean extractivism among rural communities in the Pampas.

Keeping such grievances latent involves specific practices that the women of Santa María demonstrated to me throughout my time with them: silencing, self-policing, and denial, as Julia did, saying, "No one knows," and discouraging me from any further comment. The women would also say, "There has always been cancer [cáncer siempre hubo]," to deny the increased health risks of mounting fumigations, and even, "We don't talk about that," as ways to end conversations.

These silencing acts, while individual and subjective, have a social basis. The collective uncertainty and denial of environmental hazards are socially and politically created and expressed through everyday practices and emotions.[2] "The elephant in the room" is a metaphor for what Eviatar Zerubavel calls a "conspiracy of silence," that is, the tacit agreement among a group of people "to outwardly ignore something of which they are all personally aware."[3] How do you miss an elephant in a room? The image is ludicrous and points to the fact that avoiding such a conspicuous issue requires a deliberate effort not to notice. Such is the case with the health hazards of agrochemical exposure, a problem looming over the Pampas that residents actively pretend is not there.

Seeds of Doubt

A few kilometers away from the main entrance to Santa María, scattered among farms, stand the offices and silos of several multinational grain traders and exporters, including Bunge, Cargill, and Louis Dreyfus Company. I went with Nidia to one of these offices to interview Diego at his workplace. Diego is Nidia's nephew, a young man in his early twenties who has lived his whole life in Santa María.

Most of the interview consisted of Diego showing Nidia and me around the company and explaining how grain trading and exporting works. We saw the offices, where multiple computers showed crop prices fluctuating on the major world markets. The offices were connected to a huge barn storing small tractors and other grain-handling and -storing equipment. We spent some time there talking, learning about how the barn is situated right next to the railroad tracks so that the grain can go directly from the storage silos through massive tubes into shipping containers on freight trains, directly to the port for shipping abroad.

Near the end of the interview, something unexpected happened. As we walked out of the barn, a plane flew low right in front of our eyes. A crop duster.

I looked around. On our left, about sixty feet away, was a soy field with plants that stood three feet high. Right across from us, another one. On our right, sunflower fields. We were surrounded by large-scale industrial farming.

In a split second, I saw the plane and the fields, and I thought: glyphosate. It stopped me cold. I felt my eyes widen. I heard Diego beside me say calmly, like it was nothing special, "a crop duster [un avión fumigador]." As if he was giving me a simple description of the surroundings, just like he had been doing with all the equipment and machinery he had showed me earlier.

Perplexed, I asked him, "People fumigate here with planes?"

"Yes, sure," Diego replied confidently.

"But isn't it prohibited?"

At least that was what I had been told by the CEO of Los Cardones: that fumigating by plane around Santa María was not permitted.

Diego shook his head and rolled his eyes in disbelief. "There might be regulation, but it is not enforced," he said. Then he confirmed, "Fumigations are done by airplane [Se fumiga con avión]."

I was stunned. My researcher objectivity was out the window. "But it's right there!!!" I raised my voice while I gestured toward the soy field across the fence. In my mind, there was no way for this plane to avoid spraying his workplace, surrounded as we were by agrochemical-intensive crops.

A moment of silence. I could see resignation creeping on to Diego's face.

In a very low voice, he broke our silence. "People say that a report came out, that there are malformations . . ." His voice faded before he finished his thought.

I was in shock, a mix of indignation and intense curiosity. I realized I was face-to-face with my key research question on acquiescence. And with the latent grievances that, Lukes argues, make explicit the workings of power.[4]

I snapped back. "What then??! ¿¡¿Nadie protesta?!?"

Diego paused. He tried to wield an answer. "Well . . . soy is big money [es que da mucha plata]." This was his simple answer as to why nobody protests.

Diego turned silent and lowered his head. I understood why he could not say much, particularly considering the multinational corporation that employed him. At the very least, I was sure he did not want to risk being fired.

In the midst of our very uncomfortable silence, Nidia, who had barely spoken throughout the whole interview, stepped in.

"Well, but cancer . . . there has always been cancer," she said. "No one knows if it is because of the fumigations or what."

No one, during our whole conversation, had brought up cancer or any other illness, except for Diego's timid mention of birth defects. For hours we had talked only about crop exports, prices in the Rosario and Chicago grain markets, local and global transportation, storage facilities, increasing productivity, profit margins, and the like. Clearly something else had been occupying Nidia's mind that prompted her to make that intervention. With her comment, Nidia acknowledged what the three of us thought when we saw that crop duster but did not dare to mention. The "elephant in the field," the issue that we were all personally aware of but outwardly refused to acknowledge: the toxic health effects of agrochemical spraying. Yet in the same breath she doubted its culpability and shut down the conversation.

De Eso No Se Habla (We Don't Talk about That)

Latent grievances about the health risks of agrochemical spraying emerged in the moments of closest confidence between women and me—when men had left the room, in the safety of kitchens and courtyards. As Zerubavel argues, it is these moments of social proximity between equals (in terms of power relations) that are more likely to encourage the trust and openness necessary to speak up and name "the elephant."[5]

When it first started happening, it took me by surprise. Santa María was, on arrival, no different than other soy towns I visited. Nidia and her husband, Carlos, were eager to show me how well Santa María has done in the soy boom. They drove me around town, pointing at the renovated state of downtown, at the new multistory building, "the first in town," as Nidia proudly said, and at the homes of the wealthy. "All paid for with soy money," as Carlos said. They have done well too. Carlos owns a small trucking company to transport grains to port. For years, he was a truck driver himself. "But especially in the last ten years that soybeans are so profitable [que la soja vale], I have been able to replace the older trucks," he said. "I bought two Scania, brand-new [nuevitos]." Carlos has retired from driving but not from management. His son and an employee drive the trucks now. Nidia's "main job," as she told me, is "as grandma [de abuela]." She babysits her two grandchildren daily.

When Carlos, Nidia, and I were together, the themes I explained in the previous chapters repeated. "We all live off the countryside," they said often, yet like other rural folks they also had to qualify their answer when prompted. "No, it's all large landowners [son dueños grandes]," said Nidia when I asked her who really controlled farming. "People work in the silos, in the stores and businesses," she said. "There are no factories here. If there were . . . it could help much [qué bien vendrían]." Carlos would often engage me in talking about agrarian technologies using the modernization discourse. "You should have seen this German machine they brought in to harvest! Amazing! [¡Una maravilla!]," he said, proudly miming driving the harvester, right hand on the steering wheel, left hand speaking on a cell phone. "It has a computer that gives you all the information: soil humidity, seeds, how much you harvest. . . . A beautiful machine."

Because we often talked at their home (where I was staying), Nidia was often present during these conversations. She would always agree with Carlos, either nodding or engaging on the same terms, continuing our conversations, never contradicting him. When Carlos complained against the government, for example, Nidia would agree, saying, "Yes, the Kirchners are against el campo. If we have four more years of Cristina [as president], she'll bury us [nos entierra]." Nidia would not contradict Carlos, even when speaking of agrochemicals. "They are all paranoid," he would often say when I mentioned those concerned about agrochemicals. Fumigations, to him (and to Nidia when he was present), seemed to be an issue not worth discussing as concerns were rapidly dismissed from our conversations; they were considered, as Carlos said while Nidia nodded, "irrational fears [miedos infundados]."

Yet when Carlos was not at home, Nidia's support cracked ever so slightly and shifted, particularly on the topic of agrochemicals. "People talk, say that this one or that one in town has cancer. . . . I don't know. . . . The fertilizer plant worries me sometimes, especially for the children," Nidia said, referring to her grandchildren. As I spent more time with them, my perplexity grew: I realized women's performance in front of others differed from conversations backstage.[6] I also quickly realized, however, that

I was not supposed to reveal this dissonance—and thus I too often fell in the same spiral of denial when in social gatherings.

Though Nidia and the other women of Santa María did not keep completely silent with me, their ultimate denial communicated that, for them, the grievance was not worth their mobilizing. Many, many times Nidia ended our conversations by saying, "There has always been cancer," as a way to minimize and deny harm, and she would get busy with her chores.

It happened over and over again.

One time I went to an *asado*, a barbecue, at Carolina and Martín's place for a small gathering of family and close friends. They are a young couple with two young children. Martín runs a 1,000-hectare farm, dedicated mostly to growing soybeans and raising cattle in feedlots. The meat for the barbecue dinner came from this feedlot. At the table, everyone—Martín in particular, who led the conversation on the superior quality of feedlot-raised beef—took turns extolling the quality of the meat.

During dinner we talked about el campo, and everyone seemed eager to share their knowledge and experiences in relation to my research, the reason why I was visiting in Santa María. We talked of the farms' bounties and how they spilled over into town. The men were poised to praise the speed and quality of technological innovation and its positive impact on development for Argentina. A fair amount of time was also dedicated to discussing politics, as is common at animated dinner tables in Argentina. They all took time to share their frustrations with how the Kirchners' administration policies, in their words, "hinder progress." However, overall, the mood around el campo was celebratory.

When the meal was over, the adult women cleared the table for coffee and dessert. The men stayed seated, as is still usual, around the dinner table. The kids were outside playing or asleep.

In the kitchen, behind doors, a totally different story than the one told at the table emerged. Carolina and I took charge of doing the dishes. We stood shoulder to shoulder facing the sink. She washed and I dried as she passed the clean dishes to me. Without a prompt or question on my part and completely out of the blue—not a word had been spoken on these issues at dinnertime—Carolina started talking to me about agrochemicals and health issues. First, she told me of how Martín brags that he can open herbicide jerricans with his teeth if needed. While this speaks to how confident some are of herbicides' allegedly nonharmful qualities, Carolina, while not openly disqualifying her husband, subtly wondered if this was a safe thing to do. She moved on to tell me about three cases of women in town who had to terminate their pregnancies because their babies' heads were not growing properly. Microcephaly, I knew, is a common reason for miscarriages among women exposed to pesticide drift.[7] She then mentioned the growing number of people with cancer in town. She was worried, I could tell. To dispel her own concerns, she resorted to the popular mantra of "I know, there has always been cancer." Still, she could not help adding, in an even softer voice, "Everyone says it's not the case, but I think so, that agrochemicals have something to do with this."

Carolina never asked me what my opinion was. Nidia entered the kitchen and we instantly fell silent, as if we had been caught red-handed, and we quietly finished our chores. The three of us brought dessert and coffee to the table, where we continued our previous talk as if Carolina's "confession" had never happened.

The transformation of a routine injustice into a mobilizing grievance (the process of "framing") arises in social interaction, through interpretive processes mediated by culture.[8] In conversation we find a space to link our private issues to public problems. Yet by silencing and denial, these spaces close rather than create opportunities for collective action.[9] The exchanges with the women of Santa María exemplify how policing, silencing, and denial work to contain grievance framing and to suffocate contestation. "Why don't people protest?" I asked every time I could when these issues were whispered. And every time I was met with a gesture of resignation and a sigh that killed the conversation. Every time, their silence fed the spiral of denial.

Julia's reply stood as the most symbolic of the conspiracy of silence around the health risks of agrochemical use in GM soy production in the Pampas.

When I asked her, "Why don't people protest?," she said, "We don't talk about that," and fell silent . . . as did I.

"De eso no se habla" is an iconic phrase that to any Argentine instantly recalls the terror and the complicities of silence around the disappeared during the Dirty War. Dictatorships and totalitarian police states are extreme examples of power elites disempowering and silencing populations, as happened in Argentina during the late 1970s and early 1980s.[10] During that time, Argentine society remained mostly silent while thirty thousand people were "disappeared," kidnapped by the state with no records to trace them, and while babies were stolen from women in clandestine detention centers and raised by the families of the kidnappers. Violence, Sebastián Carassai argues, is central to understanding why the Argentine middle classes created a culture of nonactivism during that time.[11] While state terror is in the past, its memory is not.[12] The phrase "de eso no se habla" is commonly used among Argentines and ties directly to the political incuriosity prevalent during the dictatorship, as happened during my conversations with the women of Santa María.

"Why is it that people don't talk about it?" I finally managed to ask Julia.

"Well . . . there are fortunes being made [es que da fortunas]." Like Diego, so too Julia pointed out high profitability as the reason for acquiescence.

Gendered Perceptions

The economic dependence on soybean production and the cultural identity created around agrarian technological innovation in rural towns like Santa María have kept most people quiet; the benefits seem to outweigh the risks. Latent grievances over the health hazards of agrochemical exposure, however, indicate a dissonance between what the public expresses outwardly (approval and support) and what people utter behind closed doors (questions and doubts), exposing the workings of power. Based on my observations in Santa María, these latent grievances are divided across gender lines. Women tapping into their identities as mothers and caregivers were more likely to question the potential harmful impact of agrochemicals on health in a context of soybean hegemony. Why is that? And how does that impact mobilization and inaction?

As social-movement scholars argue, there is a subjective component that is key to movement emergence; the subjective meanings people attach to situations that lead to collective action are the result of cognitive and emotional dimensions.[13] What we notice and perceive emerges from our roles and experiences in interaction with others. Our "cognitive bias," Barbara Risman argues, is the result of different status expectations for women and men.[14] Gendered roles lead to gendered experiences. Women's role as primary caretakers of the family leads them to be more aware of the real and potential health risks of polluting industries.[15] Feminized subjects thus present a way of knowing that arises from affective emotions (the affective bonds of love) as well as from detailed, grounded observations. Because they are in charge of their children, mothers are gathering data on their kids constantly and consistently; each day, they know how their child slept and for how long, what they ate or did not eat, how they feel and act when they are sick and sad compared with when they are happy, healthy, and cheerful. That is how mothers *know*. It is a grounded, observational and experiential, embodied and emotional cognition. This way of knowledge is contrasted with the rational (civilizing) knowledge of modern science.

Traditional gendered roles similarly (but, of course, oppositely) affect the experiences, beliefs, and ways of knowing of most of the men I met in Santa María. Following traditional European masculine expectations and arrangements, they self-defined as producers, experts, entrepreneurs, and, in the context of their families, like Martín above, also as breadwinners. So did all the other men I interviewed who were in charge of, worked in, or were trained in large-scale agricultural production, as I show across the book. It is important to underscore that, in my research, the women emphasized care while the men focused on profitability, productivity, and scientific expertise; this is not because of their different sex but because of the socially constructed definition of what it is to be male/masculine or female/feminine—in short, their gender.[16] In the Pampas, life and labor are organized according to traditional gendered arrangements; thus, gender identities tend to match one's sex assigned at birth (the definition of cisgender). In the rural areas where I did fieldwork, men tend to act masculine, women to act feminine; men marry women, who then have children that the woman will care for and the man will provide for (this is why, as I explained in the introduction, women treated me as a future wife and mother without doubt or question).

As large-scale agriculture in the Pampas maintains traditional lines of gendered labor, at the same time that it is male-dominated, masculinity in soybean production becomes hegemonic.[17] "Hegemonic masculinity," according to R. W. Connell and James Messerschmidt, refers to the various material and discursive practices that aim to produce and maintain gender-based inequalities and inequities.[18] When a woman enters into these male-dominated workspaces, she is required to behave according to the gendered (masculine) standards of the position she holds rather than to her gendered (female) identity.[19] That was the case with Mariana, the only female agronomist employed in el campo that I met during my fieldwork. She is an employee of Los Cardones, the Santa María–based agribusiness, and a colleague of Lucas and Tomás, whom I introduced in chapter 2. Like them, she is also in her late twenties and a recent graduate in agrarian engineering from a national university. When I met her, I could not hide my surprise that she was the first woman working for an agribusiness whom I could interview.

"I'm always talking with men!" I said with candid surprise.

"Yes," Mariana replied softly and half-smiled. "Yes, mostly, yes. This is the land of men [es tierra de hombres]."

I toned down my excitement to match her caution. We were, indeed, surrounded by men in Los Cardones's office.

"But there are, there are some women!" Mariana tried lifting our feminist spirits, at least for a moment. "But they're in sales," she added. "All my girlfriends [who are also] agrarian engineers, most of them are in commercial positions."

"What does that mean?" I asked.

"That is how I started, too, in Cargill, in acopio [grain storing for trading]," Mariana said. "Commercial means that you are in sales, either in grain storing or crop buying or input sales or customer relations, in charge of customer accounts. Not so much in the technical area, going out to the farms [or] during harvest time."

"And why is that?" I asked.

"Well . . . ," Mariana became cautious again, "it's that there are . . . there are certain paradigms still. It's not that simple. I work in Los Cardones because they know me. Now, if they don't know you and a position opens up for an engineer. . . . I don't know. It's not easy to get hired as a woman. At least, it happened to me. Before I started work here, in so many other places [I interviewed] they told me, 'Truth be told, yes [we would give you the job] but if you were a man.' That is, being a woman . . . it's complicated for us."

"But why not? It's not really hard work." I could have understood an argument based on the relative physical strength of men necessary to perform grueling tasks on the farm. But the repeated theme across my fieldwork was how technological innovation has made it possible to replace strenuous physical labor with computers and machines that enable farming comfortably and from a distance. Anyone with the right training and expertise could do it, regardless of their physical attributes.

"No, it's not [hard work]," Mariana agreed. "But it is still a bit machista [sexist]. Women are trying to insert themselves in el campo, but it's not easy. And compared to other countries, don't even go there! In other countries, women do the same [physical labor] as men. On the farm, exactly the same. But here . . ." She paused for a while. "But you're right, in terms of the work we do, the physical aspect has nothing to do with it, it's more the paradigm than anything else. And here even the soil is soft!" She laughed briefly at her own joke but then turned dead serious. "It's that this is a machista country," she said, and took a long breath before she continued. "The good part of it is that when you go to the field [as a woman], everyone takes care of you. The truck driver comes and offers you mates. Some other [man] comes and offers you a chair [sillita], another one [tells you], 'No, let me climb up for you!'" Mariana's voice communicated irony and annoyance at being treated so preciously, weighing the benefits of getting extra attention at the farm in her everyday work with the sexist drawbacks of the larger picture. "That is . . . along with the good comes the bad. . . . I mean, for women . . . it is much harder to break into this environment."

Of her female classmates who graduated with her at the university, "only one is doing the same job" as her, she told me, and she agreed with my observation that there are not many women in charge of agricultural production in the Pampas. "In the technical meetings Monsanto and Syngenta organize to train us, often there are only one or two of us [women]; the rest are all men."

I was curious to know what Mariana's take on glyphosate and agrochemical spraying was. Is it "a woman thing" to emphasize care over productivity and profits? Mariana, university-trained and employed as an agrarian engineer, affirmed gender scholars' claims by reproducing the masculine discourse of the new agricultural paradigm. "There are rules for fumigation," she said. "If you [as the agronomist in charge] are present during fumigations, you are complying with the law."

Mariana made it very clear that agrochemicals are safe if used according to best practices, in the same manner that powerful (male/masculine) corporate and state actors do, as shown in the previous and following chapters. She, like them, believes laypeople should trust the experts on the issue of agrochemical use and their impact. She gave me a handful of examples of how that needs to be communicated to the general public. "I was in this presentation organized by CASAFE [the Argentine association of agrochemical companies] in La Rural." La Rural is a huge agriculture and livestock fair that takes place in Buenos Aires every winter break and draws thousands of both rural and city folks. "The talk," Mariana continued, "was to raise awareness [concientizar a la gente] that what producers do is not harmful." This presentation took place during the discursive battle over glyphosate between the government and soybean producers following the conflicto del campo. In those informative talks (clearly a strategy to create acquiescence among the general population), the CASAFE experts, Mariana recounted, "showed data on how many *intoxicados* [people poisoned by agrochemicals] there have been in, say, the last twelve years. They showed like five cases of poisoning. Nothing!" Mariana repeated the hegemonic discourse: "It's that people talk and talk, but they haven't a clue!" Then she brought up another lecture. "They were showing pictures of Europe, how crops are planted up to people's front doors—you've seen European landscapes, right? There's a little house, and the rolling hills, and it's all planted out, and they fumigate there, too!—and the guy [the agribusiness representative] said, 'If you knock on the door of that house, the person who answers has no visible deformities [no sale ningún deforme]!' I mean, really, here [in Argentina] we see such ignorance in people! They [the laypeople] would have you believe that the producer is thoughtless [un inconsciente]."

My exchange with Mariana highlights that gendered roles in gendered interactions frame people's experiences and perceptions of the situation in general and of environmental hazards in particular. Her cognitive and emotional ways of knowing arise from being an expert and an engineer herself in a male-dominated environment. In this sense, while she is well aware of the structural disadvantages of being a woman in a male-dominated field, she is a masculinized subject as she frames agricultural production and agrochemical use in the terms that other self-defined male/masculine experts and producers use. Feminized subjects like the women of Santa María, on the contrary, prioritize motherhood and care, and that impacts their perception of environmental harm.

Caught in Between

Why did the women of Santa María admit that they acknowledged the potential risks of soybean production when others in Santa María solely emphasized benefits? And why are these concerned mothers not acting on their grievances and organizing into a social movement? I argue that inaction, despite the perception of risk, is the result of synergies of power at work—that is, the compound effect of multiple and intersecting axes of domination and inequality. In this case, gender is clearly the dominating axis. The women of Santa María share an important characteristic: they are all married and live in traditional gendered arrangements; their husbands are the primary breadwinners in their households, and their source of income is tied to large-scale agriculture. Therefore, they are also in that "in-between" category—caught in the middle of the power spectrum. They enjoy the wealth and privilege provided by their class position and their race (as white women of European descent), yet their gender has historically excluded them from agricultural decision-making power, even when "the family" is in the soy business (the result of two centuries of agrarian capitalism in the Pampas, as I explained in chapters 1 and 2).

Gender structures their position in society and also their ways of knowing—and here I refer to "knowing" in a broad way, as a conception and perception of risk that is simultaneously cognitive, embodied, and emotional. Self-identified as wives and mothers, in charge of children who, because of their young age, are more vulnerable to agrochemical exposure, their gendered selves lead them to prioritize care over the profitability of large-scale agriculture. Thus, they present a way of knowing based on the felt, lived experience that results from taking constant care of their loved ones in everyday life—or, as women would tell me, on "a mother's intuition" to protect her children. At the same time, they are also well aware that this intimate, experiential, gendered way of "knowing" cannot successfully establish claims to legitimacy in the cultural, political economy of soybean extractivism, which is patriarchal, capitalist, and modern. Facing the very present and real risks of losing their husbands and their source of income, the women of Santa María choose to silence themselves and others instead of speaking up against the potential risks of soybean extractivism. By doing so, they actively—though I do not think purposefully—acquiesce and reproduce injustice and the status quo.

In chapter 4, I introduce the Mothers of Barrio Ituzaingó Anexo and the women activists of Malvinas Argentinas. Unlike the women of Santa María, these women have organized in collective action to protect their children's health from toxic agrochemical risk. "When a mother's child is sick," women activists told me, not only does the mother "know" but it is, in their words, her "duty" to protect him. Female activists from Barrio Ituzaingó and Malvinas Argentinas all frequently referred to a "mother's instinct" to protect her children. This sense of "duty" and "intuition" gives women the clout to protest.[20] Drawing on motherhood as an identity is a strategy that has given women activists legitimacy and protection from those who may want to question (or silence) their activism.[21] The Mothers of Barrio Ituzaingó, for example, identify as "mothers" as a political act and in reference to the Madres de Plaza de Mayo, the Argentine mothers who organized to protest the disappearance of their children during the Dirty War.[22] They thus challenge the traditional division between the public and private spheres through a politicization of motherhood.[23] By drawing on motherhood, however, women activists get caught in a contradiction (or "trapped in a bad script," as Diana Taylor has argued about the Madres de Plaza de Mayo).[24] Because motherhood is depoliticized in the public's eye (women are just being "good mothers"), women have more freedom to protest; yet because of women's lower status in the social hierarchy, their protests are taken less seriously by those in power. This is, as Shannon Bell argues, also a barrier for men's engagement in activism. Because men's protests are always seen as political, they have less freedom to protest; they risk marginalization and loss of status if they go against the dominant economic order.[25]

Unlike the women activists I introduce next, the women in Santa María, instead of acting on their shared grievance, choose silence and denial. Could they not organize in collective action to address their concerns? The women of Santa María, I argue, are caught in another type of contradiction. Gender scholars use the concept of "emphasized femininity" in opposition to hegemonic masculinity to refer to practices in which women engage to construct gender inequality vis-à-vis men, as wives, daughters, and so on.[26] Emphasized femininity focuses on the interplay between masculinities and femininities and especially on the ways women comply with the gender hierarchy. The women of Santa María, while they tap into their gendered identities as mothers to question the potential health hazards of agrochemical use, risk their class status (as their families depend on soybean production) and likely the relation with their male partners if they do so. Thus, either because they feel powerless or because they have willingly accepted this trade-off, instead of speaking up, the women of Santa María self-police, silence, and deny.

Gendered differences and inequity, in and of themselves, do not explain the complex constellation of power that puts the women of Santa María in such a bind. Class status and class identity are also key dimensions that explain their acquiescence. Their class identity, moreover, has cultural and racial undertones that further contribute to their silence. The women of Santa María, mostly by virtue of their marriages (due to their husbands' occupations), belong to the middle class.[27] The identity of the Argentine middle class, as Ezequiel Adamovsky argues, is uniquely composed of specific racial, political, and cultural characteristics: it is at its core white (of European descent), anti-Peronist, and the promoter of modernization and civilization—in opposition to the "barbarism" brought by the Peronist working-class masses.[28] The middle class, particularly in the Pampas, is the bearer of the guiding myths of national identity I explained in chapter 1: myths that, I have argued, are key to explaining acquiescence and consent.

As part of the middle class, families in Santa María share lifestyles, values, and beliefs similar to other middle-class families in the rest of the world; these lifestyles are, as Carlos said, "paid for with soy money." Two of these shared middle-class values are consumerism and the value given to education as a means for upward mobility.[29] In their pursuit, those "in between" are often left in the bind of defending polluting industries to protect their class status even if at the expense of polluting their own land and bodies.

Environmental sociologists know well how accelerating the treadmill of consumption leads to social and ecological devastation: buying more "stuff" only means a global race for lower wages and increased resource extraction and pollution.[30] Residents in Santa María, as I explained, are very well off in comparison with people in recent decades and other rural towns. But while they have seen an increase in their comfort levels due to the soy boom, they do not overconsume as their urban counterparts might do. While I did observe expensive homes and locals driving their brand-new cars for even the most walkable of distances, I did not observe shopping malls, Amazon deliveries, fast-food drive-throughs, the latest electronic gadgets, or other signs of overconsumption. The families I met did not have air conditioning at home, did not waste food, and did not fly abroad for vacations. So, while they are protecting the soy industry to maintain their middle-class lifestyles, their ecological footprint as middle-class consumers is not as large as that of their counterparts in more affluent nations. Yet their new material affluence, in addition to a dearth of jobs in other industries, as I explained earlier, does contribute to their acquiescence.

The value given to education—in the context of contemporary Argentina, where middle-class families favor private over public schools—I found to be more telling of the ambiguous situation the women of Santa María are in.[31] Most of the time I spent alone with Nidia and Laura, her daughter-in-law, we did not converse of illnesses and fumigations but of daily routines: what to prepare for dinner, what was on TV, where on the road Laura's husband was, how the kids behaved, and, quite often, the kids' schooling. Laura is a teacher and a mother of two: a ten-year-old boy and a one-year-old girl. The boy goes to the only private school in Santa María, which is subsidized by, perhaps unsurprisingly, the philanthropic efforts of local soybean producers. It is another way in which powerful agribusiness actors garner consent from rural communities.

"In Santa María, the wealthy are not separated but integrated [in the community]," said Laura. It was an afternoon like others, when the three of us were drinking mate in Nidia's courtyard, watching over the kids while Carlos slept his siesta. "The school has a system of scholarships and sponsorships so that children of lower means [chicos humildes] can attend private school," she said. The sponsorships are personal: a producer becomes the *padrino*, the "godfather" or benefactor of the student.

Laura's child receives a scholarship to attend this private school, a school literally paid for with soy money. Those who help her child receive a better education are, while wealthy producers and landowners, not distant strangers but part of the community and neighbors of Santa María. How could one turn against your own neighbors? And turn against fumigations when soybean production provides a better future for your child? Wanting the best education for your children is caring for them too, right? Trapped in this dilemma, while occupied by daily routine, Laura, like the other women in Santa María, chooses to normalize life in the midst of toxicity.[32] That is, if and when worries emerge, she chooses denial and moves on. The trade-off, surely, is the damage to everyone's health.

The women of Santa María are caught in an ambiguous position vis-à-vis soybean production: they support it because they benefit, they doubt it in private because they see some harm, but they do not dare to publicly question the political, economic, and scientific establishments that affirm the safety of agrochemicals and the practices associated with them. Their way of knowing does not hold the same value as the official knowledge perpetuated by the synergies of power that control soybean extractivism. It is important to note, however, that these women who derive compensatory benefits from soy production are not utterly powerless but rather have significant autonomy, which reveals the dilemmas of gender hegemony and the ambiguities of domination. Inside their homes, these women have significant power over their male partners and children.[33] Sherry Ortner refers to "on-the-ground female power" to look at the ways in which women subtly resist the unequal gender hierarchy (in the manner of James Scott's "weapons of the weak").[34]

I wonder how many women in other kitchens in the Pampas region, caught in the in-between of the synergies of power, notice harm but choose silence. Chapter 4 looks into those who are the bottom of the power spectrum, who do not benefit from GM soybean production but bear its costs. They have organized to challenge soybean extractivism while more powerful actors have sought to silence that dissent.

4. Against the Grain

"Do you know what it means to lose a child?"

Marcela raised the question halfway through our conversation. It was a rhetorical question, of course. Everyone knows that the pain of losing a child is beyond words and the comprehension of anyone who has not experienced it; it must be the worst of all possible suffering. And yet for Marcela and these other mothers with whom I had the pleasure of talking—women mobilized by the grief of losing children to leukemia and other cancers—that pain compelled them to organize into a movement.

The quest to find out why their children were sick and dying brought thirteen women together in early 2002 in a movement called the Grupo de Madres de Barrio Ituzaingó Anexo. These mothers have become the symbol of the struggle against agrochemical spraying in Argentina. During our conversation, back in 2015, I heard pain and weariness in their voices. I saw it in their eyes. These women seemed heartbroken over the daily penuries of illness and the grief of loss, exhausted from going to the hospital to care for ill family members and to the health ministries to demand medical attention and the end of fumigations. I felt their anger and frustration from dealing with unresponsive public officials who promise but do not deliver. I could feel, too, past the pain, their warmth, their strength. There was a spark, a brilliance deep in their weary eyes. It was the bravery and courage to face what most do not want to face: that pesticides are to blame for the illness and lost lives of many who live and work near soy farms in Argentina.

The mothers of the Ituzaingó Anexo neighborhood are the central figures of the movements against toxic agrochemicals in Argentina. Further supporting what the literature of environmental justice has shown, mobilizations against soybean extractivism have emerged among those at the bottom of the power spectrum: those who bear its costs but reap none of the benefits.[1]

Social mobilization against GM soy in Argentina primarily centers around two main axes: the health and environmental risks of toxic agrochemical exposure, and the forced evictions and habitat devastation that come as a consequence of the northern expansion of the agrarian frontier. Broadly, the movements that have emerged in response are thus (1) citizen assemblies in defense of health and life, like the Mothers of Ituzaingó, triggered by the spread of agrochemical-induced illnesses and (2) the peasant-indigenous movement in the north of the country. Here I pay more attention to the movements against agrochemicals for the following reasons. First, this book focuses on the Pampas, and in this region mobilization against agrochemicals is the most extensive. Second, the peasant movement in the Pampas is thin in strength and numbers, the consequence of a history of invisibilization and dispossession I explained in chapter 1. Third, the impact of pesticide drift on children's health is a main catalyst for activism across actors and regions, as is the case among indigenous peasants in northern Formosa province.[2] Fourth, the anti-agrotoxins movement has been relatively more successful in its demands; for example, it has managed to get local ordinances passed to establish buffer zones, and it has increased awareness over the negative impact of GM soy production and glyphosate use in particular. Lastly, I believe that framing grievances around protecting children's health has the potential to create alliances and galvanize opposition, as the mothers in this chapter have begun to do.

While these movements' demands to defend life and livelihood are urgent and praiseworthy, they remain relatively small in numbers, and their impact on national policy is negligible. Why? What has kept local mobilization from affecting large-scale change? In addition to the fact that rural towns—and the country as a whole—are economically and ideologically tied to large-scale agricultural production (as this book has shown), here I argue that as gendered and racialized subjects in a historically disempowered position in society, these activists face structural and symbolic barriers that limit their capacity to move Argentina's development strategy away from extractivism. Furthermore, powerful corporate and state actors are not passive vis-à-vis activists. On the contrary, they mobilize a wide variety of strategies and tactics that tap into these structural and symbolic inequalities to stall, silence, and demobilize activists and their demands.

The Mothers of the Ituzaingó Anexo Neighborhood

I met the women who make up the Grupo de Madres de Barrio Ituzaingó Anexo on a cold and gray winter day in August 2015. Their stories preceded them, and so in a way I knew them already. I had read so much about their work, saw them on the news, and studied them in academic articles; I had seen them in documentaries and heard their stories while interviewing other anti-fumigation activists. Dr. Mauricio Berger, professor at the National University of Córdoba and their ally since early in the struggle, kindly offered to introduce me. That day I met up with Mauricio at the university, and we walked a few blocks to the bus stop; I had already picked up some *facturas* to bring along. In Argentina you do not show up to people's homes empty-handed, and at this time of day, the late afternoon sweet pastries go well with mates.

It is about an hour on the bus from downtown Córdoba to Ituzaingó Anexo, a working-class neighborhood in the industrial belt surrounding the city, the capital of Córdoba province. At the center of the country and the core of Pampas soybean production, Córdoba province has the second largest economy in the country, relying primarily on the agro-industry and car manufacturing, and is the second largest grower of GM soybeans after the province of Buenos Aires.[3] Córdoba city, in the heart of the province, is the second largest urban center in Argentina. Its economy is diversified across services and manufacturing. From the bus window, I could see how the tall buildings and the density of downtown transitioned into family homes, increasingly sparse, replaced by empty lots and factories. These markers that distinguish the boundaries between downtown and the industrial area of the south of Córdoba city are visual and olfactory. I could see *and smell* the difference. There was a foul stench in the air—like factory fumes. Mauricio told me the smell was a common occurrence and probably came from the car factory nearby or maybe from the GM-corn-based bio-ethanol plant established a bit farther away. The soy farms are also close by; Córdoba city is surrounded by them. Many residents in the industrial suburbs of Córdoba are thus regularly exposed to toxins. PCBs, dioxins, high levels of nitrogen and carbon dioxide from these industrial facilities, and pesticides all drift from neighboring areas.[4]

Mauricio and I got off the bus and walked the few blocks to the home of Vita, one of the leaders of the Group of Mothers. Ituzaingó Anexo is a *barrio humilde*, a "humble neighborhood," as people say in Argentina to refer to the dignified poverty of the working poor. The neighborhood has changed, and that is a consequence of the Mothers' work. One main achievement of their struggle is that the municipality of Córdoba declared the neighborhood a sanitary and environmental emergency in mid-2002.[5] This designation brought extraordinary funds for remediation, which were used to remove water-polluting electric-power transformers and to build a health clinic to treat the chronically ill and their family members (one of the movement's primary demands). On the outskirts of the neighborhood, posted in an empty field that extended for miles on end, a huge billboard advertised a projected real-estate development called Ecotierra, "Eco-earth. The key to your future." The up-and-coming community is advertised on its website as the "new" Ituzaingó and shows computer-generated images of the projected neighborhood: brand-new modern homes inhabited by young, white, middle-class families holding babies and wearing big smiles. This new neighborhood begins less than two hundred feet away from Vita's house, exactly where the neighborhood ends. We stood on the paved street that marked the boundary: houses on the right-hand side, open field with new construction on the left (figure 4.1).

"It is not just *any* field!" Mauricio snapped me out of my green bubble as I remarked positively on how the neighborhood was growing. "This was a soy field," he continued, "*the* soy field." Here was the origin of the Mothers' plight: the soy fields where they regularly saw planes spraying agrochemicals only a few hundred feet away from their homes, fields where their children used to play. In 2003, the Mothers got two city ordinances passed to ban crop dusting in that area, aerial crop dusting in urban areas in Córdoba city, and all agrochemical spraying (aerial and terrestrial) within 2,500 meters (about a mile and a half) of the Ituzaingó Anexo neighborhood.[6] Yet, in 2004, a soybean grower and a crop-duster pilot violated the local ordinance when they fumigated with chlorine and phosphorus compounds—including 2,4-D, dieldrin, and chlorpyrifos—from a plane over these fields, less than a block away from Vita's home. For these actions, the Mothers and their allies took the farmer and the pilot to court. In 2012, in a historic lawsuit, the farmer and pilot were found guilty of illegal fumigation and handed a three-year suspended sentence.[7] Ironically, it is in this buffer zone where "New Ituzaingó" will develop. How "eco-earth" is that? I wondered. I quickly realized this was not a case of greening but of greenwashing. As I was going to learn from the Mothers themselves, that is one of the many ways in which Ituzaingó is a neighborhood in denial.

Fig. 4.1. Limits of Ituzaingó Anexo, Córdoba City. This is the former site of a soybean farm and is now a real estate development. Photo by the author.

Mauricio rang the bell to Vita's home. "Through the back!" a female voice said, referring to the side gate, which opened into a narrow walkway connecting the street to the back of the house. Mauricio led the way. He knew the place well and seemed at home. Later in the day, after hours of talking and sharing mates with these women activists, I would feel at home too, thanks to the way they talked, their warmth, the way they laughed and teased each other to express support. So many had been in my place, the place of the interviewer/researcher, and yet as I introduced myself and thanked them for taking time to receive me, their responses were generous. They welcome anyone who wants to hear their story, they said, because doing so helps them amplify it—so that more people learn of the plight of the *afectados por los agrotóxicos*, as they call the victims of toxic agrochemical contamination.[8]

I vaguely recognized Vita's courtyard. Later I realized I had seen it in the background of an interview in an *Al Jazeera* documentary I had watched multiple times titled "Argentina: The Bad Seeds."[9] For all its "fame," the backyard where these women activists met was quite simple. Around a wooden table under a hanging roof that shelters meetings when it rains sat Vita, Marcela, and Norma, three of the four women who are the core of the group; Ricardo, a young man from the neighborhood who helps with organizing; Mauricio; and me.[10] In the courtyard there were plants and flowers and an orange tree that gave a faint sweet smell of early blossoms. Vita's home felt a world apart from the toxic environment outside.

The Mothers' struggle to defend health and life began in early 2002, when they became aware that children and adults in their community were getting sick and dying of cancer at an alarmingly high rate. At that time and within just a block of Vita's place, there were three cases of leukemia: a man in his early sixties and two girls. One girl was three years old, and the other was thirteen. And so a group of working-class women with no formal organizing experience decided to find out what was happening in their community. First, they blamed the water supply, as they suspected it was probably polluted by the local car factory or the electric-power transformers, the same ones that had been removed by the time I visited. They wondered if the crop dusters spraying agrochemicals over the soy fields down the street were also to blame, as they realized people commonly suffered from headaches, coughing, and skin rashes after spraying. With marches and roadblocks, they pressured the authorities to test the water and run blood studies. The results confirmed the Mothers' suspicions: there were higher-than-average residues of agrochemical and industrial pollutants in the water and their bodies.

How to link clusters of illness and death to environmental pollution? The Mothers of Ituzaingó, with help from scientific and professional experts (they mentioned biologist Raúl Montenegro in particular), surveyed the sick in their community and mapped their findings, which revealed an unusually high number of pathologies—anemia, lymphoma, and leukemia—clustered around a few particular blocks. They surveyed more than two hundred cases of cancer, respiratory and skin diseases, miscarriages, and birth defects in a neighborhood of five thousand.[11] The "map of death," *el mapa de la muerte* as they call it, hangs on the wall in a small outbuilding in the back of Vita's courtyard. This room serves as the movement's "headquarters," a place where meetings with the community and other organizations take place, and it also houses documentation. The movement's banner, pictures, and souvenirs from past visitors and activities hang on the wall (figure 4.2). There are two versions of the "map of death": the original one from 2005 and another one that is constantly being updated,

Fig. 4.2. One of the protest banners for Grupo de Madres de Barrio Ituzaingó Anexo. Photo by the author.

a sign of the relentless impact of pesticide drift as well as the absence of redress. The maps show, by number, the 127 blocks that make up the Ituzaingó Anexo neighborhood. Nearly every block has one or many tiny colored squares pasted on it: red represents a person with leukemia living on that block, blue is for cancer, green is for thyroid disease. A white dot on top of the colored square indicates a death. The visibility of the clustering of disease represented by tiny colored stickers, so many blocks showing seven, ten, fourteen people sick on just one block, so many of them topped with a deadly white dot, is shocking. It is moving and revealing, and it provides the visibility needed for consciousness transformation. Its striking simplicity is very effective in showing that something is not quite right, which is why when other victims of environmental pollution contact the Mothers for advice on how to organize, they reply: "Start with the map."

The Mothers' alliance with scientific and professional experts to make a case for the harmful environmental health effects of pesticide drift has been a powerful form of collective action. This strategy, called "popular epidemiology," refers to when laypeople partner with scientific and professional experts to investigate the patterns and causes of disease and then mobilize to ameliorate the situation.[12] It is commonly utilized during struggles for environmental justice in the United States, first mobilized in the iconic cases of Love Canal, New York, and Woburn, Massachusetts. By contesting illness, activists challenge so-called expert authority and the political economy.[13]

Stop Spraying!

The Mothers of Ituzaingó are not alone in the plight of contaminated communities. In 2006, in solidarity with their struggle, a Buenos Aires–based group of academics and activists named Grupo de Reflexión Rural (GRR) organized a campaign against agrochemical spraying, Paren de Fumigar (Stop Spraying). The campaign sought to survey the crop-sprayed towns in the provinces of Buenos Aires, Entre Ríos, Córdoba, and Santa Fe and to organize them under one umbrella, coordinating efforts and resources.[14]

At a pivotal 2008 meeting in Colonia Caroya, Córdoba, the Stop Spraying campaign developed into a collective of different chapters across the Pampas provinces. Nicolás and Micaela are members of the Córdoba chapter, Paren de Fumigar Córdoba. I met them in Córdoba city in 2011. Both were in their early twenties; he was a recently graduated engineer, and she was an advanced undergraduate in biology. They were originally from Río Carlo, a rural town an hour away from Córdoba city, and had moved to the capital to pursue their university studies.[15]

Río Carlo, Nicolás said, is "a typical soy town": a small rural town historically tied to commercial agricultural production, populated by gringos (European immigrants), and where most families are *relacionadas al campo* [dependent on the countryside]. As with other soy towns across the Pampas, large-scale GM soybean production has meant an increase in agrochemical fumigations in both quantity and scope, as farmers plant larger areas of soy to increase profitability, pushing production directly up to and even into town limits. "In Río Carlo," he continued, farmers "fumigate right up to the front door."

Concerned about the impact of agrochemicals on health, some community members, including Nicolás and Micaela, organized into a group called Vecinxs Autoconvocadxs por un Ambiente Sano (Self-Organized

Neighbors for a Healthy Environment), which was part of the Paren de Fumigar Córdoba collective. Their main goals, they told me, were "to make the problem [of the health and environmental impact of agrochemical spraying] visible" and "to keep fumigations away from homes." They signed petitions and staged protests at the field, mobilizing neighbors to the farms to stop crop dusters on the spot (that is, before they began spraying). According to Córdoba's provincial law, there is no minimum distance for the application of type 4 agrochemicals, like glyphosate. Thus, in practice and protected by law, like Nicolás said, farmers fumigate right near people's homes.[16] Encouraged by the success of other groups under the Paren de Fumigar collective, like San Jorge and Ituzaingó, the neighbors from Río Carlo demanded a municipal ordinance that sets a minimum distance for fumigations, a buffer zone between toxic agrochemicals and people's homes.

In 2009, the cry to stop spraying was heard by the national government. Due to mounting public pressure (a combination of the actions of the Paren de Fumigar campaign and the Mothers of Ituzaingó, the publication of the results of Dr. Andrés Carrasco's studies on glyphosate in *Página/12*, and the ongoing conflicto del campo), President Cristina Kirchner signed an executive order to form a national commission to study the impact of agrochemicals on human health. Known as the Comisión Nacional de Investigación sobre Agroquímicos y Salud, it was formed by scientists from CONICET, the main government agency in charge of the promotion of science and technology in Argentina.

The announcement was a brief success. In a blow to anti-agrotoxin activists, the government report denied the experiences and demands of the contaminated communities and defended corporate practices. The report concluded that "under conditions of responsible use (understood as the application of recommended doses and in accordance with best agricultural practices), glyphosate and its formulations would pose a low risk to human health or the environment."[17] Critics argue that the report was biased because CONICET did not commission its own tests but rather relied on a review of reports provisioned by Monsanto; moreover, it did not include reports that looked into the long-term impacts of exposure.[18] This shows how the state authorities use their expert advocates to legitimate production technologies and reveals the government's preference for increasing risk despite the uncertainty of the results.[19]

Malvinas Argentinas Says No to Monsanto

With some significant gains in the first half of 2012, the year promised to be a successful one for the Mothers of Ituzaingó and the Stop Spraying campaign. The Mothers won their historical lawsuit against the soy farmer and the pilot, successfully challenging the scientific establishment in proving that pesticides were guilty of environmental pollution and harmful to health, the first case of its kind in Latin America.[20] They were also recognized internationally: Sofía Gatica, another leader of the movement, was awarded the Goldman Environmental Prize, the "world's largest prize honoring grassroots environmentalists."[21]

But just like in 2009, the movement's success was met with a backlash. In June 2012, Cristina Kirchner announced from Washington, DC, Monsanto's future investment in Argentina: a GM-corn-seed plant. The news reported that during the meeting that led to the announcement, Monsanto executives "discussed with the president the importance that innovation in agriculture [would] have in the context of an exponential growth in the world demand for food during the coming years." According to the article, in this context Monsanto foresaw "a key role for Argentina."[22] This is another example of how allied corporate and state elites advance GM soy extractivism by mobilizing their economic power as well as their discursive power. Flanked by Monsanto executives, the president delivered a speech full of references to cultural and symbolic values that tap into Malthusian fears of scarcity and worldwide hunger, the ecological modernization discourse of genetically modified crops for sustainable development, and Argentina's strategic role as the granary of the world.

Monsanto's plant was designed to be a drying and conditioning facility for genetically modified corn seeds. According to the company's brochure, the plant had a planned capacity of 3.5 million tons, making it one of the largest corn-seed factories in the world. The site for the plant was the town of Malvinas Argentinas, a commuter suburb in Córdoba city's industrial belt, about ten miles away from Ituzaingó Anexo.

Malvinas Argentinas is the poorest city in the province of Córdoba. According to the 2010 census, of its 12,187 inhabitants, a quarter live in poverty, two-thirds are unemployed or underemployed, and over 70 percent have no health insurance. Like other towns on the southern periphery of Córdoba city, Malvinas is surrounded by soy fields, and thus residents are also affected by pesticide drift. Local doctors have identified a host of environmental illnesses characteristic of pesticide drift: lung disease, dermatitis, tumors, cancers, congenital malformations in children, and the highest rate of miscarriages in the country: twenty-two for every one hundred pregnancies.[23] Even so, in Malvinas, residents did not consider agrochemical pollution worth mobilizing for—until Monsanto rolled into town.

The Asamblea Malvinas Lucha por la Vida is a coalition of neighbors that organized to say "no to Monsanto" and halt the construction of Monsanto's plant.

"Why are neighbors opposed to the plant?" I asked Estela, one of the members of the AMLV, when I met her in 2015. "Because the plant will have 240 silos operating twenty-four hours a day. Seeds in the silos receive a chemical bath to dry them, and it releases polluting particles that will float over Malvinas. It is a risk to health. The health of our children." Estela had a soft and steady cadence, a patience that probably came from being a school employee and the mother of two teenagers. "The plant," she explained, "is very close to town, barely seven hundred meters from the public school and a kilometer from town. That is why the risk of contamination is high."

When we met, Estela spoke with the confidence of an expert about the impact of agrochemicals on society and the environment, but back before the plant was announced, she had no idea what Monsanto as a company did or was. And while she was aware of the farms surrounding Malvinas, agrochemicals did not concern her. The same went for Melina, another AMLV member, whom I met in Malvinas earlier that week. Melina was unemployed at the time and had never been part of a social movement before. I was curious about how and why these neighbors experienced "the click," the key moment of consciousness transformation. What made them want to know more and organize into a movement? How was it that they were so close to the struggle of the Mothers of Ituzaingó, bearing the toxic impact of pesticide drift on their own bodies, and yet so far away (intellectually and emotionally) from the consequences of the GM soy model? Maybe they weren't aware of the trial from the news? No, that was not the case. In her telling of the chronology of the movement, Melina explicitly brought up the concurrence of events, of how Monsanto's plant in Malvinas was announced at the same time that the Mothers' historic lawsuit was taking place.

"So you were aware that the trial was going on?" I asked for confirmation.

"Yes," Melina replied, "but I never related it to Monsanto. I would say, poor women! It's like I was moved by them being women, the illnesses, these poor mothers."

"But did you know this was also happening in *your* town?" I asked, referring to the fumigations with agrochemicals and the illnesses.

"No. I found out because of the trial. And then, as soon as I find out about the trial, along comes Monsanto. For me, [Monsanto] was an automotive plant, a toy factory, whatever." But then, when Melina learned about the installation of the plant in Malvinas, she realized Monsanto "is also about fumigations and then . . . it clicked! For me, you know, Ituzaingó, until Monsanto arrived, had nothing to do with me. But later I understood how the struggles were intertwined [como se entrelazaban las luchas]. To give you an example, everything that was learned from the trial of Ituzaingó, which was a process I did not experience closely, all that [knowledge] later spilled over to Malvinas, into our movement. Many *compañeros* helped us to understand that we were an assembly, from the Universidad Nacional and from political organizations, they helped us work on that. Those were the embers [las brasitas] [that sparked the movement]."

As social-movement scholars well know, social networks matter for movement formation. "The very existence of social ties between potential recruits is a prerequisite for the emergence of a social movement," write Jeff Goodwin and James Jasper in their introductory book to social movements.[24] For the neighbors in Malvinas, scientific and professional experts from the Universidad Nacional de Córdoba like Raúl Montenegro, Mauricio Berger, and Cecilia Carrizo, along with other movements, the Mothers of Ituzaingó in particular, were strategic in sparking the fire of resistance.

Estela told me how she first found out what Monsanto was, back in 2012. It was in a school meeting organized by the principal and led by biologist Raúl Montenegro where she first learned about genetically modified seeds, agrochemicals, and their impact on health and the environment. Like Estela and Melina, most of the members of the Assembly of Malvinas had neither expert knowledge of the impact of agrochemicals on health nor experience as political actors. As Vanesa, another AMLV member, said in an interview with Marina Sitrin for *TeleSur*, "If someone had told me a while back, 'Your future is this,' I would not have believed it because all of us in the assembly are just neighbors—students, teachers, housewives, and workers."[25]

Monsanto's arrival—as a concrete event—was another key catalyst for mobilization. The risks of pesticide drift, which the neighbors of Malvinas were victims of, unfolded slowly over time, making it difficult to generate the visibility necessary for grievances to form. Slow-onset, chronic problems are generally overlooked, creating acquiescence in contaminated communities. But when a problem becomes suddenly acute, when accidents occur or disaster strikes, it can lift the veil on an ongoing problem, making people more likely to frame the problem as a grievance worth mobilizing for.[26] Monsanto's arrival, for the residents of Malvinas, was just this type of sudden, acute event.

As part of their repertoire of contention, activists from Malvinas signed petitions and marched to Córdoba's capital, demanding that Monsanto comply with the Ley General de Ambiente (National Environment Law).[27] This law requires that for a development project of this magnitude, the responsible entity must submit an environmental impact assessment report, which must receive community approval for construction to begin. Community consultations have become a popular initiative for environmental justice among socioenvironmental movements in Latin America.[28] Consultations challenge power elites by demanding a transfer of decision-making power to the very community that will host the project and bear its impact. Monsanto, however, began construction before complying with this important part of the law.

As Monsanto continued with its building plans despite growing mobilization, the Malvinas activists decided to escalate their direct action and stop construction on the spot. They blockaded the entrance to the construction site, at first selectively and then permanently starting on September 19, 2013, early spring in the southern hemisphere. With the hope that springtime brings, the neighbors of Malvinas and their allies set up a festival on the construction grounds, Una Primavera sin Monsanto (Springtime without Monsanto). It was, as Estela told me, a protest-festival "for the life and health of our children, nieces, and nephews." On that day, the blockade became a permanent occupation.

I visited the occupation site, known as "el acampe de Malvinas," in 2015, in the wake of its second anniversary. Preparations for a celebration were underway. About forty people were there. In the early days of the occupation, the encampment had hosted up to two hundred people, but over time the numbers thinned, and by the time I visited they were struggling to cover shifts. Still the acampe held fast with around ten people on-site

Fig. 4.3. Abandoned Monsanto factory, Malvinas Argentinas, Córdoba.
Photo by the author.

permanently. The day I visited, August 1, was a special one, however, as
the Day of the Pachamama, a traditional Andean indigenous celebration
dedicated to Mother Earth. The acampe was bustling with young people
who had come for the celebrations, carrying guitars, capoeira drums, and
juggling clubs.

The acampe was erected at the gate of Monsanto's construction site,
strategically blocking the entrance of construction material and workers.
The camp site was made up of a handful of tents, mud and adobe construc-
tions, with flags and banners running for about three hundred feet on the
shoulder of the road. Surrounding it for protection were stacks of old tires
and rows of wire fencing, the remains of the early days of the occupation
when violence was inflicted on activists in an attempt to force them out.
The day I visited was calm, and there was a sense of a settled establishment.
Monsanto's plant, as seen from the gate, seemed abandoned (figure 4.3).
Rusting steel girders branched out from unfinished concrete. No workers,
warning signs, machinery, or construction materials were visible. There
was no movement whatsoever—all signs of halted construction.

Fig. 4.4. Anonymous parody of Grant Wood's *American Gothic* with the farmers as corpses being sprayed by a crop duster, at the site of the occupation of Monsanto's factory. Photo by the author.

"Puesto Camiones" was a mud and adobe structure at the entrance of the acampe. It served as the kitchen, with shelves of dried goods and a steel drum turned into a fire pit where two young people were making what looked like a delicious vegetable stir-fry. There were other mud and adobe structures at the acampe, including a library and a big meeting/working space filled with long tables and white plastic chairs, known as "Puesto Amaranto." At the heart of the acampe stood a large tent made of sticks and plastic sheeting, a gathering space with chairs and logs to sit on. It was filled with flags, banners, and paintings that announced, in various shapes and colors, "No to Monsanto" and "Yes to Life." One big painting caught my attention. It was a parody of *American Gothic*, Grant Wood's famous painting of a stern Quaker pair, but the farmers are corpses and a crop duster is hovering menacingly over them (figure 4.4).

The acampe was a space for alliances, a space where struggles "interweaved," like Melina said. Under Puesto Amaranto's roof, activists, journalists, filmmakers, and scientific and professional experts from

Argentina and around the world gathered to learn from each other and to help bring global visibility to the struggle against Monsanto.[29] The list is long: the Mothers of Ituzaingó and the expert allies from the Universidad Nacional de Córdoba; members of many Asambleas Ambientales from all over Argentina; journalists from BBC *Mundo* and *TeleSur*; the director of Avaaz, a global online activist network; singer Manu Chao; indigenous peoples from Ecuador and Argentina; Nobel Peace Prize winner Adolfo Pérez Esquivel; Marie-Monique Robin, film director of *The World against Monsanto*; Indian scholar-activist Dr. Vandana Shiva; and many more.

As it was a space of alliances, however, the acampe also created divisions, particularly among Malvinas's residents. While the occupation began as a spinoff of the work of the Assembly of Malvinas and its allies, with time, as it attracted people from all over, locals began to disengage. With celebrity activists also came many urban youth drawn to the struggle, "new-age hippies, vegans, complete characters," as one AMLV activist described them. With just a muttered sentence and a roll of the eyes, a second AMLV activist I was conversing with confirmed the observation. "*Hay cada loco* [Every kind of crazy]," he said, between gritted teeth. While the massive presence of "outsiders" brought visibility and success to the movement (as they provided the bodies necessary to hold the occupation), it also created a barrier to movement participation for some Malvinas residents.[30] Despite those issues, after five years of struggle, the people of Malvinas Argentinas claimed a David-over-Goliath victory. In 2017, Monsanto sold their land and abandoned town.[31]

So what do the Mothers of Ituzaingó, the Paren de Fumigar campaign, and the AMLV have in common? They all represent the grassroots struggles of self-organized community members concerned about the health and environmental risks of agrochemical use. During my fieldwork, I met mothers, students, lawyers, physicians, housewives, unemployed people, and service-sector employees who belonged to these assemblies. Most identified as "citizens" or "neighbors" (many using the -x for gender-inclusive language, as in *ciudadanxs* and *vecinxs*), and highlighted their "self-organized" status to set a clear distance between their activism and political parties and agendas. While they all lived near soy farms (and, in the case of the Malvinas residents, also close to a plant emanating toxic agrochemical fumes), none of them were economically dependent on the agro-industry. Furthermore, though many movement members were from poor and working-class communities, their alliance with professional and scientific experts brought in the necessary resources for mobilization.[32]

The groups also shared a concern over children's health, a main catalyst for mobilizing against agrotoxins, and one shared with many environmental justice movements around the world of which women are often in the lead.[33] And of course in Argentina, the health risks of and concerns about agrochemical drift are not restricted to the Pampas; they have spread all over soybean territory. In Las Palmas and La Leonesa, in the northern Chaco province, neighbors have organized to protest against glyphosate spraying.[34] Pablo Lapegna describes how peasant women in the northern province of Formosa were galvanized to organize a protest after an incident of pesticide contamination on their farms affected their children's health in particular.[35]

Peasant Movements in the Northern Chaco Region

In the north of the country, the mobilization against GM soy is led by peasant-indigenous peoples. The ever-expanding production of GM soy has pushed the agricultural frontier past the Pampas region into the northern provinces of Chaco, Formosa, Santiago del Estero, and Salta. This is where the monocultures of GM soy have taken their heaviest toll.

The northern Chaco forest is the largest forest ecosystem and the largest biomass reservoir in Argentina and extra-tropical South America.[36] *El monte*, as locals call the forest, is being rapidly destroyed by bulldozing and fire to clear land for mechanized large-scale crop production and cattle ranching. In its 2016 report *State of the World's Forests*, the Food and Agriculture Organization of the United Nations ranked Argentina highest in the rate of deforestation in South America and the world.[37]

Deforestation in the northern provinces started long before the expansion of soybeans, a fact often espoused by promoters of GM biotechnology to deflect criticism of the spread of the new technology.[38] Many authors agree, however, that the rate of deforestation has *accelerated* with the introduction of GM soy.[39] A government report on deforestation in Argentina also points at the expansion of the monocultures of GM soy as the main accelerator of deforestation and forest degradation in the last decades, and claims that these are the highest rates of deforestation in Argentine history.[40] Between 1998 and 2008, 1.7 million hectares of native forests were lost in the northern provinces of Salta, Santiago del Estero,

Chaco, and Jujuy. The Forest Law, passed in 2007 to limit the clearing of the native forest, has failed to slow the pace of deforestation.[41] In Argentina, as in Brazil, Paraguay, and Bolivia, the expansion of commercial crops (mainly soybeans) and cattle ranching continues to be the main driver of deforestation.[42] Deforestation is also a main driver of climate change, a fact that counters the hegemonic discourse of GM crops for sustainable development.[43]

The expansion of the agricultural frontier also threatens the lives and livelihoods of rural inhabitants, many of whom are indigenous and peasants. "We live this, the encroachment of the frontier by agribusiness, of soy, of GM crops," the leaders of MOCASE, the peasant movement of Santiago del Estero, told me when I interviewed them in their headquarters in Quimilí in August 2011. "It is a permanent threat to [our] territory, to the lands of peasant-indigenous communities: the environmental pollution from the products of the technological package that come with transgenic crops, the threat to biodiversity, the loss of our seeds, the criminalization of our struggles to defend the territory."[44]

MOCASE is the largest and most important peasant movement in Argentina.[45] Peasant organization in Santiago del Estero started in the late 1970s in response to forced evictions by agribusinesses. In the 1990s, at the height of Argentina's neoliberal restructuring, the movement organized as MOCASE. The group is an active member of peasant-indigenous organizations articulated at the national, regional, and international levels: the Movimiento Nacional Campesino Indígena (MNCI), the Coordinadora Latinoamericana de Organizaciones del Campo, and the transnational peasant movement La Vía Campesina.[46]

MOCASE is part of a new wave of indigenous activism in Argentina that started in the late 1980s; by 1992 it had gained national visibility with the protests against the quincentennial celebrations of Columbus's "discovery" of the Americas.[47] The 1990s were rife with mobilizations over land conflicts across the country, from Neuquén in the south, led by Mapuches, to Salta and Jujuy in the north, led by Kollas, Tobas, and Wichís. Many of these local conflicts gained national visibility. In 1998, for example, *Diario Clarín* published a story on MOCASE members resisting a forced eviction by an agribusiness entrepreneur, which became the first story of peasant resistance to be published in a mainstream outlet since the return of democracy in 1983.[48] These mobilizations led to an ethnic reemergence of groups that had been previously rendered invisible and marginal since the

1870s' "conquest of the desert" campaign (see chapter 1).[49] Their legal victory came with the inclusion of indigenous rights in the Argentine Constitution of 1994 (article 75, section 17), which guarantees respect for their languages and culture, the collective possession of the lands they traditionally occupy, and their right to participation in decision-making processes over their natural resources. This constitutional reform opened up the possibility of demanding legal control over lands being encroached by the expansion of agribusinesses.[50]

More than nine thousand families compose MOCASE, and most of them are at risk of dispossession. Thus, the movement's most important and urgent goal is, as their leaders told me, "that families remain on their land." In order to gain land titles, the movement actively pursues legal actions to protect the families who have lived on the same land over generations, calling for constitutional indigenous rights to communal property. They also call for the application of the Ley Veinteañal, a law that grants property rights to anyone who has lived and worked on rural territory for twenty years or more.[51]

"The Argentine Code says that to own a plot of land a person must meet two conditions," Cariló, a MOCASE member, explains in *Toda esta sangre en el monte*, a documentary about the movement made in 2012. "One," he continues, "is to have the title of property, and the other, to have effective ownership. In the case of entrepreneurs, they get the title of domain. What they lack is effective ownership." Agribusiness entrepreneurs who may have never even stepped foot in the province (most of them come from the provinces of Córdoba and Salta) buy land in Santiago del Estero to produce soy.[52] The conflict arises because the land is effectively occupied by peasant families. Wielding land titles, foreigners set out to fence their plot. "That is the meaning of fencing [eso implica el alambrado]," Cariló says. "The perimeter fence implies the possession of the entrepreneur who has purchased the domain." By enclosing the commons, barbed wire and fences thus become another technology of accumulation by dispossession.[53]

Land evictions are often forced and violent.[54] To stop entrepreneurs from fencing lots and thus displacing and dispossessing the people already there, MOCASE members put their bodies on the line to defend their homes and land. Several MOCASE members who have tried to stop evictions have been murdered by security guards hired by agribusinessmen; Cristian Ferreyra in 2011 and Miguel Galván in 2012 are only two of the most notorious deaths.[55] Violence thus becomes an important strategy that corporate actors wield to dispossess peasants of their land and to quell activism. Peasants are relatively powerless to resist agribusiness. The Red Agroforestal Chaco Argentina documented 224 land conflicts during 2013, disputing 2.8 million hectares in the northern Chaco region. These conflicts affected close to 18,000 peasant and indigenous families, almost half of which hold 50 hectares or less.[56]

After the 2001 crisis and in the midst of the soy boom, various peasant movements gathered strength riding on the wave of social unrest across the country. "Movements with a focus on land appeared on the scene as one of the many movements that rejected the neoliberal program in its various facets," Patricia Collado explains.[57] Joining with MOCASE in the struggle for the land are the peasant movement of Formosa (MOCAFOR), Jujuy (MOCAJU), and others who make common cause under both the national network (MNCI) and La Vía Campesina. What these movements have in common are a discourse against extractivism and the desire for an alternative project for society-environment relations. MOCASE is leading the pursuit of an agenda for agrarian reform, environmental justice, agroecology, and food sovereignty.[58]

Divert, Delegitimize, Demobilize

Anti-GM-soy activists' calls to protect lives and livelihoods are urgent and praiseworthy. Yet the corporate and state actors who reap the benefits of GM soy refuse to hear them. What are the barriers to local grassroots struggles affecting large-scale change? As I have been arguing throughout this book, powerful actors stop these smaller mobilizations from bringing about meaningful social change.

A major barrier that anti-agrotoxin activists face is recruiting local residents to join the movement.[59] Movements remain small in numbers, and activists express how difficult it is to get neighbors to join in the struggle. The main barrier to consciousness transformation and solidarity building, factors integral to participation, is the fact that, as we have seen, rural towns are economically and ideologically tied to soybean production. In other words, activists' frames do not resonate with the "cultural economy."[60] As I have shown, residents' assertions that they "all live off the countryside" point to the cultural and economic dependence on capitalist agrarian production in general and historically, with the reliance now being on GM soybeans in particular. As Nicolás and Micaela from Paren de Fumigar Córdoba said, in "a typical soy town" like Río Carlo, it is hard to get other neighbors on board because "the town sees progress in the countryside," which affects the visibility of the problem required for consciousness transformation. In a town where most families have historically relied on commercial farming and where, in Nicolás's words, "we know that we can't touch the profitability issue" (meaning demanding farmers shift decision-making parameters away from the profit motive), the potential for recruitment, as well as the potential for transformation, is limited.

In peri-urban areas like Ituzaingó Anexo and Malvinas Argentinas, while not exclusively dependent on agricultural production, economic need stifled mobilization too.[61] In Malvinas, Monsanto's plant promised four hundred jobs in a community desperate for work. This pitted neighbors against activists, as many residents supported construction because it promised to provide much-needed jobs. In a strategy to further divide the community, Monsanto, through an NGO called Inclusión Social (Social Inclusion), set up a job-training program. Indeed, Melina told me how NGO representatives would knock on people's doors and ask, "So, what are you interested in working on? We have courses on cell phone repair, baking, plumbing, dressmaking. . . ." According to Melina, who mimicked the NGO representative's hyped-up marketing tone, if the neighbor showed interest, the rep would say, "We are looking to train people, bring people skills, because what we are lacking are jobs and training. Did you know that new industries are coming to town?"

"Then," Melina continued in her normal voice, "if you said 'no,' they would respond, [again in a patronizing tone], 'Did you know that Monsanto is coming to town!?'" Melina then suddenly stopped smiling and became indignant: "And right away, they would pull out a brochure!!! Along with the foundation's brochure and the course inscription form, they would give you Monsanto's brochure!! Which said that Monsanto was a good company, that it brought prosperity to town, well, all that." Called a program of corporate social responsibility (or CSR), this is a commonly used corporate strategy to buy acquiescence from local populations for extractivist projects.[62] Other agribusinesses have prospered from this cleavage (and because people need to work). When I visited Malvinas Argentinas in 2015, Bimbo (the world's largest baking company, according to its US website) was planning on establishing a baking facility in town. AMLV activists supported the construction of the plant because of the potential for job creation. Bimbo is, like Monsanto, another representative of the corporate concentration of food production; for example, Bimbo holds half of the bread market in the United States. The company is a driver of the agro-industry.[63] This just goes to show how limited residents' demands will be as long as they are structurally constrained by high rates of poverty and unemployment in the community.

Political elites prey on the material needs of affected people to create acquiescence and consent, particularly through the strategic allocation of *planes sociales*, the cash-transfer subsidies implemented by the Kirchner administration, either by promising handouts or by threating to withdraw. Studying why peasants from the northern province of Formosa mobilized in 2003 and then did not in 2009 after two similar events of agrochemical exposure, Lapegna exposes how networks of patronage and clientelism cause demobilization and acquiescence. With his study, he also shows that peasants' relationship to GM crops is contested and more nuanced than peasant leaders suggest. In the case of members of MOCAFOR in Formosa, objections against transgenic crops were raised not in terms of the technology per se but against the negative impact it may have had on their daily survival, particularly as agrochemicals kill their crops and sicken their animals and children.[64]

For social change to happen, people need to organize in collective action *and* the state needs to respond favorably to activists' demands by passing laws, policies, or regulations that address these claims.[65] The Kirchner governments seemed at times to be responsive to activists' claims, most notably when Cristina Kirchner instructed CONICET to form a national commission on the impact of agrochemicals on health in 2009. But instead, the state used the report to contest anti-agrotoxin activists' claims of environmental illness and to diffuse dissent. How so? Political power in a democracy needs legitimation, meaning that the state needs to ensure the support of the people in order to maintain its authority.[66] When opposition grows, the state must provide some avenues for civil society to express discontent to show that it is responsive to citizens' demands. In what David Meyer calls the "paradoxical insight" of democratic governments, the political system diffuses dissent by embracing it. That is, by providing some avenues to bring it to the open, dissent can be more easily managed instead of crushed with violence.[67]

For social change to occur, the most important thing states can do is to enact laws.[68] Despite activists' demands, however, the Argentine government has yet to pass a federal law that bans glyphosate fumigations within town limits; SENASA continues to classify glyphosate as having low toxicity; and new GM seed varieties are in the pipeline for approval. The problem is that, along with legitimation, states need to fulfill another primary function: accumulation.[69] The state, thus, will pursue policies that foster the economic growth necessary for its own reproduction and to gather support from corporations and from civil society, which benefit from the provision of public goods and services.[70] Activists, however, target the production technologies that sustain accumulation and the logic of growth itself.[71] Anti-GM-soy mobilization is met with such strong resistance because it is attacking the foundation of the state's political and economic power.

A very effective strategy power elites deploy to suppress contestation has been to demand proof of harm to the contaminated communities, shifting blame and responsibility to the victims.[72] Working-class mothers with sick children have been forced to show proof of the links between fumigations and illnesses when instead the precautionary principle should be followed; corporations that develop and profit from these technologies should be required to fully test for potentially harmful impacts *before* such technologies are released. Laypeople have been forced to become experts on the chemical, biological, and health aspects of agrochemicals and genetically modified seeds as well as on their legal aspects, like ordinances, laws, and due process. This long and exhausting learning process took place while also rallying and organizing and in the halls of health ministries, waiting for public officials to hear their demands, after long days of work, all while caring for family members, some of whom are also sick. These intellectual, physical, and emotional demands are a heavy strain that bring many down.[73] As Vita told me after yet another joke as the Mothers teased each other, "We laugh at life like this because it's so exhausting." Marcela agreed: "Yes, you have to have some humor. . . . I have thought of quitting many times. Work, family, lots of daily things and chores, plus this [referring to their activism]. It all takes lots of time and lots of energy." Norma nodded in confirmation: "Yes, sometimes it's overwhelming." As women are more likely to care for children and the family, scholars recognize that activist women often take what is called the "triple burden" of paid, domestic, and political work.[74] This is one way that gender structures the uneven distribution of the burden of environmental injustice.

Forcing activists to wait forever and neglecting them throughout long bureaucratic procedures are good strategies for stalling and tiring activists hoping they quit their struggle. Law 26160 calls for protection against forced evictions until the completion of a census of indigenous lands. It was sanctioned in 2006 and presented by the Kirchner administration as part of "historical reparations" for indigenous peoples. However, the law has only ever been partially implemented and the census never completed.[75] In 2012, after the killings of the peasant leaders Ferreyra and Galván, peasant movements organized demonstrations in Buenos Aires to demand its urgent enforcement.[76] As land conflicts and violence against peasants continue, activists have been forced to demand extensions to the protections afforded by this law, now known as Ley Cristian Ferreyra. Such extensions are set to expire once again in November 2021, a full fifteen years after the law was first passed, with no clear signs of the state's willingness to enforce it.[77]

The Mothers of Ituzaingó have been waiting for fifteen years for their demands to be addressed. They continue to demand medical treatment for those affected in the neighborhood because the health center in Ituzaingó, despite "promises and more promises" from politicians, as they told me, receives "less and less funding." They had to wait for five years for the Supreme Court to ratify, in 2017, a three-year suspended sentence for the farmer and crop-duster pilot accused in the historic trial of 2012 (for fumigations that date back to 2004).[78] They continue to wait and demand that the criminal trial begin, which they refer to as the *causa madre* (original case). Unlike the 2012 trial, where the sentence was for violating a civil ordinance, this is a call for a trial aimed at convicting the farmer and crop-duster pilot for willful environmental pollution, and it seeks to establish a direct link between fumigations and illness and death in Ituzaingó Anexo.

But sick people cannot wait, as Vita said in a 2017 interview with *Ecos Córdoba* at the rally to mark the fifteenth anniversary of their struggle.[79] Regarding how the Mothers were dealing with the long years of delay for the causa madre, a journalist at the event asked, "Are you being patient?" Vita replied, "We are not patient. You see, those who were plaintiffs in 2002, most of them have passed. So, you cannot have patience if you know you have cancer. Time plays against people. Our idea of time is not the same as the judicial system's [El tiempo nuestro no es el tiempo de la justicia]." By not providing much-needed medical services and by pushing the start of the trial further and further into the future, those in power diffuse dissent by literally waiting for activists to die.

The mobilization of scientific expertise to contest activists' claims is another common tactic to quell dissent. Science is presented as an objective and neutral truth and laypeople are required to trust experts blindly, based solely on their credentials.[80] Denying the problem on the basis of scientific evidence is the ultimate way to silence activists and create acquiescence among the rest. In the United States, climate-change deniers have used this tactic to stall action, and the same has been employed in cases against lead, asbestos, and tobacco.[81] The Argentine state uses it through its expert-advocate institutions, among them CONICET and SENASA, as I explained above. Norberto Yauhar, the former minister of agriculture under Cristina Kirchner's administration, exemplified this institutional denial. When he was interviewed by *Al Jazeera*, he said, "We don't place our population at risk. Argentina has some of the world's most stringent environmental safeguards thanks to strict restrictions on fertilizers and pesticides."[82]

Those who dare to question the alleged scientifically proven safety of agrochemicals or transgenic seeds are then demonized. Characterizing them as antiscience zealots, luddites, and know-nothings against progress and development is another well-used strategy for demobilization.[83] To dismiss the Mothers of Ituzaingó, public officials have relied on stereotypical gendered insults, calling them hysterical, irrational, and ignorant housewives.[84] To silence peasants, the corporate-state elite and their expert allies often rely on the colonial civilizing discourse and wield stereotypical racist insults.[85] "They say peasants don't know how to organize resources to produce, they are *negros* [black], they are poor, they are backwards," Cariló from MOCASE says in the documentary *Toda esta sangre en el monte*, talking of the politicians and entrepreneurs who promote the agribusiness model. Lapegna narrates how MOCAFOR members have been disrespected and ignored as health officials called them "dirty," diagnosing skin rashes and eye and throat soreness due to agrochemical drift as "a lack of proper hygiene" and "the clothes they wore" and proposing they wash with water and lye soap.[86]

The leadership of the corporate-state elite give the loudest voice to the "activists are anti-development" discourse. Gustavo Grobocopatel, CEO of Los Grobo, said in an interview, "People that are against pesticides are against poor people. Agriculture needs a lot of pesticides to produce more. When you produce more you reduce the cost, you reduce the food price, and then a lot of poor people can eat."[87] Lino Barañao, minister of science and technology from 2007 to 2019, denied Dr. Andrés Carrasco's findings in 2009 and is responsible for famously saying "glyphosate is just like water with salt."[88] In 2018, Barañao said, "The difference between an ecologist and an environmentalist is the same as a wine expert and a wino," and he thus called for fighting "a battle against fundamentalists."[89] This represents a call for the Argentine scientific establishment to discipline and punish socioenvironmental activists who dare to challenge the political economy of extractivism.

Last but certainly not least, the most important strategy for demobilizing activists has been the use of violence. Activists from Malvinas recall several events when violence was used to forcibly remove them and put an end to the occupation of Monsanto's construction site. But the first one, in particular, sticks in their minds. It was September 30, 2013, the early days of the occupation. Sofía Gatica, one of the Mothers of Ituzaingó and an ally of the AMLV, recalled that day: "The problems had started three days earlier with UOCRA workers [the construction workers' union]. They claimed that people were being fired and that the union was coming to their defense. They barged in pushing and shoving, smashing tents and banners." Violence later escalated: "Then the police came, and the infantry, they threw away the tire barriers and broke our flags, so we defended ourselves. That was because the trucks with the construction materials were arriving. But we had said that the materials were not to come in, that Monsanto was not to build." To stop the action, Sofía and two other women activists lay in front of the trucks. This image mirrors the struggle for environmental justice in Warren County, North Carolina, in 1973, when protestors lay down in front of dump trucks to stop them from taking soil contaminated with PCB to the local landfill. It did not last. Gatica continued, "The police picked me up and threw me on the asphalt. They hit me five or six times. I ended up in the emergency room because of dizziness and pain."[90]

Peasant families bear the brunt of the violence. They must deal with threats and the reality of forced evictions and the violence that comes with them, as agribusiness entrepreneurs, with the support of their government allies, go so far as to murder the peasants who dare to stop evictions. This is one of the main strategies for dispossessing people and quelling dissent, a legacy of the colonizing project of the nineteenth century. This is a fate that peasant and indigenous people share with members of other socioenvironmental movements in Latin America, which is becoming one of the most dangerous forms of activism.[91]

"What was it that poisoned him?"

Carla shrugged her shoulder again.

"It happens, Amanda. We're in the country, there are sown fields all around us. People come down with things all the time, and even if they survive they end up strange. You see them on the street. Once you learn to recognize them you'll be surprised how many there are."

—Samanta Schweblin, *Fever Dream*

In 2014, Argentine fiction writer Samanta Schweblin published *Distancia de rescate* (Rescue distance). The book was translated into English as *Fever Dream* and short-listed for the prestigious International Man Booker Prize in 2017.[1] Schweblin tells the story of Amanda, an urban mother who is spending her summer holiday in the countryside with her daughter, Nina, while her husband is working in the city and visiting over weekends. They are from Buenos Aires, the city of "noise, the grime, the congestion of everything"; the countryside is the Pampas, where "the soy fields stretch out to either side," and "it's all very green, a perfumed green." Amanda, we discover, is lying in bed in an emergency room speaking deliriously through a fever. Her interlocutor is David, Carla's son. Why is Amanda ill? Why is David also ill, his face and body covered with white spots, and his personality strange? What explains birds and horses dying mysteriously, and why are rural children like David and Abigail sick or living with severe malformations? Of Abigail we learn that "one of her legs is very short, it barely goes past her knee, but she still has a foot" and "her enormous forehead . . . takes up more than half her face." David tells us that "the worms" hold the answer.[2]

The resonances between Schweblin's book and mine are remarkable. Like the women of Santa María in chapter 3, who notice potential harms arising from agrochemical spraying yet keep their grievances latent, the characters in Schweblin's story know that the "sown fields all around" them and the poisoning of their community are connected. Yet, like the women of Santa María, they also keep silent, shrugging their shoulders. The matter-of-fact response, "It happens, Amanda," closes a conversation that could, otherwise, turn their latent grievances into a public issue.[3] In Schweblin's book, suspense builds through not knowing exactly what is going on. David interrogates Amanda to find out "the exact moment when the worms come into being." But what we readers learn as the story continues—and horror grows—is that the afflictions have nothing to do with worms. We read of poisoned river streams, of "the breeze moving through the soy," and of "men," clearly agribusiness employees in the context of the story, "unloading the barrels" (bidones, or jerricans) and smiling at Amanda at the exact moment when she realizes her daughter is all wet from playing in the grass—"but it's not from dew, is it?" Amanda asks David.[4] In Schweblin's story, agrochemicals are never directly mentioned or blamed, yet they are a real presence. Indeed, they are a conspicuous absence: like an elephant in the room, as I explain in chapter 3. In fiction, as in Santa María, mothers in the Pampas worry about their children's health yet keep silent over toxic agrochemical contamination.

Why are rural inhabitants of the Pampas acquiescent in the face of soybean expansion when they are the ones who bear the toxic burden of agrochemical exposure? Why are most, on the contrary, complacent and supportive of large-scale production of GM soy? A powerful synergy of state and corporate actors has adeptly mobilized uses of and attached meanings to GM biotechnology that build on historical and structural inequalities as well as on cultural myths of national identity to create acquiescence and consent over GM soy extractivism as a national model for socioeconomic development. Actors who wield power at the higher levels of politics and the economy—heads of government alongside agribusiness executives and entrepreneurs—promote the GM soy model on the promise of ecological modernization for sustainable development: that is, the promise of technological innovation for economic growth and social well-being in an environmentally sustainable manner. These powerful actors have tailored what is otherwise a broad and abstract promise to fit the Argentine context: Argentina's historical dependence on a gendered and racialized political economy of Pampas agro-extractivism. Moreover, they have used Argentina's cultural myths of national identity to legitimate the unequal and unjust dimensions and consequences of soybean extractivism.

To understand how the "synergies of power" operate to create acquiescence and consent, I have broken down the multiple dimensions of power, privilege, and inequality that create, compound, and legitimate social and environmental injustice. I have shown how structural inequities of class, gender, and race operate across the macro-, meso-, and micro-levels of the Argentine political economy of soybean extractivism. This has benefited wealthy, highly educated men of European descent (and the handful of women who must adopt masculine standards when entering these male-dominated fields, like former president Cristina Kirchner), while excluding the poor and working class as well as feminized and racialized subjects from decision-making power over large-scale farming. These dimensions not only intersect at a point in time to impact any group of individuals, but they also compound over time and space. I have highlighted how two centuries of Argentine history have shaped—and, with time, exacerbated—the exploitation of nature, the domination of gendered and racialized subjects, and the preeminence of urban over rural lifestyles and landscapes. Finally, I have illustrated how culture, in particular the guiding myths of national identity (Argentina as "the granary of the world"; Argentina as a modern, European nation), has served to shape and ultimately legitimate inequitable and unjust dimensions and outcomes. While these dimensions can be broken down analytically, it is in their historical, overlapping, and intersecting reality that power compounds so as to go unchallenged (that is, to legitimate the status quo to create acquiescence, or subjects' willful compliance). I have used "synergies of power" to capture in one concept these various and simultaneous forces.

Powerful state and corporate actors introduced genetically modified, herbicide-resistant soybeans in a social, cultural, and ecological context that resulted from a historical process that shaped the present political economy of the Pampas. I traced this history to the origins of the Argentine nation: I showed how the intellectual elite of the time—the Generation of 1837—shaped the Pampas after their interests, goals, and ideals. This nineteenth-century elite wielded their discursive, political, and military power to dispossess and invisibilize indigenous peoples and to populate the

Pampas with Europeans in the name of modernization and progress. They set out to tame and to civilize the ecology and the people of the Pampas to make the region efficient and productive in capitalist terms. And they succeeded. By the turn of the twentieth century, Argentina had become the granary of the world, a top global exporter of agricultural and livestock products, thanks to the establishment of a type of large-scale capitalist agriculture controlled, managed, and labored by European immigrant men. The pursuit of Argentina's comparative advantage in the name of modernity and civilization encouraged the exploitation of the Pampas region, of its vast, fertile prairies, ideally suited for growing temperate commercial crops for export. It encouraged rapid urbanization too, as machinery and agrochemicals replaced rural labor in large mechanized farms; and as the city, identified as the home of modernity, had—and continues to have— pull with rural inhabitants.

It is into this context—of an urban, modern Argentina, for a century reliant on large-scale commercial agriculture for exports—that genetically modified, herbicide-resistant soybeans were introduced in 1996. In the present moment of soybean extractivism, state and corporate actors—the Menem and Kirchner administrations allied with leaders of national and transnational agribusinesses—wielded their political, economic, and legal power to make large-scale GM soybean production possible and profitable. They did so most significantly by passing the Deregulation Decree in 1991 and by maintaining a weak regulation framework for the commercialization and use of genetically modified seeds. They also wielded their discursive power—through the mobilization of scientific expertise and the media—to disseminate a hegemonic discourse that GM soybean production is beneficial to society and the environment. The technological package of Roundup Ready soy, according to this discourse, promotes environmental sustainability (as no-tilling methods conserve the soil and glyphosate is a relatively low-toxicity agrochemical) as well as economic sustainability, by turning the farming business profitable. Most significantly, the adoption of cutting-edge agrarian technologies represents Argentina's reclamation of its global status as the world's granary. A century after the first agro-export boom, and part and parcel of a proud history of agrarian technological innovation in the Pampas, the green revolution of GM crops at the turn of the twenty-first century has made possible a soy boom that brings billions in foreign income while allegedly serving the humanitarian purpose of "feeding the world."

How do the synergies of power operate on the ground, in the rural communities in the Pampas? Inhabitants of large rural towns in the Pampas tend to emphasize the claimed positives of large-scale GM soy farming, touting "we do the best agriculture in the world" and "we all live off the countryside." Why are they supportive of GM soy production when most of them do not profit from farming as a business? How do they manage to ignore the negative impact of GM soy production? To understand how power operates to create acquiescence, I have zoomed in on the everyday life of the Pampas and have found that rural folks are not dupes of power but instead are caught in a complex, ambiguous situation of perceived positives and invisibilized negatives and that they often actively create their own acquiescence and consent (like the women of Santa María do). I emphasized the need to look into those positioned "in between" on the power spectrum in order to disentangle the relational and synergistic qualities of power dynamics to reproduce power, privilege, and injustice. Those "in between" are Pampas inhabitants who do not wield decision-making power over natural resources or technological innovation, although, while not profiting from it, they still reap some benefits from the GM soy model. These benefits are economic (in terms of higher earnings, rent, or family income) and cultural, ingrained in their modern, European national identity. Living in rural towns surrounded by sown fields, however, they also bear the health and environmental costs of pesticide drift. Male actors "in between," such as agronomists and agribusiness employees (like Leo, Lucas and Tomás, and Antonio), rank relatively high in the hierarchy of power due to their class, gender, and race. They identify with the hegemonic discourse of GM soy and, from their relatively higher status, help reproduce it. So does Mariana, who as the sole female agronomist in a male-dominated office, behaves according to the masculine standards of her position, framing agrochemical use as safe based on her expert credentials and claiming "ignorance" for those who question scientific expertise.

Middle-class women who identify primarily as wives and mothers (the women of Santa María) are particularly caught in between. They know, like Pampas inhabitants say, that everyone in town "lives off the countryside." This "living off of the countryside," as shown, means that rural inhabitants reap the trickle-down benefits of soybean production—for example, through job creation in the input and service sectors of the agro-industry and through the increased consumption of the agro-related class (which activates the real estate sector, for example). With no alternative economic sources other than agricultural production, the economic dependence of rural towns on soybeans does not create a conducive context to protest or change. Neither does the degree to which the health and environmental risks of agrochemical use are invisibilized. This is seen in the example of Bernetti, a soybean producer who, so certain about the low toxicity of glyphosate spraying and while having power over his farming business, enthusiastically chooses to plant 1,000 hectares of herbicide-resistant soybeans in his own backyard. The women of Santa María are aware of this context and are powerless to create a viable alternative, as they are economically dependent on their husbands and, due to their gender, are beneath them in the hierarchy of power. Despite the fact that they do perceive potential health risks in large-scale agrochemical use, instead of speaking up, they actively construct their acquiescence with doubt, silence, and denial.

Lastly, I have shown that not everyone is acquiescent in the face of the tremendous harm brought by GM soy expansion. Movements have emerged among those at the bottom of the power spectrum: those who do not reap the benefits but bear the costs of soybean extractivism. These movements against toxic agrochemicals in the Pampas have been led by women concerned about the health and environmental risks of agrochemical exposure. Peasant-indigenous movements have emerged as well, organized to resist violent and forced evictions and widespread deforestation in the north of the country.

The Mothers of Ituzaingó Anexo, in the city of Córdoba, continue to lead the anti-agrotoxin movement in Argentina, having inspired mobilization to "stop spraying" in other rural soy towns as well as the AMLV, a coalition of neighbors organized against the establishment of a Monsanto GM seed factory in their city, Malvinas Argentinas. Broadly, the anti-agrotoxin activists' main demand is to protect health by regulating agrochemical use, particularly by banning fumigation within town limits based on the precautionary principle. Though it did not require buffer zones, the AMLV also called for applying the precautionary principle to potential agrochemical drift, as it required Monsanto to produce an environmental impact assessment report for its plant before construction. Beyond regulations, one major achievement of these self-named "citizen assemblies for health and life" has been the creation of an advocacy network of laypeople and experts that has built a set of epidemiological data showing the links between illnesses and fumigations.[5] Another major achievement has been the passing of local ordinances that regulate agrochemical use within town limits; these have increased in number, from only three local ordinances banning glyphosate within town limits in 2006 to 104 by 2013.[6] However, while ordinances are increasing, this is only happening in a very small number of towns affected by the same problem. Movements have remained localized and unable to advance regulation at the provincial and national levels. Moreover, while there are exchanges among groups and assemblies (by email, listservs, and meetings) there is no national anti-agrotoxin network in place. The majority of Argentine rural towns remain acquiescent even when agrochemical drift is perceived as a hazard.

Why are these movements not more successful in enacting large-scale change? Activists face as barriers the very structural and cultural dynamics that create acquiescence among the general population. These barriers are the long-term economic and cultural dependence (of rural towns in particular and the country in general) on large-scale industrial agriculture for export, as well as the activists' structurally disempowered positions as poor and working-class feminized and racialized subjects. Furthermore, the pro–GM soy corporate and state actors have not remained quiet vis-à-vis these activists' challenges but have mobilized their power to quell dissent. Among other strategies to delegitimize activists, government officials and agribusiness leaders have mobilized the discourse of scientific expertise to deny activists' claims to agrochemical toxicity, calling activists who question so-called expert science "fundamentalists" against progress and development. They also often recur to stereotypical gendered and racialized insults to silence activists and their claims, and, not unusually, to violence as well. By doing so, powerful actors have managed to diminish the power of social movements that might otherwise move Argentina's development trajectory away from soybean extractivism.

At Distance to Care

A second theme in Schweblin's book strongly resonates with mine: the role of mothers as their children's primary caretakers, as constant and close guardians of their health and well-being.

The main protagonist in Schweblin's story is Amanda, an anxious mother. Amanda's worries have her constantly calculating the "rescue distance" to save her daughter from harm (hence, the book's title).[7] In the story, Amanda and Carla bond over worrying about their children's well-being. And while they do not exactly know or understand what is harming them (the unnamed agrochemicals), they take being alarmed as a given for mothers: "Yes, it's an instinct that comes with being a mother," Carla says to Amanda.[8]

There are women concerned with children's health who are subtly and overtly raising alarm over the health risks of agrochemical spraying. Both the women who protest, like the Mothers of Ituzaingó, and those who silence themselves, in Santa María, call on their "instinct" and "intuition" as mothers to question (out loud or in whispers) corporate and state science and expert advocates' claims about glyphosate's nontoxicity.

To claim motherhood as a strategy could open a window of opportunity for activism—as feminized subjects relegated to the private sphere can legitimately claim a space in the public sphere out of their "duty" to protect children. But this opportunity is short-lived and, ultimately, a trap. Because of women's lower status in the social hierarchy, their claims are taken less seriously by those in power, who often dismiss them on a gendered basis, calling women who protest "hysterical" and "uneducated housewives."

Though they are often unheard, significantly, these women bring to the table a way of "knowing" risk that is different than that of modern, corporate-sponsored science. Their way of knowing is both a rational conception and an embodied perception; that is, it is simultaneously cognitive, embodied, and emotional. It emerges from the felt, lived experience of taking care of their loved ones, of gathering data constantly on their children.

Still, the women of Santa María know that under present conditions— that is, a cultural economy of soybean extractivism that is patriarchal, capitalist, and modern—this way of knowing cannot uphold any claims to legitimacy. Therefore, in their relative powerlessness, the women of Santa María choose silence and denial. In an ironic twist, this serves also as a way to protect their families, as this very denial ensures their marriage and their families' income.

But what if we radically reconsidered whose knowledge and which ways of knowing become validated and valued? Women calling on motherhood bring forward a way of knowing that emerges from grounded observations and a preference for long-term sustainability, broadly defined as the survival of their progeny in the healthiest and happiest of conditions. That is, *they value long-term care at close distance.* Corporate actors, on the contrary, push for maximizing both short-term profitability and distance from the farm and the natural conditions that make farming possible.

At the extreme level of these efforts to distance and disembed, Argentine agribusiness leaders claim that "knowledge," as immaterial scientific and technological innovation, holds the future of agriculture and the promise of sustainable development: to grow more food to address world hunger and poverty with minimum ecological impact. Discursively, the spin is remarkable. For Argentina, in particular, it makes it possible to fully and proudly embrace the countryside, historically the land of barbarism, as now the Pampas can be farmed from a distance, with the aid of satellites and high-tech instruments, by professionals and entrepreneurs who "farm" from the comfort of urban settings and IT offices. It is the transcendence of the urban/rural divide by the modernization of the countryside. The oxymoron of an urban country that has historically turned its back on the countryside, yet embraced dependency on agricultural exports, has been made a reality.

In general, "farming with knowledge" would ideally rid agriculture of its tumultuous past and intrinsically contentious nature. Land (and, soon, water) is a scarce resource and has historically been at the core of world revolutions.[9] Knowledge, ideally, is not diminished by sharing. In reality, however, corporate-sponsored scientific and technological developments in genetically modified crops are neither free nor free to share. Patents and contracts protect corporate investments and limit farmers' capacity to freely adopt, share, and reproduce new seed varieties. Powerful actors— from the corporate world to state authorities and global sustainable development scholars—argue that genetically modified crops are necessary "to feed the world." Yet soybean producers (like Bernetti in chapter 2) will not feed themselves or their families with their harvest. As the figures I presented in the first chapters show, global food productivity has increased continuously over decades and yet millions continue to be hungry around the world. The United Nations estimates that one in every nine people suffers from chronic undernourishment and that global hunger is on the rise.[10] Achieving social well-being and justice in an ecologically sustainable manner requires going beyond technological solutions to take a deep and complex look into the power dynamics that guide technological innovation and control natural resources—and into the very definition of "development." Whose and which goals, knowledge, and values matter?

I am certainly not proposing that we dismiss scientific expertise on the basis of feelings and intuitions. As I write these concluding lines, in March 2019, a measles outbreak in the Pacific Northwest is underway partly as a result of many highly educated Americans who distrust science and the government refuse to vaccinate their children, justifying this with the argument that parents know better.[11] These behaviors endanger public health instead of protecting it. Vaccines have decades of testing and public funding to support them, with public health—not profit—as its main goal.[12] Very much to the contrary, glyphosate-based herbicides, the agrochemical companion to genetically modified soybeans, have been developed and mostly tested by the same company that profits from them.

In December 2017, a US federal scientific advisory panel to the EPA, on the evaluation of the carcinogenic potential of glyphosate, concluded that "there is no reliable evidence" of an association between glyphosate exposure and tumors, leukemia, or Hodgkin's lymphoma. Yet immediately after this statement, the very same experts raised the red flag of "critical data-gaps," warning that "all available epidemiologic studies of glyphosate-users are not really studies of glyphosate over-exposed workers."[13] If impact testing on glyphosate does not include those who are chronically exposed to it, then the EPA conclusions are, to say the least, questionable.

From learning about the practices of the tobacco, lead, and asbestos industries, civil society has become more wary of corporate-funded research and testing.[14] Ever since Rachel Carson published *Silent Spring* in 1962, the toxic impact of agrochemicals on health and environment has become part of public consciousness as well as public fears.[15] Glyphosate is currently in the eye of the media as possibly the next corporate scandal. Journalists and lawyers have begun to uncover Monsanto's internal documents that allegedly show Roundup could harm health, and yet these findings have been intentionally hidden from public view. "Does the World's Top Weed Killer Cause Cancer?" was a top headline in the midst of the world's first Roundup-related cancer trial.[16] In August 2018, a California jury ordered Monsanto to pay close to $300 million in damages to a school groundskeeper suffering from non-Hodgkin's lymphoma, who alleged that chronic exposure to the glyphosate-based weed killer caused his cancer.[17] Earlier, in July 2018, the European Union had voted down the latest generation of genetically engineered CRISPR crops, subjecting them—under the principle of precaution—to the same strict regulations that GMOS are under.[18] Meanwhile, in Argentina, as in the United States, promoters of GM biotechnology rapidly defended glyphosate-based herbicides and genetically modified crops.[19]

It remains to be seen what will happen next. Power is entrenched and even those who bear the costs of soybean extractivism often help perpetuate social and environmental injustice. Yet I believe that what these stories do—those published in the news, Schweblin's, mine—is help uncover grievances kept latent by the synergies of power. They reveal the elephant in the field. They show that care of and precaution for people and the environment are being diminished and shortchanged in the name of profits and growth. Those in power will surely aim to veil the elephant again. But as the saying goes, what has once been seen cannot ever be unseen.

NOTES

Introduction

1. Leguizamón, "Modifying Argentina"; Newell, "Bio-Hegemony."

2. "Sólo la biotecnología salvará al mundo," *Clarín*, January 29, 2001.

3. See Aranda, *Tierra arrasada*; Cáceres, "Accumulation by Dispossession"; Lapegna, *Soybeans and Power*; Leguizamón, "Modifying Argentina"; Pengue, "Transgenic Crops in Argentina."

4. Magdoff and Tokar, *Agriculture and Food in Crisis*; R. Motta, "Social Disputes over GMOs"; Stone, "Anthropology of Genetically Modified Crops."

5. R. Motta, *Social Mobilization*; Schurman and Munro, *Fighting for the Future of Food*; Scoones, "Mobilizing against GM Crops in India, South Africa and Brazil"; Patel, *Stuffed and Starved*.

6. Fitting, *Struggle for Maize*; Kinchy, *Seeds, Science, and Struggle*.

7. On India, see Patel, *Stuffed and Starved*. On France, see Heller, *Food, Farms, and Solidarity*.

8. On European Union regulations, see Qaim, "GM Crop Regulation"; and National Academies of Sciences, Engineering, and Medicine (NAS), *Genetically Engineered Crops*. Reports of bans are from the European Commission; see "Several European Countries Move to Rule Out GMOs," accessed April 16, 2019, http://ec.europa.eu/environment /europeangreencapital/countriesruleoutgmos.

9. Harrison, *Pesticide Drift*; Alkon, "Food Justice and the Challenge to Neoliberalism."

10. Lapegna, *Soybeans and Power*; Leguizamón, "Environmental Injustice in Argentina"; R. Motta, *Social Mobilization*; Newell, "Bio-Hegemony."

11. Coronil, *Magical State*.

12. By "perspectives on the political economy of the environment," I mean sociological work that focuses on the power dynamics over the control of material resources that sustain life. See Rudel, Roberts, and Carmin, "Political Economy of the Environment."

13. I am certainly not the first sociologist to ask why communities remain acquiescent in the face of social and environmental injustice. See, for example, the important work of Auyero and Swistun, *Flammable*; Beamish, *Silent Spill*; Bell, *Fighting*

King Coal; Crenson, *Un-Politics of Air Pollution*; Cable, Shriver, and Mix, "Risk Society and Contested Illness"; Gaventa, *Power and Powerlessness*; Lapegna, *Soybeans and Power*; Lukes, *Power*; Norgaard, *Living in Denial*; Roscigno, "Power, Revisited"; and Shriver, Adams, and Messer, "Power, Quiescence, and Pollution." Yet the number of studies on acquiescence is quite limited, and "attention to inaction remains the exception rather than the core of what most [sociological] analyses do" (Roscigno, "Power, Revisited," 354).

14. Pigna, *Los mitos de la historia argentina*, vol. 2; Shumway, *Invention of Argentina*.

15. See, among others, Bullard, *Dumping in Dixie*; Cole and Foster, *From the Ground Up*; Mohai, Pellow, and Roberts, "Environmental Justice."

16. Foster, Clark, and York, *Ecological Rift*; Gould, Pellow, and Schnaiberg, *Treadmill of Production*; Rudel, Roberts, and Carmin, "Political Economy of the Environment"; Schnaiberg and Gould, *Environment and Society*.

17. Auyero and Swistun, *Flammable*; Bell, *Fighting King Coal*; Gaventa, *Power and Powerlessness*; Lukes, *Power*; Shriver, Adams, and Messer, "Power, Quiescence, and Pollution."

18. Gould, Pellow, and Schnaiberg, *Treadmill of Production*; Pellow and Brulle, *Power, Justice, and the Environment*; Pellow, *What Is Critical Environmental Justice?*

19. I use the terms *genetically modified*, *genetically engineered*, and *transgenic* interchangeably to refer to plants that result from gene splicing recombinant DNA (in particular, to herbicide-tolerant and insect-resistant GM crops: soybeans, corn, cotton, and canola). While supporters of the technology argue that conventional plant breeding and modern genetic modification are equivalent as they both result in a plant with altered genomes, critics argue that these are *qualitatively different* processes. In traditional plant and animal breeding, breeders can only mix species that are sexually compatible. GM biotechnology is different from the traditional process because transgenic mixing cannot be realized in natural settings and is possible only in the lab. Kloppenburg, *First the Seed*.

20. On the potential of Golden Rice, see the Golden Rice Project website, accessed October 27, 2018, http://www.goldenrice.org. The crop had not been approved as of October 2018; see International Service for the Acquisition of Agri-Biotech Applications (ISAAA), GM Approval Database, accessed October 27, 2018, http://www.isaaa .org/gmapprovaldatabase/event/default.asp?EventID=528. For a critique, see Stone and Glover, "Disembedding Grain."

21. In addition to soybeans, corn accounts for 31 percent of global crops planted; cotton, 13 percent; and canola, 5 percent. The remaining 1 percent of commercially planted GM crops is made up of alfalfa, sugar beets, papayas, potatoes, eggplants, and apples. ISAAA, *Global Status of Commercialized Biotech/GM Crops in 2017*, 91.

22. For more on *Bacillus thuringiensis* crops, see "What Is Insect Resistance in Crops?," UC Davis Seed Biotechnology Center website, accessed November 11, 2018, http://sbc.ucdavis.edu/files/191415.pdf.

23. Glover, "Corporate Shaping of GM Crops"; Gillam, *Whitewash*.

24. Qaim and Traxler, "Roundup Ready Soybeans in Argentina"; Trigo, "Fifteen Years of Genetically Modified Crops in Argentine Agriculture."

25. On "superweeds," see Gilbert, "Case Studies"; Livingston et al., *Economics of Glyphosate Resistance Management in Corn and Soybean Production*. On bollworms in Brazil, see Oliveira and Hecht, "Sacred Groves," 256; Pinto, Mattos, Silva, Rocha, and Elliot, "Spread of *Helicoverpa armigera*." On the increasing use of agrochemicals, see Binimelis, Pengue, and Monterroso, "'Transgenic Treadmill.'"

26. Benbrook, "Trends in Glyphosate Herbicide Use"; Catacora-Vargas et al., "Soybean Production in the Southern Cone of the Americas." In Argentina, the rate of glyphosate use per hectare has more than doubled since the adoption of herbicide-tolerant soybeans, from 2.05 kilograms per hectare in 1996 to 4.45 kilograms per hectare in 2014. Benbrook, "Trends in Glyphosate Herbicide Use," appendix.

27. International Agency for Research on Cancer, *Evaluation of Five Organophosphate Insecticides and Herbicides*.

28. Paraquat is a highly toxic poison with associated risks of neurologic disease. 2,4-D was a main component in the infamous Agent Orange used by the United States during the Vietnam War, and research shows an association of non-Hodgkin lymphoma with high exposure to 2,4-D. Atrazine is a potent endocrine disruptor. Centers for Disease Control and Prevention, "Facts about Paraquat," April 2, 2013, https://emergency.cdc.gov/agent/paraquat/basics/facts.asp. Kim, Kabir, and Jahan, "Exposure to Pesticides"; Smith et al., "2,4-Dichlorophenoxyacetic Acid (2,4-D) and Risk of Non-Hodgkin Lymphoma"; Hayes et al., "Atrazine Induces Complete Feminization and Chemical Castration in Male African Clawed Frogs (*Xenopus laevis*)."

29. Binimelis, Pengue, and Monterroso, "'Transgenic Treadmill'"; Leguizamón, "Modifying Argentina."

30. Jacobsen et al., "Feeding the World," 652.

31. In 1996, the United States, Argentina, Canada, China, and Mexico together planted 1.7 million hectares of GM crops, the vast majority across the United States and Argentina. In 2017, the United States planted 75 million hectares of GM crops (40 percent of the global total); Brazil, 50.2 million hectares (26 percent); Argentina, 23.6 million hectares (12 percent); Canada, 13.1 million hectares (7 percent); India, 11.4 million hectares (6 percent); and Paraguay and Pakistan, 3 million hectares each (2 percent each). ISAAA, *Global Status of Commercialized Biotech/GM Crops*.

32. Glover, "Corporate Shaping of GM Crops"; R. Motta, "Social Disputes over GMOs"; Schnurr, "Can Genetically Modified Crops Help the Poor?"; Schurman and Munro, *Fighting for the Future of Food*; Oliveira and Hecht, "Sacred Groves."

33. In India, GM crops cover 6 percent of total agricultural area; in Pakistan, they cover 8 percent. Calculated from data listed in ISAAA, *Global Status of Commercialized Biotech/GM Crops*; and Food and Agriculture Organization of the United Nations (FAO), "Country Profiles, Estimates for 2014," accessed October 23, 2018, http://www.fao.org/countryprofiles.

34. On Japan, see the US Department of Agriculture Foreign Agricultural Service (USDA FAS), "Japan. Agricultural Biotechnology Annual: Japan's Regulatory System for GE Crops Continues to Improve," Global Agricultural Information Network (GAIN) Report JA5024 (Washington, DC: USDA), July 13, 2015, https://gain.fas.usda.gov/Recent%20GAIN%20Publications/Agricultural%20Biotechnology%20

Annual_Tokyo_Japan_7-13-2015.pdf. On second-generation GM crops in Africa, see Schnurr, "Can Genetically Modified Crops Help the Poor?"; Dowd-Uribe, "GMOs and Poverty"; Schurman, "Micro (Soft) Managing a 'Green Revolution' for Africa."

35. Dowd-Uribe, "GMOs and Poverty"; Glover, "Corporate Shaping of GM Crops"; Schnurr, "Can Genetically Modified Crops Help the Poor?"

36. United Nations, Sustainable Development Goals, "Zero Hunger: Why It Matters" (New York: United Nations, 2016), accessed October 23, 2018, https://www.un.org /sustainabledevelopment/wp-content/uploads/2018/09/Goal-2.pdf; FAO, *Crop Prospects and Food Situation*, Global Quarterly Report 3, September 2018, http://www.fao.org /documents/card/en/c/CA1487EN.

37. ISAAA, *Global Status of Commercialized Biotech/GM Crops*, 1.

38. Sachs, *Age of Sustainable Development*, 317.

39. Friedman, *Hot, Flat, and Crowded*; Pinker, *Enlightenment Now*.

40. Sachs, *Age of Sustainable Development*, 317. Malthus's famous thesis, as developed in *An Essay on the Principle of Population*, is that population growth increases geo-metrically while food production increases arithmetically, thus leading to chronic food shortages.

41. Sachs, *Age of Sustainable Development*.

42. Sachs, *Age of Sustainable Development*, 10.

43. Intergovernmental Panel on Climate Change (IPCC), *Climate Change 2014*; IPCC, *Global Warming of 1.5°C* (Geneva: IPCC, 2018), https://www.ipcc.ch/sr15/.

44. Buttel, "Ecological Modernization as Social Theory"; Givens, Clark, and Jorgenson, "Strengthening the Ties"; Pinker, *Enlightenment Now*.

45. Gudynas, "Debates on Development"; Peet and Hartwick, *Theories of Development*.

46. USDA FAS, "World Agricultural Production," accessed August 26, 2018, https:// apps.fas.usda.gov/psdonline/circulars/production.pdf.

47. For the United States, see Jim Barrett, "USDA Reports Soybean, Corn Acreage Down," news release (Washington, DC: National Agricultural Statistics Service, United States Department of Agriculture), June 29, 2018, https://www.nass.usda.gov /Newsroom/2018/06-29-2018.php. For Argentina, see Trigo, "Fifteen Years of Genetically Modified Crops."

48. US United Soybean Board, "Soybean Oil for the Food Industry," accessed October 24, 2018, https://www.soyconnection.com/foodindustry. Soybean-based milk formula is used for infants who are believed to be lactose intolerant. "Soy Infant Formula," National Institute of Environmental Health Sciences website, December 28, 2018, https://www.niehs.nih.gov/health/topics/agents/sya-soy -formula/index.cfm.

49. USDA, "USDA Coexistence Fact Sheets: Soybeans," February 2015, https://www .usda.gov/sites/default/files/documents/coexistence-soybeans-factsheet.pdf.

50. The $86 billion in global soy exports breaks down as follows: $51.7 billion in beans, $9.45 billion in soybean oil, and $24.8 billion in soybean meal. Soybean meal is a byproduct of the extraction of soybean oil and is used as a protein source to feed

cattle, poultry, and hogs. In 2016, Argentina was the top global exporter of soybean meal (40 percent of global exports, export value of USD $9.95 billion) and the top exporter of soybean oil (44 percent of global exports, valued at USD $4.14 billion). China imported 62 percent of global soybeans in 2016, and India, 27 percent of global soybean oil; 39 percent of soybean meal is destined for countries in the European Union. Observatory of Economic Complexity (OEC), "Products," accessed November 15, 2018, https://atlas.media.mit.edu/.

51. Patel, *Stuffed and Starved*; Rosa et al., "Human (Anthropogenic) Driving Forces."

52. York and Gossard, "Cross-National Meat and Fish Consumption," 294.

53. Jorgenson, "Global Warming and the Neglected Greenhouse Gas."

54. Oliveira and Hecht, "Sacred Groves," 252.

55. Pat Mooney and the ETC Group, "Blocking the Chain: Industrial Food Chain Concentration, Big Data Platforms and Food Sovereignty Solutions" (Val David, QC: ETC Group, GLOCON, INKOTA-netzwerk, and Rosa Luxemburg Stiftung, 2018), http://www.etcgroup.org/sites/www.etcgroup.org/files/files/blockingthechain_english_web .pdf; Elsadig Elsheikh and Hossein Ayazi, *The Era of Corporate Consolidation and the End of Competition: Bayer-Monsanto, Dow-DuPont, and ChemChina-Syngenta*, research brief (Berkeley: Haas Institute for a Fair and Inclusive Society at the University of California, Berkeley), October 2018, https://haasinstitute.berkeley.edu/sites/default/files/haas _institute_shahidi-_era_of_corporate_consolidation_end_of_competition_publish.pdf.

56. IPES Food, "Too Big to Feed: Exploring the Impacts of Mega-Mergers, Consolidation and Concentration of Power in the Agri-Food Sector" (Brussels: IPES Food, 2017), http://www.ipes-food.org/_img/upload/files/Concentration_FullReport.pdf; Oliveira and Hecht, "Sacred Groves," 257.

57. Clapp, "Financialization, Distance and Global Food Politics"; Fairbairn, "'Like Gold with Yield'"; Isakson, "Food and Finance."

58. Leguizamón, "Disappearing Nature?"; Turzi, *Political Economy of Agricultural Booms*.

59. McMichael, *Food Regimes*; Teubal, "Genetically Engineered Soybeans."

60. Data on soybean production are from the Argentine Ministry of Agriculture, Livestock, and Fisheries (MAGYP). Secretaría de Agroindustria, "Datos abiertos de agroindustria," accessed October 4, 2016, http://www.siia.gov.ar/index.php/series-por -tema/agricultura.

61. Argentine exports are calculated from data listed in OEC, "Products."

62. Leguizamón, "Disappearing Nature?"; Oliveira and Hecht, "Sacred Groves." On research and development funding, see Schnaiberg, *Environment*.

63. McMichael, "Food Regime Genealogy"; McMichael, *Food Regimes*. On flex crops, see Borras et al., "Land Grabbing"; Oliveira and Hecht, "Sacred Groves," 256.

64. Schnaiberg, *Environment*; Gould, Pellow, and Schnaiberg, *Treadmill of Production*.

65. Otero, "Neoliberal Food Regime."

66. Dowd-Uribe, "GMOs and Poverty"; Glover, "Corporate Shaping of GM Crops"; Leguizamón, "Modifying Argentina"; Leguizamón, "Disappearing Nature?"; Schnurr, "Can Genetically Modified Crops Help the Poor?"

67. I develop the concept of "synergies of power" from reading Gould, Pellow, and Schnaiberg (*Treadmill of Production*, 59), who invite scholars to think about how power operates synergistically to reinforce power and powerlessness.

68. For a critical review of classic EJ literature, see Pellow, *What Is Critical Environmental Justice?*; Pellow and Nyseth Brehm, "Environmental Sociology for the Twenty-First Century"; and Pellow and Brulle, *Power, Justice, and the Environment*, chap. 1.

69. Pellow, *What Is Critical Environmental Justice?*, 19. See also Pellow and Brulle, *Power, Justice, and the Environment*.

70. Sundberg, "Tracing Race."

71. For exceptions to the focus on collective action, see Auyero and Swistun, *Flammable*; Beamish, *Silent Spill*; Bell, *Fighting King Coal*; Lapegna, *Soybeans and Power*; Norgaard, *Living in Denial*; and Shriver, Adams, and Messer, "Power, Quiescence, and Pollution."

72. Gould, Pellow, and Schnaiberg, *Treadmill of Production*; Mohai, Pellow, and Roberts, "Environmental Justice"; Rudel, Roberts, and Carmin, "Political Economy of the Environment"; Pellow and Nyseth Brehm, "Environmental Sociology for the Twenty-First Century."

73. Shriver, Adams, and Messer, "Power, Quiescence, and Pollution."

74. Bullard, *Dumping in Dixie*; Cole and Foster, *From the Ground Up*; Mohai, Pellow, and Roberts, "Environmental Justice."

75. Pellow and Nyseth Brehm, "Environmental Sociology for the Twenty-First Century." A relatively small but important body of work expands this limited focus on environmental disadvantage toward exploring environmental privilege. See, for example, Mascarenhas, *Where the Waters Divide*; Norgaard, *Living in Denial*; Park and Pellow, *Slums of Aspen*; Pulido, "Rethinking Environmental Racism"; D. Taylor, *Environment and the People in American Cities*.

76. Roscigno, "Power, Revisited," 350.

77. Lukes, *Power*, 28.

78. Bértola and Ocampo, *Economic Development of Latin America since Independence*; Cardoso and Faletto, *Dependency and Development in Latin America*; Kay, *Latin American Theories*.

79. Weber, *Protestant Ethic*; Gramsci, *Selections from the Prison Notebooks*.

80. Sorensen, *"Facundo" and the Construction*; Shumway, *Invention of Argentina*.

81. Gordillo and Hirsch, "Indigenous Struggles"; Halperin Donghi, *Nación para el desierto*.

82. Shumway, *Invention of Argentina*; Pigna, *Mitos de la historia argentina*.

83. "Mobilization of bias" refers to the set of predominant values, beliefs, and institutional procedures that operate systematically to the benefit of political and economic elites. See Bachrach and Baratz, "Two Faces of Power"; Gaventa, *Power and Powerlessness*; Lukes, *Power*.

84. de la Cadena, "Indigenous Cosmopolitics in the Andes."

85. Alberto and Elena, "Introduction." On indigenous marginalization, see Gordillo and Hirsch, "Indigenous Struggles"; Lapegna, *Soybeans and Power*.

86. Stølen, "Agricultural Change in Argentina"; Stølen, *La decencia de la desigualdad*; Ferro, *Género y propiedad rural*.

87. See Auyero and Swistun, *Flammable*; Beamish, *Silent Spill*; Bell, *Fighting King Coal*; Crenson, *Un-Politics of Air Pollution*; Gaventa, *Power and Powerlessness*; Gould, "Pollution and Perception"; Gould, "Sweet Smell of Money."

88. Bachrach and Baratz, "Two Faces of Power"; Gaventa, *Power and Powerlessness*; Lukes, *Power*.

89. Newell, "Bio-Hegemony"; Gras and Hernández, "Hegemony, Technological Innovation, and Corporate Identities."

90. Herman and Chomsky, *Manufacturing Consent*; Lukes, *Power*; McChesney, *Rich Media*.

91. Schurman and Munro, *Fighting for the Future of Food*, xvi–xvii.

92. Foster, "Marx's Theory of Metabolic Rift"; Foster, Clark, and York, *Ecological Rift*; O'Connor, *Natural Causes*; Pellow and Nyseth Brehm, "Environmental Sociology for the Twenty-First Century"; Rudel, Roberts, and Carmin, "Political Economy of the Environment."

93. Schnaiberg, *Environment*; Schnaiberg and Gould, *Environment and Society*; Gould, Pellow, and Schnaiberg, *Treadmill of Production*.

94. McAdam, *Political Process*; McCarthy and Zald, "Resource Mobilization and Social Movements."

95. Goodwin, Jasper, and Polletta, "Emotional Dimensions of Social Movements"; Jasper, "Emotions and Social Movements"; Benford and Snow, "Framing Processes and Social Movements."

96. Polletta and Ho, "Frames and Their Consequences," 190.

97. Bell, *Fighting King Coal*, 3–4; McAdam, *Political Process*.

98. Bell, *Fighting King Coal*; Norgaard, *Living in Denial*.

99. Auyero and Swinstun, *Flammable*; Beamish, *Silent Spill*; Bell, *Fighting King Coal*; Norgaard, *Living in Denial*; Gould, "Pollution and Perception"; Gould, "Sweet Smell of Money"; Stauber and Rampton, *Toxic Sludge Is Good for You!*.

100. Brown, "Popular Epidemiology"; Cable, Shriver, and Mix, "Risk Society and Contested Illness"; Harrison, *Pesticide Drift*; Kinchy, *Seeds, Science, and Struggle*.

101. Beamish, *Silent Spill*.

102. Gaventa, *Power and Powerlessness*; Lukes, *Power*.

103. Zerubavel, *Elephant in the Room*.

104. Shriver, Adams, and Messer, "Power, Quiescence, and Pollution."

105. These are common strategies identified in the sociology of denial literature; see, for example, Auyero and Swistun, *Flammable*; Norgaard, *Living in Denial*; and Zerubavel, *Elephant in the Room*.

106. Roscigno, "Power, Revisited."

107. Gaventa, *Power and Powerlessness*; Lukes, *Power*.

108. Schurman and Munro, "Targeting Capital."

109. Walton, "Making the Theoretical Case," 124.

110. Gaventa, *Power and Powerlessness*; Lukes, *Power*; Roscigno, "Power, Revisited."

111. Paige, *Agrarian Revolution*.

112. Data are for 2016. Secretaría de Agroindustria, "Datos abiertos agroindustria."

113. Pengue, "Transgenic Crops in Argentina"; Gasparri, Grau, and Manghi, "Carbon Pools."

1. The Roots of the Soy Model

1. Data are listed in Chazarreta and Rosati, "Cambios en la estructura," 92. The 2008 Rural Census (Censo Nacional Agropecuario) is, as of December 2018, the most recently available. In September 2018, INDEC began surveying for a new Rural Census. For updates, see the 2018 Censo Nacional Agropecuario website, https://cna2018.indec .gob.ar/.

2. James M. MacDonald and Robert A. Hoppe, *Large Family Farms Continue to Dominate US Agricultural Production* (Washington, DC: US Department of Agriculture, Economic Research Service, 2017), https://www.ers.usda.gov/amber-waves/2017/march /large-family-farms-continue-to-dominate-us-agricultural-production/.

3. The total number of farms in Argentina has decreased from 378,357 farms in 1988 to 256,773 in 2008. Large farms (larger than 1,000 hectares) accounted for 7.3 percent of farms in 1988 and 10.2 percent in 2008. Data are calculated from 2008 Rural Census data, listed in Chazarreta and Rosati, "Cambios en la estructura," 92.

4. Roberts and Thanos, *Trouble in Paradise*; Restall and Lane, *Latin America in Colonial Times*.

5. Acosta, "Extractivism and Neoextractism." According to Eduardo Galeano, in 1650, Potosí had a population of 160,000, ten times larger than Boston at the time. "They say that even the horses were shod with silver in the great days of the city of Potosí," he writes (Galeano, *Open Veins of Latin America*, 20). For the wondrous story of Potosí, see Lane, *Potosí*.

6. Boyer, "Latin American Environmental History."

7. Brailovsky and Foguelman, *Memoria verde*.

8. South of the Caribbean, the Spanish Empire spread over the Andean region, which provided great mineral riches but no access to the Atlantic and, thus, no access to European markets. (Recall that the Portuguese dominated Brazil at the time.) The Spanish had no access to South America from the Atlantic, except in the north, in Cartagena and Caracas, and the far south, entering the Río de la Plata, the river that separates Buenos Aires and Montevideo. See Restall and Lane, *Latin America in Colonial Times*.

9. Rock, *Argentina*.

10. Benítez-Rojo, "Nineteenth-Century Spanish American Novel."

11. Benítez-Rojo, "Nineteenth-Century Spanish American Novel"; Sorensen, *"Facundo" and the Construction*; Shumway, *Invention of Argentina*.

12. Shumway, *Invention of Argentina*, xi.

13. Clark, "Emergence and Transformation of Positivism."

14. Pigna, *Mitos de la historia argentina*; Shumway, *Invention of Argentina*.

15. Burns, *Poverty of Progress*; Clark, "Emergence and Transformation of Positivism."

16. See Coronil, *Magical State*; García Canclini, *Culturas híbridas*; Larraín, *Identity and Modernity in Latin America*. Beatriz Sarlo refers to this version of Latin American modernity as "subordinate" or "peripheral." See Sarlo, *Una modernidad periférica*.

17. Benítez-Rojo, "Nineteenth-Century Spanish American Novel"; Halperin Donghi, *Nación para el desierto*; Larraín, "Modernity and Identity."

18. Shumway, *Invention of Argentina*; Sorensen, *"Facundo" and the Construction*. The original titles in Spanish are *Facundo o civilización y barbarie en las Pampas Argentinas*

and *Bases y puntos de partida para la organización política de la República Argentina*. Facundo is for Facundo Quiroga (1788–1835), the caudillo leader of the northern province of La Rioja, also known as El Tigre de los Llanos, or the Tiger of the Plains.

19. To understand the mentality of the Generation of 1837, it is important to understand their historical context. In the 1840s, Argentina was divided in two factions: the Unitarios, liberals who wanted to have a centralized government seated in Buenos Aires; and the Federales, conservatives who wanted a decentralized government (which would give more power to the provinces). At this time, power was in the hands of the Federales. Juan Manuel de Rosas, the caudillo of the province of Buenos Aires, was the de facto ruler of the country. Rosas was an hacendado and had strong popular support from the rural masses. The men of the Generation of 1837 opposed Rosas, and thus many of them were forced into exile. They were able to return to the country only after Rosas's rule ended in 1852. See Luna, *Breve historia de los argentinos*; Rock, *Argentina*.

20. The nineteenth-century elite's analysis of society was imbued with the spirit of the times, particularly French positivism and functionalism. From this sociological perspective, as first developed by Auguste Comte and later by Émile Durkheim, society is understood as a living body, an organism where each part (that is, every institution in society, such as the economy, politics, education, and the family) has a specific function. Just like a living organism, when organs/institutions do not work well, they become ill and affect the rest of the (social) body. See Durkheim, *Division of Labor in Society*; Parsons, *Evolution of Societies*.

21. Pigna, *Mitos de la historia argentina*; Shumway, *Invention of Argentina*.

22. Sarmiento's civilization/barbarism dichotomy resembles a classical dichotomy in sociological theory: Ferdinand Tönnies's *Gemeinschaft* and *Gesellschaft* (community and society). Tönnies's classical analysis of the transition from traditional/feudal society (Gemeinschaft) into modern/capitalist society (Gesellschaft) is at the core of the modernization paradigm: this transition is conceptualized as a linear movement toward progress, modernity, and higher rationalization. Tönnies, *Community and Society*. While both Tönnies and Sarmiento were writing roughly contemporaneously, there is an important difference between them. For Tönnies, as well as for other European scholars after him, such as Karl Marx, Émile Durkheim, and Max Weber (and even Talcott Parsons in the United States in the mid-twentieth century), the traditional Gemeinschaft is in the past. It had already been—or was rapidly being—superseded by industrial capitalist society. In their writings, thus, these authors at times mourn the loss of traditional community values. Durkheim's and Weber's writings, in particular, often show the romantic traces of a lost past. In the Argentina of the early nineteenth century, however, the two categories coexist in time. The Generation of 1837 cannot afford romanticism; nothing had been lost yet. For them, on the contrary, the "barbarism" arising from the Pampas was felt like the plague. They thus set out to exterminate it.

23. Clark, "Emergence and Transformation of Positivism," 63.

24. Brailovsky and Foguelman, *Memoria verde*.

25. Sarmiento, *Facundo*, 46.

26. Brailovsky and Foguelman, *Memoria verde*. As these authors note, indigenous tribes also used the guanaco's leather for clothing and to build the *toldos*, covers for shelters. That is why natives' settlements in Argentina are called *tolderías*.

27. Brailovsky and Foguelman, *Memoria verde*.

28. Rosal, "Exportación de cueros," 568. The main destination for Argentine leather was Great Britain. Wool was mostly destined for the United States, France, and Germany. Salted meat was considered too low quality to feed European industrial workers and was used instead to feed slaves, thus exported mostly to Cuba and Brazil.

29. Mumford, *Technics and Civilization*.

30. Mumford, *Technics and Civilization*; Pinker, *Enlightenment Now*.

31. Shumway, *Invention of Argentina*; Sorensen, *"Facundo" and the Construction*.

32. In the Pampas region, five small national parks protect a total of fewer than 50,000 hectares: Campos del Tuyú and Ciervo de los Pantanos in Buenos Aires province; Lihué Calel in La Pampa; and Islas de Santa Fe and Predelta in the province of Santa Fe. Parques Nacionales de la Argentina, accessed December 29, 2018, https://www.parquesnacionales.gob.ar/.

33. Alberdi, *Bases y puntos de partida*.

34. Brailovsky and Foguelman, *Memoria verde*.

35. Shumway, *Invention of Argentina*, 156.

36. Sabato, *Historia de la Argentina*.

37. Three other laws passed under Roca's administration were strategic in consolidating the Argentine nation. First, the law that made Buenos Aires the nation's capital; second, the Law of Monetary Unification (1881), which gave the national government the sole power to issue currency; and, third, a law that oversaw the creation of a national army. Gallo, *República en ciernes*.

38. Stølen, *Decencia de la desigualdad*, 45–46.

39. Ludmer, "Gaucho Genre."

40. C. Taylor, *Rural Life in Argentina*; de Cristóforis, *Inmigrantes y colonos*.

41. Gallo, *República en ciernes*, 36.

42. de Cristóforis, *Inmigrantes y colonos*; Avni, "Agricultura judía." For the history of colonias, see Djenderedjian, *Gringos en las Pampas*.

43. Halperin Donghi, *Nación para el desierto*.

44. Boyer, "Latin American Environmental History"; Restall and Lane, *Latin America in Colonial Times*. Brailovsky and Foguelman, in *Memoria verde*, call the destruction of the Inca system of terraced agriculture in the Argentine northwest one of the worst ecological catastrophes the country has endured.

45. The colonial institutions of forced indigenous labor in the Spanish mines are known as *mita* and *encomienda*. While neither was technically a slave system, Restall and Lane (*Latin America in Colonial Times*, 155–56) argue they "came close to it," due to the forceful drafting of indigenous subjects and the harsh labor conditions, which sickened, killed, or maimed most of them. In the Argentine northeast, in the province of Misiones in particular, Guaraníes aiming to escape the slave-raiding *bandeirantes*, who were seeking labor for the sugar plantations in Brazil, found refuge in the Jesuit

missions, who subdued them by other means. See Ganson, *Guaraní*; Restall and Lane, *Latin America in Colonial Times*, 160–61.

46. Gordillo and Hirsch, "Indigenous Struggles," 4; Rock, *Argentina*.

47. Hasbrouck, "Conquest of the Desert"; Rock, *Argentina*, 154. A boleadora is a weapon consisting of "two or three round stones wrapped in leather and lashed together with thongs two yards long." "One of these weights was held in the hand while the weapon was whirled about the head and then hurled at the enemy or the animal hunted. So great was the skill of the Indians in hurling the [boleadoras] that they could strike the head of their quarry with one of the stones or wrap the thongs about its neck or legs, no matter how fast it was running" (Hasbrouck, "Conquest of the Desert," 200).

48. Pigna, *Mitos de la historia argentina*; Gordillo and Hirsch, "Indigenous Struggles."

49. Harvey, *New Imperialism*.

50. Pigna, *Mitos de la historia argentina*, 370–73.

51. Gordillo, *Rubble*; Gordillo, "Savage Outside of White Argentina."

52. Domínguez, "Lucha por la tierra."

53. Binstock and Cerrutti, *Niños, niñas y adolescentes*, 13. According to the 2004–5 Encuesta Complementaria de Poblaciones Indígenas de la Argentina, 457,363 people identified as indigenous (the number increases to 600,329 if including people who did not identify as indigenous but were first-generation indigenous descent). The largest groups are Mapuche (113,680 people), Kolla (70,505), Toba (69,452), and Wichí (40,036). In the 2010 census, 955,135 people identified as of indigenous descent. Binstock and Cerrutti, "Población y la estructura social," 46. See also INDEC, *Censo nacional de población, hogares y viviendas*, 2010, https://www.indec.gob.ar.

54. Binstock and Cerrutti, *Niños, niñas y adolescentes*; Binstock and Cerrutti, "Población y la estructura social."

55. Lapegna, *Soybeans and Power*, 35.

56. Gordillo, "Savage Outside of White Argentina"; Gordillo and Hirsch, "Indigenous Struggles"; Alberto and Elena, "Introduction."

57. Barsky and Gelman, *Historia del agro argentino: Desde la conquista hasta fines del siglo XX*; Pigna, *Mitos de la historia argentina*; Shumway, *Invention of Argentina*.

58. Friedmann and McMichael, "Rise and Decline of National Agricultures."

59. Barsky and Gelman, *Historia del agro argentino: Desde la conquista hasta fines del siglo XX*.

60. McMichael, "Food Regime Genealogy," 141.

61. Sanz-Villarroya, "Convergence Process."

62. Hora, "Evolución del sector," 153.

63. At $4,367 in 1990 PPP (purchasing power parity) adjusted dollars. Sanz-Villarroya, "Convergence Process," 441.

64. Palacio, *Chacareros pampeanos*, 41.

65. Palacio, *Chacareros pampeanos*.

66. Avni, "Agricultura judía," 543; my translation.

67. Carl Taylor was a major figure of the study of rural life in the United States and the thirty-sixth president of the American Sociological Association. American Socio-

logical Association, "Carl C. Taylor," accessed July 19, 2018, http://www.asanet.org/carl-c-taylor; C. Taylor, *Rural Life in Argentina*, 6 (quotations), 7–8.

68. C. Taylor, *Rural Life in Argentina*, 7–8.

69. Djenderedjian, *Gringos en las Pampas*; C. Taylor, *Rural Life in Argentina*.

70. Avni, "Agricultura judía," 546.

71. Stølen, *Decencia de la desigualdad*.

72. Between 1870 and 1915, the percentage of the urban population went up from 29 to 52 percent. Binstock and Cerrutti, "Población y la estructura social," 41. Only Uruguay and Chile experienced a dynamic of rapid urbanization similar to Argentina's. Prévôt-Schapira and Velut, "Sistema urbano."

73. Avni, "Agricultura judía"; Ferro, *Género y propiedad rural*; Hora, "Evolución del sector agroexportador"; Stølen, *Decencia de la desigualdad*.

74. Avni, "Agricultura judía"; Hora, "Evolución del sector."

75. Ferro, *Género y propiedad rural*; Stølen, *Decencia de la desigualdad*.

76. I take Gustavo Grobocopatel's family history from interviews he gave to Rodolfo González Arzac. See González Arzac, *¡Adentro!*; and Alexandre Roig and Graciela Mochkofsky, "El rico que se cree Steve Jobs," *Revista Anfibia* 8, accessed July 25, 2018, http://revistaanfibia.com/cronica/el-rico-que-se-cree-steve-jobs/.

77. Barsky and Gelman, *Historia del agro argentino: Desde la conquista hasta comienzos del siglo XXI*, 361–74.

78. Bértola and Ocampo, *Economic Development of Latin America*.

79. Shumway, *Invention of Argentina*, 299.

80. Horowitz, "Populism and Its Legacies in Argentina."

81. Between 1947 and 1960, the rural population in Argentina declined in both relative and absolute terms, down from 37.8 percent of the total population (accounting for 6 million) to 28 percent (5.6 million) at the end of the period. In the Pampas the decline was steeper, as the rural population declined from 27.8 percent to 18.5 percent. Recchini de Lattes, "Proceso de urbanización," 870. In Buenos Aires province, the trend of rural depopulation was starker: by 1960, the rural population accounted for barely 13 percent of the total population. The urban population was concentrated in the Greater Buenos Aires area, which grew at a pace five times higher than the rest of the province, an area that, by 1980, contained 25 percent of the total Argentine population. Hora, *¿Cómo pensaron?*, 161.

82. Barsky and Gelman, *Historia del agro argentino: Desde la conquista hasta comienzos del siglo XXI*, 389–99.

83. Patel, "Long Green Revolution."

84. Asociación de Semilleros Argentinos website, accessed April 3, 2011, http://www.asa.org.ar.

85. Patel, "Long Green Revolution," reports increases in production due to higher yields across the developing world. For example, maize production in Chile grew by 200 kilograms per hectare per year after 1964. In Asia, food supply doubled in twenty-five years with only a 4 percent increase in planted area.

86. Barsky and Gelman, *Historia del agro argentino: Desde la conquista hasta fines del siglo XX*, 368.

87. Chazarreta and Rosati, "Cambios en la estructura"; Rosati, "Patrones espaciales."

88. Chazarreta and Rosati, "Cambios en la estructura"; Rosati, "Patrones espaciales."

89. Teubal, "Expansión del modelo sojero."

90. Some policies implemented included an emphasis on the fiscal sector at the expense of the productive sector; the privatization of state-run companies; and the gradual undermining of the welfare state, lowering government expenditures on social security. Neffa, *Modos de regulación.*

91. Vanden and Prevost, *Politics of Latin America.*

92. Paige, *Agrarian Revolution*; Skocpol, "What Makes Peasants Revolutionary?"; Wickham-Crowley, *Guerrillas and Revolution*; Wolf, *Peasant Wars.*

93. Green and Branford, *Faces of Latin America*; Kay, "Latin America's Agrarian Reform."

94. Shiva, *Violence of the Green Revolution*; Patel, "Long Green Revolution," 5.

95. Gillespie, *Soldiers of Perón*; May, "Theories and Experiences of Guerrilla Warfare."

96. Giberti et al., *Sociedad, economía y reforma agraria.*

97. Kay, "Latin America's Agrarian Reform."

98. Hora, *¿Cómo pensaron?*

99. In the 1970s, peasant mobilization was strong in the north of the country, as exemplified by the Ligas Agrarias in Formosa. Galafassi, "Conflicto por la tierra." Members of the Ligas Agrarias, as well as rural workers from the sugar industry in Tucumán, were often the targets of state violence during this period, and many of their members were disappeared. Giarracca and Teubal, "Del desarrollo agroindustrial," 353–54.

100. Bértola and Ocampo, *Economic Development of Latin America*, 199.

101. Argentina's social and economic crisis in the 1980s worsened with hyperinflation, which peaked in 1989 at 3079 percent and 2314 percent in 1990. Between 1981 and 1990, GDP per capita fell, on average, by 2.1 percent yearly, and foreign debt rose to 70 percent of GDP. Poverty, which was at 16 percent early in the decade, increased yearly to peak in 1989 at 47.4 percent of the total population. Novaro, *Historia de la Argentina*, 225–26.

102. Menem was elected in 1989 on a classic Peronista platform, promising a revolution in the manufacturing sector and wage increases (thus, his campaign slogan, "Revolución productiva y salariazo"). He did not deliver. Fewer than two years after taking power, he turned Argentina into the poster child of neoliberalism. Stokes, *Mandates and Democracy.*

103. Carranza, "Poster Child"; Barsky and Gelman, *Historia del agro argentino: Desde la conquista hasta fines del siglo XX*; Teubal, "Genetically Engineered Soybeans."

104. Harvey, *Brief History of Neoliberalism.*

105. Green, *Silent Revolution.*

106. Gudynas, "Debates on Development."

107. McMichael, *Development and Social Change.*

108. Otero, "Neoliberal Food Regime."

109. Horacio Verbitsky, "Verano del '96," *Página/12*, April 26, 2009.

110. See Tokar, *Redesigning Life?*.

111. Solá signed Resolution 167 even though he did not have the legal right to do so at the time. This permission would come three days later. Verbitsky, "Verano del '96."

112. SENASA's parallel institution in the United States would be the FDA, but in the United States, the Office of Pesticide Programs under the EPA is in charge of pesticide regulation. These institutions' mandate is to design regulations for agrochemical use that would keep the ambient concentration of each pesticide below a level of public-health concern. In order to determine these safety levels, these institutions run a variety of risk assessments. Then those regulations are specified on the product label, which also includes safety handling and use guidelines and instructions to be followed by the applicator. The label language constitutes the federal law for each product. As another strategy to mitigate risk, these institutions may also establish buffer zones around sensitive areas. Harrison, *Pesticide Drift*.

113. See the Argentine label for Roundup on Monsanto's website, accessed December 7, 2017, http://www.monsantoglobal.com/global/ar/productos/documents/roundup-ultramax.pdf.

114. Arancibia, "Challenging the Bioeconomy"; Aranda, *Tierra arrasada*.

115. The studies run by the research teams of Dr. Séralini in France and Dr. Carrasco in Argentina are among the most widely cited by critics as scientific evidence that links illness and exposure. Antoniou et al., *Roundup and Birth Defects*; Antoniou, Robinson, and Fagan, GMO *Myths and Truths*; Gillam, *Whitewash*.

116. Sández, *Argentina fumigada*.

117. Chudnovsky, "Argentina"; Newell, "Bio-Hegemony"; Pengue, "Transgenic Crops in Argentina"; Qaim and Traxler, "Roundup Ready Soybeans"; Teubal, "Expansión del modelo sojero."

118. Kloppenburg, *First the Seed*; Patel *Stuffed and Starved*; Shiva, *Stolen Harvest*.

119. Delvenne, Vasen, and Vara, "'Soy-ization' of Argentina." On contract requirements, see Pierri and Abramovsky, "Legislaciones de patentes."

120. Glyphosate-tolerant soybeans were first released commercially in Argentina under license by Nidera, not by the owner Monsanto. Nidera had access to Monsanto's RR gene through the acquisition of Asgrow Argentina. Nidera could not apply for patent rights for RR soy because it did not own the rights to the RR gene. When Monsanto sought to revalidate the patent in 2001, the petition was rejected on the grounds that the RR-tolerant plants were not a new variety and they were already widespread on Argentine soil. Delvenne, Vasen, and Vara, "'Soy-ization' of Argentina."

121. The use of saved seeds combined with illegal seed trading accounts for 65 to 80 percent of the total herbicide-tolerant soybean market. Feeney and Berardi, "Seed Market Segmentation."

122. Trigo and Cap, "Impact of the Introduction of Transgenic Crops."

123. Kelly Hearn, "Is Monsanto Playing Fast and Loose with Roundup Ready Soybeans in Argentina?" GRIST, September 22, 2006, https://grist.org/article/hearn1/.

124. Pengue, "Transgenic Crops in Argentina."

125. Bisang, "Apertura económica," 437.

126. Novaro, *Historia de la Argentina*.

127. See Carranza, "Poster Child."

128. Grugel and Riggirozzi, "Post-Neoliberalism in Latin America."

129. Wilpert, *Changing Venezuela*.

130. Bither-Terry, "Zero Hunger."

131. Lustig and Pessino, "Social Spending." The introduction of the noncontributory pension program in 2004–5, which extended retirement benefits to those who had completed fewer than thirty years of social contributions, had a significant impact on the reduction of poverty and income inequality. However, this "golden picture of Argentine redistribution policies," Lustig and Pessino argue, "becomes significantly tarnished when one takes note of two things" (321). First, the payment for noncontributory pensions is partially funded by tax-paying retirees, generating unfair losses for lower- and middle-class retirees. And, second, social spending has been financed by distortionary taxes and unorthodox revenue-raising mechanisms. Thus, the Kirchners' program for social spending might not be fiscally sustainable.

132. Lustig et al., "Deconstructing the Decline." The incidence of total poverty rate is defined as the percentage of the population earning daily incomes of USD $4 PPP or less. Extreme poverty in Latin America (defined as earnings below USD $2.50 PPP) also dropped, from 24.9 to 16.3 percent in the same time period. A significant percentage of poverty reduction is due to a decline in income inequality (43 percent on average and up to 88 percent in countries like El Salvador and Mexico). Across the region, the Gini coefficient for household income (the index measurement for inequality) dropped from 0.548 in the late 1990s to 0.488 in the late 2000s. While income inequality in Latin America continues to be among the highest in the world, the reduction in inequality during this decade is impressive in a context of rising income inequality in other regions of the world.

133. Lustig and Pessino, "Social Spending," 311. Poverty rates measure disposable income below the USD $4 PPP/day threshold. Disposable income equals net market income (wages and salaries) plus government cash transfers. Social spending—which increased by 13.5 percent between 2003 and 2009 to reach 40.6 percent of GDP— includes main cash transfers, noncontributory pensions, and public spending on education and primary health care. See Lustig and Pessino for details on how concepts are constructed and measured.

134. Acosta, "Extractivism and Neoextractism"; Arsel, Hogenboom, and Pellegrini, "Extractive Imperative in Latin America"; Farthing and Fabricant, "Open Veins Revisited."

135. Gudynas, "Diez tesis urgentes."

136. Lewis, *Ecuador's Environmental Revolutions*.

137. Secretaria de Agricultura, Pesca y Alimentos (SAGPYA), *Plan estratégico 2005–2015*, 5, 13.

138. "Plan estratégico agroalimentario y agroindustrial participativo y federal, 2010–2016," accessed December 20, 2013, www.minagri.gob.ar/site/areas/PEA2/index.php.

139. Bello, *Food Wars*.

140. Barsky and Dávila, *Rebelión del campo*; Hora, "Crisis del campo."

141. See, e.g., "No End in Sight for Argentine Farmers' Strike," *CNN*, March 27, 2008; "Argentine Farmers Vow to Press Strike over Tax," *New York Times*, March 27, 2008; "Argentine Farm Tax Crisis Worsens," *BBC News*, March 27, 2008.

142. "Crisis política tras el sorpresivo voto del vicepresidente Cobos contra las retenciones móviles kirchneristas," *Clarín*, July 16, 2008.

143. Mangonnet and Murillo, "El *boom* sojero"; Svampa, "End of Kirchnerism."

144. "El discurso presidencial: 'Son piquetes de la abundancia,'" *Clarín*, March 26, 2008.

145. "Discurso de Cristina Fernández el 31 de marzo de 2008," transcript of speech, https://es.wikisource.org/wiki/Discurso_de_Cristina_Fern%C3%A1ndez_el_31_de_marzo_de_2008.

146. "Al gran yuyo argentino, ¡salud . . . !" *Clarín*, April 5, 2008.

147. Vommaro and Gené, "Argentina."

2. Revolution in the Pampas

1. Gras, "Changing Patterns in Family Farming"; Lódola, *Contratistas*.

2. Early modernization theorists like Lewis Mumford (*Technics and Civilization*) and even Karl Marx (*Manifesto of the Communist Party*) had an optimistic belief in the potential of the machine to free people from hard labor, creating time for learning and leisure to fulfill our human potential. Steven Pinker (*Enlightenment Now*) and Thomas Friedman (*Hot, Flat, and Crowded*) echo this liberating potential of the machine.

3. Schnaiberg, *Environment*; Schnaiberg and Gould, *Environment and Society*.

4. Weber, *Protestant Ethic*.

5. Wedeen, *Ambiguities of Domination*, xvii.

6. I developed this argument first in Leguizamón, "Disappearing Nature?."

7. Foster, "Marx's Theory of Metabolic Rift"; Foster, Clark, and York, *Ecological Rift*; Schnaiberg and Gould, *Environment and Society*.

8. Grosso and Albaladejo, "Ingenieros agrónomos."

9. Shiva, *Violence of the Green Revolution*.

10. Interview with an agronomist, a main advisor on agrochemical use and legislation for the province of Córdoba (Córdoba city, August 2011).

11. Gras and Hernández, *Agro como negocio*.

12. Gras and Hernández, "Hegemony." See also Gras and Hernández, "Agribusiness and Large-Scale Farming."

13. David E. Bell and Cintra Scott, "Los Grobo: Farming's Future?" *Harvard Business School Case*, no. 511–088, December 2010.

14. Alejandro Bercovich, "'Yo soy un sin tierra': Entrevista a Gustavo Grobocopatel," *Página/12*, April 25, 2004.

15. Hernández, "Ruralidad globalizada."

16. The five largest agribusinesses operating in Argentina—MSU, Los Grobo, El Tejar, Cresud, and Adecoagro—control, via landownership or leasing, close to 3 million hectares of farmland in Argentina and neighboring Uruguay, Bolivia, Paraguay, and

Brazil. In 2011, Los Grobo harvested 320,000 hectares. Leguizamón, "Disappearing Nature?," 9–10.

17. Gras, "Changing Patterns in Family Farming."

18. Cáceres, "Accumulation by Dispossession"; Murmis and Murmis, "Land Concentration."

19. Borras et al., "Land Grabbing"; Oliveira and Hecht, "Sacred Groves."

20. Hernández, "Ruralidad globalizada," 53–54.

21. Clapp, "Financialization, Distance and Global Food Politics"; Isakson, "Food and Finance."

22. Fairbairn, "'Like Gold with Yield,'" 16.

23. Expoagro, accessed May 13, 2013, http://expoagro.com.ar.

24. Grosso and Albaladejo, "Ingenieros agrónomos."

25. Newell, "Bio-Hegemony."

26. "Norberto Yauhar en lanzamiento de nueva tecnología en soja Intacta RR2 de Monsanto—Discursos Ministro Norberto Yauhar," Ministry of Agriculture website, accessed April 28, 2013, http://www.minagri.gob.ar/site/institucional/prensa/index.php?edit_accion=noticia&id_info=120822171448.

27. See Monsanto's website for Argentina, accessed July 10, 2019, https://www.monsantoglobal.com/global/ar/quienes-somos/Pages/default.aspx.

28. "Monsanto ya se aseguró el cobro de las regalías por su nueva súper soja," *Clarín*, August 22, 2012; "La soja del futuro ya está en el país," *La Nación*, March 30, 2013.

29. Herman and Chomsky, *Manufacturing Consent*; McChesney, *Rich Media*; Stauber and Rampton, *Toxic Sludge Is Good for You!*

30. "Media Ownership and Concentration in Argentina," in *Who Owns the World's Media? Media Concentration and Ownership around the World*, ed. Eli M. Noam and the International Media Concentration Collaboration, Oxford Scholarship Online, January 2016, doi:10.1093/acprof:oso/9780199987238.003.0019.

31. "La soja impulsó un récord de las exportaciones," *Clarín*, May 31, 2004; "La soja no tiene freno: Llegó a los $900," *La Nación*, December 27, 2007; Fernando Bertello, "Mejor, imposible: La soja de 60 quintales," *La Nación*, April 27, 2013.

32. "Sólo la biotecnología salvará al mundo," *Clarín*, January 29, 2001; "Soja, el maná del siglo XXI," *Clarín*, December 30, 2006.

33. Mario Santucho, Diego Genoud, Alejandro Bercovich, and Javier Scheibengraf, "El tecnócrata mesiánico," *Revista Crisis*, March 3, 2013.

34. "El granero del mundo," *Clarín*, October 17, 2002.

35. "Vergüenza y polémica en Argentina por la muerte de cuatro niños desnutridos," *El País*, November 15, 2002.

36. Barruti, *Mal comidos*; Teubal, "Genetically Engineered Soybeans."

37. "La soja es un arma cargada de futuro," *Clarín*, February 2, 2002.

38. "A falta de carne barata, buena resulta ser la soja," *Clarín*, April 22, 2002.

39. "Confirman que la soja reduce el colesterol y protege el corazón," *La Nación*, November 19, 2007.

40. Herman and Chomsky, *Manufacturing Consent*; McChesney, *Rich Media*.

41. McAdam, *Political Process*.

42. The full headline was "La mancha venenosa" ("The Poisonous Stain"); *Página/12*, January 12, 2009. *Página/12* is known for its ironic, punning covers. Here it denotes agrochemicals as poisonous while playing on the name of a popular children's game similar to tag, in which the goal is to run away from the child who is the *mancha*, who has to spread (spray) out his "poison" to beat the other kids.

43. Darío Aranda, "El tóxico de los campos," *Página/12*, April 13, 2009.

44. Paganelli et al., "Glyphosate-Based Herbicides."

45. The episode, entitled "Soja" (Soy), aired at midnight on August 26, 2008. Around 1.2 million people watched it. Alfredo Zaiat, "La soja la ligó," *Página/12*, August 28, 2008.

46. Fabián Tomasi would later become an outspoken advocate against agrochemical spraying. In the show, he explained how he handled agrochemicals without protective equipment and showed the harmful impact of glyphosate on his own body. He suffered from severe toxic polyneuropathy. His image, his torso often bare, appeared in multiple national and international media outlets. See, e.g., "Argentines Link Health Problems to Farming Chemicals," *USA Today*, October 20, 2013; the photographs by Jordi Ruiz Cirera in "The United Soya Republic," accessed June 11, 2019, https://phmuseum.com /jordi/story/the-united-soya-republic-74222faeba; and Pablo Piovano, "The Human Cost," accessed June 11, 2019, http://www.pablopiovano.com/human-cost/the-human -cost.html. Tomasi died on September 7, 2018, at the age of fifty-three. "Murió Fabián Tomasi, símbolo de la lucha contra el glifosato," YouTube C5N, accessed June 11, 2019, https://youtu.be/SeJq2Q5akUU.

47. Arancibia, "Challenging the Bioeconomy."

48. "Para el SENASA, el herbicida cumple con todas las normativas," *La Nación*, April 25, 2009.

49. "Los cables utilizados," *Página/12*, March 9, 2011.

50. See also Kloppenburg, *First the Seed*.

51. In 2012, Cristina Kirchner and Grupo Clarín were embroiled in a bitter legal and discursive battle; see Simon Romero and Emily Schmall, "Battle between Argentine Media Empire and President Heats Up over a Law," *New York Times*, November 30, 2012. The "battle" was over a law aimed at dismantling corporate media concentration (popularly called the Ley de Medios). President Mauricio Macri overturned the law by executive decree in 2016 (Vommaro and Gené, "Argentina"). Despite this legal battle, corporations and the state continued to be allies in sustaining a positive discourse about the soy model as a development strategy.

52. See Stølen, *Decencia de la desigualdad*.

53. In 1970, the rural population in Argentina was 5.1 million people, or 21.3 percent of the total population (compared to 43.3 percent in Latin America). By 1980, the rural population had declined to 17.1 percent (4.81 million) and, by 1995, to 11.9 percent of the total population (4.17 million people). By 2015, the rural population was only 3.55 million people, or 8.2 percent of the total population. CEPAL, "CEPALSTAT—Statistics and Indicators, Demographic and Social" database, accessed January 21, 2019, http://estadisticas.cepal.org/cepalstat/WEB_CEPALSTAT /estadisticasIndicadores.asp?idioma=i.

54. According to the rural national censuses of 1998, 2002, and 2008, there was a loss of 78,900 farms between 1988 and 2008, a plunge of 41.7 percent. Between 2002 and 2008, in the Pampas region there has been a reduction of 24,405 farms: an 18 percent decrease in farm numbers. Data are from the CNA 1998, 2002, and 2008. Data for 2008 are preliminary, as most of its data were not yet released at the time of this writing. The "Pampas region" includes the provinces of Buenos Aires, Entre Ríos, Santa Fe, Córdoba, and La Pampa. "North" includes Chaco, Santiago del Estero, and Salta. "Censo Nacional Agropecuario 2008: Resultados provisorios," accessed January 12, 2018, https://www.indec.gob.ar/ftp/cuadros/publicaciones/cna08_10_09.pdf.

55. Barruti, *Mal comidos*.

56. Ministerio de Agricultura, Ganadería y Pesca, "Mercado de granos: Informe diario," June 3, 2011, https://www.agroindustria.gob.ar/new/0-0/programas/dma/informe_diario/2011/infogra_2011-06-03.pdf. These are pretax prices at port (FOB, "free of board"). Producers must pay taxes, most significantly export taxes, which for soybeans rose to 35 percent, on top of their expenses (including transportation). Producers do not get nearly as much as the FOB prices, which is why they were so antagonistic to the Kirchner administrations and their taxation policy.

57. Theft and vandalism are not uncommon. In 2014, several producers reported their silobolsas being ripped, the repercussions of the bitter social division following the conflicto del campo. Fernando Bertello, "Silobolsas: La revolución del agro que obsesiona al gobierno," *La Nación*, June 24, 2015.

58. Paris covers 105 square kilometers (12,000 hectares is equal to 120 square kilometers). "Paris," *Encyclopedia Britannica*, accessed June 20, 2019, https://www.britannica.com/place/Paris.

59. Gustavo Grobocopatel, "El modelo del poroto," *Página/12*, April 11, 2010.

60. Gras, "Changing Patterns in Family Farming."

61. Grosso et al., "Impactos de los 'pools de siembra'"; Murmis and Murmis, "Land Concentration."

62. Academia Argentina de las Letras, *Diccionario*.

63. Catacora-Vargas et al., "Soybean Production in the Southern Cone."

64. In 1996, farmers applied 821,000 kilograms of glyphosate over 6.67 million hectares of GM soy, compared to 88.03 million kilograms over 19.78 million hectares in 2014. Benbrook, "Trends in Glyphosate Herbicide Use," appendix.

65. Paganelli et al., "Glyphosate-Based Herbicides"; Séralini et al., "Republished Study."

66. REDUAS, *Informe del primer encuentro*; Ruderman et al., "Análisis de la salud colectiva."

67. International Agency for Research on Cancer, *Evaluation of Five Organophosphate Insecticides and Herbicides*.

68. Harrison, *Pesticide Drift*.

69. Auyero and Swistun, *Flammable*.

70. Bell, *Fighting King Coal*; Beamish, *Silent Spill*; Crenson, *Un-Politics of Air Pollution*; Gaventa, *Power and Powerlessness*; Gould, "Pollution and Perception"; Gould, "Sweet Smell of Money."

71. On the environmental and health risks of slum dwelling, see Auyero and Swistun, *Flammable.*

72. Walsh, Warland, and Smith, "Backyards."

3. The Elephant in the Field

1. Lukes, *Power.*

2. Auyero and Swistun, *Flammable*; Norgaard, *Living in Denial.*

3. Zerubavel, *Elephant in the Room*, 2.

4. Lukes, *Power.*

5. Zerubavel, *Elephant in the Room.*

6. See Goffman, *Presentation of Self in Everyday Life.*

7. REDUAS, *Informe del primer encuentro.*

8. Benford and Snow, "Framing Processes."

9. Mills, *Sociological Imagination*; Norgaard, *Living in Denial.*

10. Zerubavel, *Elephant in the Room*, 41.

11. Carassai, *Argentine Silent Majority.*

12. Human-rights violations were prosecuted following 1983 with the return to democracy (as seen with the Trial of the Juntas [Juicio a las Juntas] and *Nunca Más*, a report created by the National Commission on the Disappearance of Persons) and during the Kirchner administrations (see Novaro, *Historia de la Argentina*).

13. McAdam, *Political Process*; Goodwin, Jasper, and Polletta, "Emotional Dimensions of Social Movements"; Jasper, "Emotions and Social Movements."

14. Risman, "Gender as a Social Structure."

15. Bell, *Our Roots Run Deep*; Brown and Ferguson, "'Making a Big Stink'"; Krauss, "Women and Toxic Waste Protests."

16. See Kimmel, *Gendered Society.*

17. I first developed this argument in Leguizamón, "Gendered Dimensions."

18. Connell and Messerschmidt, "Hegemonic Masculinity."

19. Kimmel, *Gendered Society.*

20. Bell, *Our Roots Run Deep*; Brown and Ferguson, "'Making a Big Stink'"; Krauss, "Women and Toxic Waste Protests."

21. Like one Mother of Ituzaingó said, "No one could challenge us with, 'Who authorized you [to protest]?!' The fact of being a mother already authorized you to speak up. No one could question you, if my son is sick, if I want to denounce [what happened to] him, [or] take him wherever I want." Leguizamón, "Gendered Dimensions," 209.

22. Torrado, "Madres en contra de la soja." On the Madres de Plaza de Mayo, see Navarro, "Personal Is Political."

23. Mason-Deese, "Unemployed Workers' Movements"; S. Motta and Seppälä, "Feminized Resistances."

24. Diana Taylor, *Disappearing Acts.*

25. Bell, *Fighting King Coal.*

26. Connell and Messerschmidt, "Hegemonic Masculinity"; Schippers, "Recovering the Feminine Other."

27. Because I do not have data on their incomes, I determined their class status based on their occupation. Occupational structure is a proxy for (income-based) class structure. In Argentina, the social groups considered to be "middle class" are business managers, university professionals and technicians, small business owners, and public employees. Sautu, "Formación."

28. Adamovsky, *Historia*.

29. Sautu, "Formación."

30. Gould, Pellow, and Schnaiberg, *Treadmill of Production*.

31. On middle-class families and education, see Sautu, "Formación."

32. As in Auyero and Swistun, *Flammable*; and in Norgaard, *Living in Denial*.

33. Stølen, *Decencia de la desigualdad*; Risman, "Gender as a Social Structure."

34. Ortner, "Gender Hegemonies," 38; Scott, *Weapons of the Weak*.

4. Against the Grain

1. Bullard, *Dumping in Dixie*; Cole and Foster, *From the Ground Up*; Mohai, Pellow, and Roberts, "Environmental Justice."

2. See, respectively, Rauchecker, "¿Sustentabilidad de qué?," 71; Cáceres, "Accumulation by Dispossession," 16; and Lapegna, *Soybeans and Power*.

3. "Provincia: Economía," Gobierno de la Provincia de Córdoba, accessed October 23, 2017, http://www.cba.gov.ar/provincia/economia/.

4. REDUAS, "Plantas de bioetanol." PCBs (Polychlorinated Biphenyls) are highly toxic chemicals, banned in the United States since 1979. EPA website, accessed January 13, 2019, https://www.epa.gov/pcbs/learn-about-polychlorinated-biphenyls-pcbs/.

5. Carrizo and Berger, *Estado incivil*; Torrado, "Madres en contra de la soja."

6. Torrado, "Madres en contra de la soja," 177.

7. For details of the trial, see Juicio a la Fumigación, "La Causa," accessed June 1, 2018, http://www.juicioalafumigacion.com.ar/la-causa/.

8. See Berger, "Afectados ambientales."

9. "Argentina: The Bad Seeds," *Al Jazeera English*, March 13, 2013, https://youtu.be/JxATngnqgv8.

10. The original group of thirteen has divided as Grupo de Madres de Barrio Ituzaingó and as Madres de Ituzaingó Anexo Línea Fundadora, led by Sofía Gatica.

11. Berger and Ortega, "Poblaciones expuestas a agrotóxicos," 133.

12. Brown, "Popular Epidemiology"; Brown and Mikkelsen, *No Safe Place*.

13. Brown, Morello-Frosch, and Zavestoski, *Contested Illnesses*, 3–15.

14. Grupo de Reflexión Rural, *Pueblos fumigados*.

15. Río Carlo is a pseudonym, as are the names of the activists I mention in this chapter, except for the Mothers of Ituzaingó, who are public figures.

16. Rauchecker, "Estructura territorial," 182–83.

17. CONICET, *Evaluación de la información científica*.

18. Berger, "Afectados ambientales"; Skill and Grinberg, "Controversias socio-técnicas."

19. Cable, Shriver, and Mix, "Risk Society."

20. Arancibia, "Regulatory Science and Social Movements."

21. "Sofia Gatica: 2012 Goldman Prize Recipient South and Central America," Goldman Environmental Prize website, accessed June 13, 2013, https://www.goldmanprize.org/recipient/sofia-gatica/.

22. "Monsanto invertirá $1.500 millones," *La Voz del Interior*, June 16, 2012.

23. Ruderman et al., "Análisis de la salud."

24. Goodwin and Jasper, *Social Movements Reader*, 12.

25. Marina Sitrin, "If We Can Stop Monsanto, We Can Change the World," *TeleSur* TV, March 1, 2015.

26. Steven Lukes, "Questions about Power: Lessons from the Louisiana Hurricane," Understanding Katrina website, June 11, 2006, http://understandingkatrina.ssrc.org/Lukes/.

27. For a detailed account of the AMLV, see Agosto, *Malvinas*.

28. Walter and Urkidi, "Community Consultations."

29. Interview with Cecilia Carrizo and Mauricio Berger, researchers at the Universidad Nacional de Córdoba, August 2015.

30. For a similar situation, see Bell, *Fighting King Coal*.

31. "Conflictos socioambientales: Monsanto en Malvinas, una insignia," *La Voz del Interior*, April 23, 2017.

32. McCarthy and Zald, "Resource Mobilization and Social Movements"; Brown, "Popular Epidemiology"; Brown, *Toxic Exposures*; Brown and Mikkelsen, *No Safe Place*.

33. Bell, *Fighting King Coal*; Bell, *Our Roots Run Deep*; Brown and Ferguson, "'Making a Big Stink'"; Krauss, "Women and Toxic Waste Protests"; Levine, *Love Canal*; Toledo, Garrido, and Barrera-Bassols, "Struggle for Life."

34. Aranda, *Tierra arrasada*.

35. Lapegna, *Soybeans and Power*, 89–92.

36. Gasparri, Grau, and Manghi, "Carbon Pools."

37. FAO, *State of the World's Forests*.

38. Trigo, "Fifteen Years of Genetically Modified Crops."

39. Gasparri, Grau, and Manghi, "Carbon Pools"; Paolasso, Krapovickas, and Gasparri, "Deforestación"; Pengue, "Transgenic Crops in Argentina."

40. Unidad de Manejo del Sistema de Evaluación Forestal (USDEF), *Informe sobre deforestación en Argentina*, 4.

41. USDEF, *Pérdida de bosque nativo*, 10. The 2008 report maps the process of deforestation in the northern provinces; see http://www.ambiente.gov.ar/archivos/web/UMSEF/File/Mapas/deforestacion07–08_ley26331_130x90.jpg.

42. FAO, *State of the World's Forests*; De Sy et al., "Land Use Patterns."

43. Blanco et al., "Drivers, Trends, and Mitigation."

44. Quoted in Leguizamón, "Environmental Injustice in Argentina," 686.

45. Barbetta, "Movimiento campesino."

46. Movimiento Campesino de Santiago del Estero—Via Campesina, *Recorriendo caminos polvorientos*.

47. Gordillo and Hirsch, "Indigenous Struggles"; Teubal, "Agrarian Reform."

48. Barbetta, Domínguez, and Sabatino, "Ausencia campesina."

49. Gordillo and Hirsch, "Indigenous Struggles"; Barbetta, Domínguez, and Sabatino, "Ausencia campesina."

50. Collado, "Social Conflict in Argentina."

51. "According to the Argentine Civil Code (Articles 4015 and 4016), any person can claim landownership after 20 years of uninterrupted occupation and effective use of the land" (Cáceres, "Accumulation by Dispossession," 14).

52. Interview with real estate agent, Santiago del Estero, August 2011.

53. Akram-Lodhi, "Land, Markets, and Neoliberal Enclosure"; Cáceres, "Accumulation by Dispossession."

54. Aranda, *Tierra arrasada*; Lapegna, *Soybeans and Power*.

55. Lapegna, "Expansion of Transgenic Soybeans."

56. Red Agroforestal Chaco Argentina (REDAF), *Conflictos sobre la tenencia*, 42–43.

57. Collado, "Social Conflict in Argentina," 12.

58. Barbetta, Domínguez, and Sabatino, "Ausencia campesina."

59. As in Bell, *Fighting King Coal*.

60. See Schurman and Munro, *Fighting for the Future of Food*; Schurman and Munro, "Targeting Capital."

61. See Auyero and Swistun, *Flammable*; Bell, *Fighting King Coal*; Gaventa, *Power and Powerlessness*; Gould, "Pollution and Perception"; and Gould, "Sweet Smell of Money."

62. See Wilson Becerril, "How Gold Mining Companies Stifle Opposition in Peru."

63. Howard, "AFHVS 2016 Presidential Address."

64. Lapegna, *Soybeans and Power*.

65. Konefal, "Forces of Social Change," 258–59.

66. Habermas, *Legitimation Crisis*.

67. Meyer, *Politics of Protest*, 2.

68. Konefal, "Forces of Social Change."

69. Habermas, *Legitimation Crisis*; Konefal, "Forces of Social Change."

70. Schnaiberg, *Environment*.

71. Shriver, Cable, and Kennedy, "Mining for Conflict."

72. Brown, *Toxic Exposures*.

73. Brown, *Toxic Exposures*; Brown and Mikkelsen, *No Safe Place*; Levine, *Love Canal*.

74. Auyero and Swistun, *Flammable*, 17; S. Motta, "'We Are the Ones We Have Been Waiting For.'"

75. Darío Aranda, "Hecha la ley, hecho el desalojo," *Página/12*, August 22, 2011.

76. Lapegna, *Soybeans and Power*, 29.

77. Infobae, "El gobierno oficializó la prórroga de la ley que suspende el desalojo de tierras indígenas," November 23, 2017, https://www.infobae.com/politica/2017/11/23/el-gobierno-oficializo-la-prorroga-de-la-ley-que-suspende-el-desalojo-de-tierras-indigenas/; Mariel Bleger, "En el nombre de la Lay (26.160)," *Al Márgen*, July 12, 2018, https://almargen.org.ar/2018/07/12/en-el-nombre-de-la-ley-26-160/.

78. Consuelo Cabral, "Quedó firme el fallo de Ituzaingó: 'Fumigar es delito y los agrotóxicos son peligrosos,'" La Nueva Mañana, September 13, 2017.

79. Lea Ross, "15 años de las Madres de barrio Ituzaingó Anexo: Lucha y espera," ANRed, March 23, 2017, https://www.anred.org/?p=63108.

80. Brown, Toxic Exposures; Cable, Shriver, and Mix, "Risk Society"; Kinchy, Seeds, Science, and Struggle.

81. Norgaard, Living in Denial; Oreskes and Conway, Merchants of Doubt.

82. "Argentina: The Bad Seeds."

83. Kinchy, Seeds, Science, and Struggle.

84. Carrizo and Berger, Estado incivil; Leguizamón, "Gendered Dimensions."

85. Gordillo, "Savage Outside of White Argentina."

86. Lapegna, Soybeans and Power, 92–94.

87. "Argentina: The Bad Seeds." The quotation is slightly edited for English grammar: Grobocopatel spoke in English, not in his native Spanish.

88. "Ministro and Modelo," Lavaca, December 11, 2015, http://www.lavaca.org/mu95/ministro-modelo/. Lino Barañao was appointed minister of science and technology in 2007 by Cristina Kirchner. He was one of the few public officials to transition into Mauricio Macri's administration. His term ended with Macri's in December 2019. "Barañao y Robledo: dos ministros de ciencia se van," La Voz del Interior, December 5, 2019, https://www.lavoz.com.ar/ciudadanos/baranao-y-robledo-dos-ministros-de-ciencia-se-van/.

89. "La ciencia argentina llama a una batalla contra los fundamentalismos," La Gaceta, April 11, 2018.

90. Agosto, Malvinas, 36–37, my translation.

91. "New Data Reveals 197 Land and Environmental Defenders Murdered in 2017," Global Witness website, February 2, 2018, https://www.globalwitness.org/en-gb/blog/new-data-reveals-197-land-and-environmental-defenders-murdered-2017/.

Conclusion

1. For reviews of Fever Dream, see Chris Power, "Fever Dream by Samanta Schweblin Review—Terrifying but Brilliant," Guardian, March 24, 2017; "Samanta Schweblin's Blistering Debut Novel," Economist, April 22, 2017; Jia Tolentino, "The Sick Thrill of 'Fever Dream,'" New Yorker, January 4, 2017.

2. Schweblin, Fever Dream: on the city and the countryside, 93; on Abigail, 50–51; "the worms," 1–2.

3. In a similar exchange of denial, Carla tells Amanda how rural inhabitants often consult "the woman in the green house" when they need a doctor:

> She can tell if someone is sick, and where in the body the negative energy is coming from. She cures headaches, nausea, skin ulcers, and cases of vomiting blood. If your reach her in time, she can stop miscarriages.
>
> Are there that many miscarriages?
>
> She says that everything is energy.
>
> My grandmother always said that. (Schweblin, Fever Dream, 21)

Carla, like the women of Santa María, brought up a list of health risks of agrochemical exposure, yet, when directly questioned about them, Carla diffused the problem with denial ("She says that everything is energy"). Amanda, as an urban resident unaware of the problem of pesticide drift, took her response for granted, continuing their conversation as if nothing had happened.

4. Schweblin, *Fever Dream*: "the exact moment," 2; "the breeze," 117; "men unloading the barrels" but "not dew," 105.

5. Arancibia, "Challenging the Bioeconomy"; Skill and Grinberg, "Controversias socio-técnicas."

6. Rauchecker, "Estructura territorial," 182.

7. Amanda says to herself as she learns from Carla of David's poisoning: "I'm wondering whether what happened to Carla could happen to me. I always imagine the worst-case scenario. Right now, for instance, I'm calculating how long it would take me to jump out of the car and reach Nina if she suddenly ran and leapt into the pool. I call it the 'rescue distance': that's what I named the variable distance separating me from my daughter, and I spend half the day calculating it, though I always risk more than I should" (Schweblin, *Fever Dream*, 18–19).

8. Schweblin, *Fever Dream*, 97.

9. Paige, *Agrarian Revolution*; Skocpol, "What Makes Peasants Revolutionary?"; Wolf, *Peasant Wars*.

10. WHO, "Global Hunger Continues to Rise, New UN Report Says," WHO Newsroom, September 11, 2018, https://www.who.int/news-room/detail/11-09-2018-global-hunger-continues-to-rise-new-un-report-says.

11. "Measles Outbreak in Pacific Northwest about Half of US Cases," *New York Times*, March 1, 2019; "Teen Tells Senate Why He Defied His Mom to Get Vaccinated," *New York Times*, March 5, 2019.

12. Donald G. McNeil, Jr., "Why Don't We Have Vaccines against Everything?," *New York Times*, November 19, 2018.

13. FIFRA Scientific Advisory Panel Meeting Minutes and Final Report No. 2017-01, "A Set of Scientific Issues Being Considered by the Environmental Protection Agency Regarding: EPA's Evaluation of the Carcinogenic Potential of Glyphosate December 13–16, 2016," pp. 5, 16, https://www.epa.gov/sites/production/files/2017-03/documents/december_13-16_2016_final_report_03162017.pdf.

14. Markowitz and Rosner, *Deceit and Denial*; Oreskes and Conway, *Merchants of Doubt*.

15. Harrison, *Pesticide Drift*; Szasz, *Shopping Our Way to Safety*.

16. Gillam, *Whitewash*; Peter Waldman, Lydia Mulvany, Tiffany Stecker, and Joel Rosenblatt, "Does the World's Top Weed Killer Cause Cancer? Trump's EPA Will Decide," *Bloomberg Businessweek*, July 13, 2017.

17. "Monsanto Ordered to Pay $289 Million in World's First Roundup Cancer Trial," *New York Times*, August 10, 2018.

18. Jason Daley, "Europe Applies Strict Regulations to CRISPR Crops," *Smithsonian*, July 27, 2018, https://smithsonianmag.com/smart-news/europe-applies-strict-regulations-gene-edited-crops-180969774; "CRISPR and Co Are GMOs, Says EU

Court," *European Biotechnology, Life Science and Industry Magazine*, July 25, 2018, https://european-biotechnology.com/up-to-date/latest-news/news/crispr-co-are-gmos -says-eu-court.html.

19. See Eduardo Ferreyra, "La batalla contra el glifosato no tiene fundamentos científicos ni legales," *La Nación*, June 30, 2018; "Sin el glifosato, la alternativa sería catastrófica," *Clarín Rural*, October 14, 2018; "Publican online más de 300 resúmenes de estudios sobre la seguridad del glifosato," *Clarín Rural*, November 12, 2018.

BIBLIOGRAPHY

Academia Argentina de las Letras. *Diccionario del habla de los argentinos*. Buenos Aires: Espasa, 2003.

Acosta, Alberto. "Extractivism and Neoextractism: Two Sides of the Same Curse." In *Beyond Development: Alternative Visions from Latin America*, edited by Miriam Lang and Dunia Mokrani, 61–86. Quito: Fundación Rosa Luxemburg; Amsterdam: Transnational Institute, 2013.

Adamovsky, Ezequiel. *Historia de la clase media argentina: Apogeo y decadencia de una ilusión, 1919–2003*. Buenos Aires: Planeta, 2009.

Agosto, Patricia. *Malvinas: Un pueblo en lucha contra Monsanto*. Buenos Aires: América Libre, 2014.

Akram-Lodhi, A. "Land, Markets, and Neoliberal Enclosure: An Agrarian Political Economy Perspective." *Third World Quarterly* 28, no. 8 (2007): 1437–56.

Alberdi, Juan Bautista. *Bases y puntos de partida para la organización política de la República Argentina*. 1852. Buenos Aires: Biblioteca del Congreso de la Nación, 2017. https://bcn.gob.ar/uploads/BasesAlberdi.pdf.

Alberto, Paulina, and Eduardo Elena. "Introduction: The Shades of the Nation." In *Rethinking Race in Modern Argentina*, 1–22. Cambridge: Cambridge University Press, 2016.

Alkon, Alison Hope. "Food Justice and the Challenge to Neoliberalism." *Gastronomica: The Journal of Critical Food Studies* 14, no. 2 (2014): 27–40.

Antoniou, Michael, Mohamed Habib, C. Vyvyan Howard, Richard C. Jennings, Carlo Leifert, Rubens Onofre Nodari, Claire Robinson, and John Fagan. *Roundup and Birth Defects: Is the Public Being Kept in the Dark?* London: Earth Open Source, 2011.

Antoniou, Michael, Claire Robinson, and John Fagan. *GMO Myths and Truths: An Evidence-Based Examination of the Claims Made for the Safety and Efficacy of Genetically Modified Crops*. London: Earth Open Source, 2012.

Arancibia, Florencia. "Challenging the Bioeconomy: The Dynamics of Collective Action in Argentina." *Technology in Society* 35, no. 2 (2013): 79–92.

Arancibia, Florencia. "Regulatory Science and Social Movements: The Trial against the Use of Pesticides in Argentina." *Theory in Action* 9, no. 4 (2016): 1–21.

Aranda, Darío. *Tierra arrasada: Petróleo, soja, pasteras y megaminería. Radiografía de la Argentina del siglo XXI*. Buenos Aires: Sudamericana, 2015.

Arsel, Murat, Barbara Hogenboom, and Lorenzo Pellegrini. "The Extractive Imperative in Latin America." *Extractive Industries and Society* 3, no. 4 (2016): 880–87.

Auyero, Javier, and Débora A. Swistun. *Flammable: Environmental Suffering in an Argentine Shantytown*. Oxford: Oxford University Press, 2009.

Avni, Haim. "La agricultura judía en la Argentina, ¿éxito o fracaso?" *Desarrollo Económico* 22, no. 88 (1983): 535–48.

Bachrach, Peter, and Morton S. Baratz. "Two Faces of Power." *American Political Science Review* 56, no. 4 (1962): 947–52.

Barbetta, Pablo. "El movimiento campesino de Santiago del Estero: Luchas y sentidos en torno a la problemática de la tierra." In *El campo argentino en la encrucijada*, edited by Norma Giarracca and Miguel Teubal, 423–48. Buenos Aires: Alianza Editorial, 2005.

Barbetta, Pablo, Diego Domínguez, and Pablo Sabatino. "La ausencia campesina en la Argentina como producción científica y enfoque de intervención." *Mundo Agrario* 13, no. 25 (2012). Accessed June 6, 2019. https://www.mundoagrario.unlp.edu.ar/article /view/2032.

Barruti, Soledad. *Mal comidos: Cómo la industria alimentaria argentina nos está matando*. Buenos Aires: Planeta, 2013.

Barsky, Osvaldo, and Mábel Dávila. *La rebelión del campo: Historia del conflicto agrario argentino*. Buenos Aires: Editorial Sudamericana, 2008.

Barsky, Osvaldo, and Jorge Gelman. *Historia del agro argentino: Desde la conquista hasta fines del siglo XX*. Buenos Aires: Grijalbo Mondadori, 2001.

Barsky, Osvaldo, and Jorge Gelman. *Historia del agro argentino: Desde la conquista hasta comienzos del siglo XXI*. 3rd ed. Buenos Aires: Sudamericana, 2009.

Beamish, Thomas. *Silent Spill: The Organization of an Industrial Crisis*. Cambridge, MA: MIT Press, 2002.

Bell, Shannon. *Fighting King Coal: The Challenges to Micromobilization in Central Appalachia*. Cambridge, MA: MIT Press, 2016.

Bell, Shannon. *Our Roots Run Deep as Ironweed: Appalachian Women and the Fight for Environmental Justice*. Urbana: University of Illinois Press, 2013.

Bello, Walden F. *The Food Wars*. London: Verso, 2009.

Benbrook, Charles M. "Trends in Glyphosate Herbicide Use in the United States and Globally." *Environmental Sciences Europe* 28, no. 1 (2016). doi:10.1186/ s12302-016-0070-0.

Benford, Robert, and David Snow. "Framing Processes and Social Movements: An Overview and Assessment." *Annual Review of Sociology* 26, no. 1 (2000): 611–39.

Benítez-Rojo, Antonio. "The Nineteenth-Century Spanish American Novel." In *The Cambridge History of Latin American Literature*, vol. 1, edited by R. González Echevarría and E. Pupo-Walker, 417–89. Cambridge: Cambridge University Press, 1996.

Berger, Mauricio. "Afectados ambientales: Hacia una conceptualización en el contexto de luchas por el reconocimiento." *Debates en Sociología* 42 (2016): 31–53.

Berger, Mauricio, and Francisco Ortega. "Poblaciones expuestas a agrotóxicos: Autoorganización ciudadana en la defensa de la vida y la salud, ciudad de Córdoba, Argentina." *Physis: Revista de Saúde Coletiva* 20, no. 1 (2010): 119–43.

Bértola, Luis, and José Antonio Ocampo. *The Economic Development of Latin America since Independence*. Oxford: Oxford University Press, 2012.

Binimelis, Rosa, Walter Pengue, and Iliana Monterroso. "'Transgenic Treadmill': Responses to the Emergence and Spread of Glyphosate-Resistant Johnsongrass in Argentina." *Geoforum* 40, no. 4 (2009): 623–33.

Binstock, Georgina, and Marcela Cerrutti. "La población y la estructura social." In *La sociedad argentina hoy: Radiografía de una nueva estructura*, edited by Gabriel Kessler, 37–59. Buenos Aires: Siglo Veintiuno, 2016.

Binstock, Georgina, and Marcela Cerrutti. *Los niños, niñas y adolescentes indígenas de Argentina: Diagnóstico socioeducativo basado en la ECPI*. Buenos Aires: UNICEF, 2010.

Bisang, Roberto. "Apertura económica, innovación y estructura productiva: La aplicación de biotecnología en la producción agrícola pampeana argentina." *Desarrollo Económico* 43, no. 171 (2003): 413–42.

Bither-Terry, Russell. "Zero Hunger: The Politics of Anti-Hunger Policy in Brazil." PhD diss., University of North Carolina, Chapel Hill, 2013. https://cdr.lib.unc.edu /indexablecontent/uuid:e08c8ad6-7f71-4d71-ab88-9d6297a67866.

Blanco, Gabriel, Reyer Gerlagh, Sangwon Suh, et al. "Drivers, Trends, and Mitigation." In *AR5 Climate Change 2014: Mitigation of Climate Change*. Report of the Intergovernmental Panel on Climate Change. https://www.ipcc.ch/site/assets/uploads/2018/02 /ipcc_wg3_ar5_chapter5.pdf.

Borras, Saturnino M., Jr., Jennifer C. Franco, Sergio Gómez, Cristóbal Kay, and Max Spoor. "Land Grabbing in Latin America and the Caribbean." *Journal of Peasant Studies* 39, nos. 3–4 (2012): 845–72.

Boyer, Christopher R. "Latin American Environmental History." In *Oxford Research Encyclopedia of Latin American History*. Oxford: Oxford University Press, 2016. Accessed December 27, 2018. doi:10.1093/acrefore/9780199366439.013.295.

Brailovsky, Antonio, and Dina Foguelman. *Memoria verde: Historia ecológica de la Argentina*. Buenos Aires: Debolsillo, 2009.

Brown, Phil. "Popular Epidemiology and Toxic Waste Contamination: Lay and Professional Ways of Knowing." *Journal of Health and Social Behavior* 33, no. 3 (1992): 267–81.

Brown, Phil. *Toxic Exposures: Contested Illnesses and the Environmental Health Movement*. New York: Columbia University Press, 2007.

Brown, Phil, and Faith I. T. Ferguson. "'Making a Big Stink': Women's Work, Women's Relationships, and Toxic Waste Activism." *Gender and Society* 9, no. 2 (1995): 145–72.

Brown, Phil, and Edwin J. Mikkelsen. *No Safe Place: Toxic Waste, Leukemia, and Community Action*. Berkeley: University of California Press, 1990.

Brown, Phil, Rachel Morello-Frosch, and Stephen Zavestoski, eds. *Contested Illnesses: Citizens, Science, and Health Social Movements*. Berkeley: University of California Press, 2012.

Bullard, Robert. *Dumping in Dixie: Race, Class, and Environmental Quality*. Berkeley: University of California Press, 1990.

Burns, E. Bradford. *The Poverty of Progress: Latin America in the Nineteenth Century*. Berkeley: University of California Press, 1980.

Buttel, Frederick H. "Ecological Modernization as Social Theory." *Geoforum* 31, no. 1 (2000): 57–65.

Cable, Sherry, Thomas E. Shriver, and Tamara L. Mix. "Risk Society and Contested Illness: The Case of Nuclear Weapons Workers." *American Sociological Review* 73, no. 3 (2008): 380–401.

Cáceres, Daniel M. "Accumulation by Dispossession and Socio-Environmental Conflicts Caused by the Expansion of Agribusiness in Argentina." *Journal of Agrarian Change* 15, no. 1 (2015): 116–47.

Carassai, Sebastián. *The Argentine Silent Majority: Middle Classes, Politics, Violence, and Memory in the Seventies.* Durham, NC: Duke University Press, 2014.

Cardoso, Fernando Henrique, and Enzo Faletto. *Dependency and Development in Latin America.* Berkeley: University of California Press, 1979.

Carranza, Mario E. "Poster Child or Victim of Imperialist Globalization? Explaining Argentina's December 2001 Political Crisis and Economic Collapse." *Latin American Perspectives* 32, no. 6 (2005): 65–89.

Carrizo, Cecilia, and Mauricio Berger. *Estado incivil y ciudadanos sin estado: Paradojas del ejercicio de derechos en cuestiones ambientales.* Unquillo, Argentina: Narvaja Editor, 2008.

Carson, Rachel. *Silent Spring.* Boston: Houghton Mifflin, 1962.

Catacora-Vargas, Georgina, Pablo Galeano, Sarah Zanon Agapito-Tenfen, Darío Aranda, Tomás Palau, and Rubens Onofre Nodari. "Soybean Production in the Southern Cone of the Americas: Update on Land and Pesticide Use." Cochabamba, Bolivia: GenØk of the Federal University of Santa Catarina; REDES-AT; BASE-IS, 2012. http://genok.no/wp-content/uploads/2013/03/Soybean-Production-in-the-Southern -Cone-of-the-Americas-Update-on-Land-and-Pesticide-Use.pdf.

Chazarreta, Adriana, and Germán Rosati. "Los cambios en la estructura social agraria argentina." In *La sociedad argentina hoy: Radiografía de una nueva estructura,* edited by Gabriel Kessler, 85–110. Buenos Aires: Siglo Veintiuno, 2016.

Chudnovsky, Daniel. "Argentina: Adopting RR Soy, Economic Liberalization, Global Markets, and Socio-Economic Consequences." In *Gene Revolution: GM Crops and Unequal Development,* edited by S. Fukuda-Parr, 85–103. London: Earthscan, 2006.

Clapp, Jennifer. "Financialization, Distance and Global Food Politics." *Journal of Peasant Studies* 41, no. 5 (2014): 797–814.

Clark, Meri. "The Emergence and Transformation of Positivism." In *A Companion to Latin American Philosophy,* edited by Susana Nuccetelli, Ofelia Schutte, and Otávio Bueno, 53–67. Oxford: Wiley-Blackwell, 2013.

Cole, Luke W., and Sheila R. Foster. *From the Ground Up: Environmental Racism and the Rise of the Environmental Justice Movement.* New York: New York University Press, 2001.

Collado, Patricia A. "Social Conflict in Argentina: Land, Water, Work." *Latin American Perspectives* 42, no. 2 (2015): 125–41.

CONICET. *Evaluación de la información científica vinculada al glifosato en su incidencia sobre la salud humana y el ambiente.* Report of the Comisión Nacional de Investigación sobre Agroquímicos. Buenos Aires: CONICET, July 2009. http://www .fundacion-campo.org/userfiles/prensa/glifosatoinfoconicet09.pdf.

Connell, R. W., and James Messerschmidt. "Hegemonic Masculinity: Rethinking the Concept." *Gender and Society* 19, no. 6 (2005): 829–59.

Coronil, Fernando. *The Magical State: Nature, Money, and Modernity in Venezuela.* Chicago: University of Chicago Press, 1997.

Crenson, Matthew A. *The Un-Politics of Air Pollution: A Study of Non-Decisionmaking in the Cities.* Baltimore, MD: Johns Hopkins University Press, 1971.

de Cristóforis, Nadia. *Inmigrantes y colonos en la provincia de Buenos Aires: Una mirada de largo plazo (siglos XIX–XXI).* Buenos Aires: Editorial de la Facultad de Filosofía y Letras Universidad de Buenos Aires, 2016.

de la Cadena, Marisol. "Indigenous Cosmopolitics in the Andes: Conceptual Reflections beyond 'Politics.'" *Cultural Anthropology* 25 (2010): 334–70.

De Sy, V., M. Herold, F. Achard, R. Beuchle, J. G. P. W. Clevers, E. Lindquist, and L. Verchot. "Land Use Patterns and Related Carbon Losses Following Deforestation in South America." *Environmental Research Letters* 10 (2015). doi:10.1088/1748-9326/10/12/124004.

Delvenne, Pierre, Federico Vasen, and Ana María Vara. "The 'Soy-ization' of Argentina: The Dynamics of the 'Globalized' Privatization Regime in a Peripheral Context." *Technology in Society* 35, no. 2 (2013): 153–62.

Djenderedjian, Julio. *Gringos en las Pampas: Inmigrantes y colonos en el campo argentino.* Buenos Aires: Editorial Sudamericana, 2008.

Domínguez, Diego I. "La lucha por la tierra en Argentina en los albores del siglo XXI: La recreación del campesinado y de los pueblos originarios." PhD diss., Universidad de Buenos Aires, 2009.

Dowd-Uribe, Brian. "GMOs and Poverty: Definitions, Methods, and the Silver Bullet Paradox." *Canadian Journal of Development Studies* 38, no. 1 (2017): 129–38.

Durkheim, Émile. *The Division of Labor in Society.* 1893. New York: Simon and Schuster, 1997.

Fairbairn, Madeleine. "'Like Gold with Yield': Evolving Intersections between Farmland and Finance." *Journal of Peasant Studies* 41, no. 5 (2014): 777–95.

Farthing, Linda, and Nicole Fabricant. "Open Veins Revisited: Charting the Social, Economic, and Political Contours of the New Extractivism in Latin America." *Latin American Perspectives* 45, no. 5 (2018): 4–17.

Feeney, Roberto, and Valeria Berardi. "Seed Market Segmentation: How Do Argentine Farmers Buy Their Expendable Inputs?" *International Food and Agribusiness Management Review* 16, no. 1 (2013): 17–40.

Ferro, Silvia. *Género y propiedad rural: República Argentina.* 2nd ed. Buenos Aires: MAGyP, 2013.

Fitting, Elizabeth. *The Struggle for Maize: Campesinos, Workers, and Transgenic Corn in the Mexican Countryside.* Durham, NC: Duke University Press, 2011.

Food and Agriculture Organization of the United Nations (FAO). *State of the World's Forests, 2016. Forests and Agriculture: Land-Use Challenges and Opportunities.* Rome: FAO, 2016. http://www.fao.org/3/a-i5588e.pdf.

Foster, John Bellamy. "Marx's Theory of Metabolic Rift: Classical Foundations for Environmental Sociology." *American Journal of Sociology* 105, no. 2 (1999): 366–405.

Foster, John Bellamy, Brett Clark, and Richard York. *The Ecological Rift: Capitalism's War on the Earth*. New York: New York University Press, 2011.

Friedman, Thomas L. *Hot, Flat, and Crowded: Why We Need a Green Revolution—And How It Can Renew America*. New York: Farrar, Straus and Giroux, 2008.

Friedmann, Harriet, and Philip McMichael. "The Rise and Decline of National Agricultures, 1870 to the Present." *Sociologia Ruralis* 29, no. 2 (1989): 93–117.

Galafassi, Guido. "Conflicto por la tierra y movimientos agrarios en el nordeste argentino en los años setenta: La unión de ligas campesinas formoseñas." *Perfiles Latinoamericanos* (FLACSO, Mexico) 26 (2006): 159–84.

Galeano, Eduardo. *Open Veins of Latin America: Five Centuries of the Pillage of a Continent*. New York: Monthly Review Press, 1974.

Gallo, Ezequiel. *La república en ciernes: Surgimiento de la vida política y social pampeana, 1850–1930*. Buenos Aires: Siglo Veintiuno, 2013.

Ganson, Barbara. *The Guaraní under Spanish Rule in the Río de la Plata*. Stanford, CA: Stanford University Press, 2003.

García Canclini, Néstor. *Culturas híbridas: Estrategias para entrar y salir de la modernidad*. Mexico City: Grijalbo, 1990.

Gasparri, N. Ignacio, H. Ricardo Grau, and Eduardo Manghi. "Carbon Pools and Emissions from Deforestation in Extra-Tropical Forests of Northern Argentina between 1900 and 2005." *Ecosystems* 11, no. 8 (2008): 1247–61.

Gaventa, John. *Power and Powerlessness: Quiescence and Rebellion in an Appalachian Valley*. Urbana: University of Illinois Press, 1982.

Giarracca, Norma, and Miguel Teubal, eds. *Actividades extractivas en expansión: ¿Reprimarización de la economía argentina?* Buenos Aires: Antropofagia, 2013.

Giarracca, Norma, and Miguel Teubal. "Del desarrollo agroindustrial a la expansión del 'agronegocio': El caso argentino." In *Norma Giarracca: Estudios rurales y movimientos sociales: Miradas desde el Sur. Antología esencial*, 349–80. Buenos Aires: CLACSO, 2017.

Giberti, Horacio C., Aldo E. Solari, Gino Germani, and Jorge A. Ochoa de Eguileor. *Sociedad, economía y reforma agraria*. Buenos Aires: Libera, 1965.

Gilbert, Natasha. "Case Studies: A Hard Look at GM Crops." *Nature News* 497, no. 7447 (2013): 24.

Gillam, Carey. *Whitewash: The Story of a Weed Killer, Cancer, and the Corruption of Science*. Washington, DC: Island Press, 2017.

Gillespie, Richard. *Soldiers of Perón: Argentina's Montoneros*. Oxford: Oxford University Press, 1982.

Givens, Jennifer, Brett Clark, and Andrew K. Jorgenson. "Strengthening the Ties between Environmental Sociology and Sociology of Development." In *The Sociology of Development Handbook*, edited by Greg Hooks, 69–94. Berkeley: University of California Press, 2016.

Glover, Dominic. "The Corporate Shaping of GM Crops as a Technology for the Poor." *Journal of Peasant Studies* 37, no. 1 (2010): 67–90.

Goffman, Erving. *The Presentation of Self in Everyday Life*. New York: Doubleday, 1959.

González Arzac, Rodolfo. *¡Adentro! Millonarios, chacareros y perdedores en la nueva Argentina rural*. Buenos Aires: Marea, 2009.

Goodwin, Jeff, and James M. Jasper, eds. *The Social Movements Reader: Cases and Concepts*. Malden, MA: Blackwell, 2003.

Goodwin, Jeff, James Jasper, and Francesca Polletta. "Emotional Dimensions of Social Movements." In *The Blackwell Companion to Social Movements*, edited by David Snow, Sarah Soule, and Hanspeter Kriesi, 413–32. Malden, MA: Blackwell, 2004.

Gordillo, Gastón. *Rubble: The Afterlife of Destruction*. Durham, NC: Duke University Press, 2014.

Gordillo, Gastón. "The Savage Outside of White Argentina." In *Rethinking Race in Modern Argentina*, edited by Paulina Alberto and Eduardo Elena, 241–67. Cambridge: Cambridge University Press, 2016.

Gordillo, Gastón, and Silvia Hirsch. "Indigenous Struggles and Contested Identities in Argentina: Histories of Invisibilization and Reemergence." *Journal of Latin American Anthropology* 8, no. 3 (2003): 4–30.

Gould, Kenneth. "Pollution and Perception: Social Visibility and Local Environmental Mobilization." *Qualitative Sociology* 16, no. 2 (1993): 157–78.

Gould, Kenneth. "The Sweet Smell of Money: Economic Dependency and Local Environmental Political Mobilization." *Society and Natural Resources* 4, no. 2 (1991): 133–50.

Gould, Kenneth, David Pellow, and Allan Schnaiberg. *The Treadmill of Production: Injustice and Unsustainability in the Global Economy*. Boulder, CO: Paradigm, 2008.

Gramsci, Antonio. *Selections from the Prison Notebooks of Antonio Gramsci*. New York: International, 1971.

Gras, Carla. "Changing Patterns in Family Farming: The Case of the Pampa Region, Argentina." *Journal of Agrarian Change* 9, no. 3 (2009): 345–64.

Gras, Carla, and Valeria Hernández. "Agribusiness and Large-Scale Farming: Capitalist Globalisation in Argentine Agriculture." *Canadian Journal of Development Studies* 35, no. 3 (2014): 339–57.

Gras, Carla, and Valeria Hernández. *El agro como negocio: Producción, sociedad y territorios en la globalización*. Buenos Aires: Editorial Biblos, 2013.

Gras, Carla, and Valeria Hernández, eds. *La Argentina rural: De la agricultura familiar a los agronegocios*. Buenos Aires: Editorial Biblos, 2009.

Gras, Carla, and Valeria Hernández. "Hegemony, Technological Innovation, and Corporate Identities: 50 Years of Agricultural Revolutions in Argentina." *Journal of Agrarian Change* 16, no. 4 (2016): 675–83.

Green, Duncan. *Silent Revolution: The Rise and Crisis of Market Economics in Latin America*. New York: New York University Press, 2003.

Green, Duncan, and Sue Branford. *Faces of Latin America*. 4th ed. New York: Monthly Review Press, 2012.

Grosso, Susana, and Christophe Albaladejo. "Los ingenieros agrónomos y la 'nueva agricultura': Des/reterritorialización de la profesión." In *La Argentina rural: De la agricultura familiar a los agronegocios*, edited by Carla Gras and Valeria Hernández, 117–34. Buenos Aires: Editorial Biblos, 2009.

Grosso, Susana, María Eva Bellini, Laura Qüesta, Martine Guibert, Silvia Lauxmann, and Fabiana Rotondi. "Impactos de los 'pools de siembra' en la estructura social agraria: Una aproximación a las transformaciones en los espacios centrales de la provincia de Santa Fe (Argentina)." *Revista de estudios regionales y mercado de trabajo* 26 (2010): 115–38. http://www.memoria.fahce.unlp.edu.ar/art_revistas/pr.4537/pr .4537.pdf.

Grugel, Jean, and Pía Riggirozzi. "Post-Neoliberalism in Latin America: Rebuilding and Reclaiming the State after Crisis." *Development and Change* 43, no. 1 (2012): 1–21.

Grupo de Reflexión Rural. *Pueblos fumigados: Informe sobre la problemática del uso de plaguicidas en las principales provincias sojeras de la Argentina.* Buenos Aires: Grupo de Reflexión Rural, 2009. http://www.rapaluruguay.org/agrotoxicos/Prensa/Pueblos _Fumigados_GRR.pdf.

Gudynas, Eduardo. "Debates on Development and Its Alternatives in Latin America: A Brief Heterodox Guide." In *Beyond Development: Alternative Visions from Latin America*, edited by Miriam Lang and Dunia Mokrani, 15–40. Amsterdam: Transnational Institute; Quito: Rosa Luxemburg Foundation, 2013.

Gudynas, Eduardo. "Diez tesis urgentes sobre el nuevo extractivismo: Contextos y demandas bajo el progresismo sudamericano actual." In *Extractivismo, política y sociedad*, 187–225. Quito: Centro Andino de Acción Popular, 2009.

Habermas, Jürgen. *Legitimation Crisis.* Boston: Beacon, 1973.

Halperin Donghi, Tulio. *Una nación para el desierto argentino.* Buenos Aires: Prometeo Libros, 2010.

Harrison, Jill Lindsey. *Pesticide Drift and the Pursuit of Environmental Justice.* Cambridge, MA: MIT Press, 2011.

Harvey, David. *A Brief History of Neoliberalism.* New York: Oxford University Press, 2005.

Harvey, David. *The New Imperialism.* Oxford: Oxford University Press, 2005.

Hasbrouck, Alfred. "The Conquest of the Desert." *Hispanic American Historical Review* 15, no. 2 (1935): 195–228.

Hayes, Tyrone B., Vicky Khoury, Anne Narayan, Mariam Nazir, Andrew Park, Travis Brown, Lillian Adame, et al. "Atrazine Induces Complete Feminization and Chemical Castration in Male African Clawed Frogs (*Xenopus laevis*)." *Proceedings of the National Academy of Sciences of the United States of America* 107, no. 10 (2010): 4612–17.

Heller, Chaia. *Food, Farms, and Solidarity: French Farmers Challenge Industrial Agriculture and Genetically Modified Crops.* Durham, NC: Duke University Press, 2013.

Herman, Edward S., and Noam Chomsky. *Manufacturing Consent: The Political Economy of the Mass Media.* New York: Pantheon, 2002.

Hernández, Valeria. "La ruralidad globalizada y el paradigma de los agronegocios en las pampas gringas." In *La Argentina rural: De la agricultura familiar a los agronegocios*, 39–64. Buenos Aires: Editorial Biblos, 2009.

Hora, Roy. *¿Cómo pensaron el campo los argentinos? Y cómo pensarlo hoy, cuando ese campo ya no existe.* Buenos Aires: Siglo Veintiuno Editores, 2018.

Hora, Roy. "La crisis del campo del otoño de 2008." *Desarrollo económico* 50, no. 197 (2010): 81–111.

Hora, Roy. "La evolución del sector agroexportador argentino en el largo plazo, 1880–2010." *Historia agraria* 58 (2012): 145–81.

Horowitz, Joel. "Populism and Its Legacies in Argentina." In *Populism in Latin America*, edited by Michael L. Conniff, 23–47. Tuscaloosa: University of Alabama Press, 1999.

Howard, Philip H. "AFHVS 2016 Presidential Address: Decoding Diversity in the Food System: Wheat and Bread in North America." *Agriculture and Human Values* 33, no. 4 (2016): 953–60.

Intergovernmental Panel on Climate Change (IPCC). *Climate Change 2014: Synthesis Report. Contribution of Working Groups I, II, and III to the Fifth Assessment Report of the Intergovernmental Panel on Climate Change.* Geneva: IPCC, 2014. https://www.ipcc.ch/report/ar5/syr/.

International Agency for Research on Cancer. *Evaluation of Five Organophosphate Insecticides and Herbicides.* IARC Monographs no. 112. Lyon: International Agency for Research on Cancer, 2015.

International Service for the Acquisition of Agri-biotech Applications (ISAAA). *Global Status of Commercialized Biotech/GM Crops in 2017: Biotech Crop Adoption Surges as Economic Benefits Accumulate in 22 Years.* ISAAA Brief no. 53. Ithaca, NY: ISAAA, 2017. https://www.isaaa.org/resources/publications/briefs/53/download/isaaa-brief -53-2017.pdf.

Isakson, S. Ryan. "Food and Finance: The Financial Transformation of Agro-Food Supply Chains." *Journal of Peasant Studies* 41, no. 5 (2014): 749–75.

Jacobsen, Sven-Erik, Marten Sørensen, Søren Marcus Pedersen, and Jacob Weiner. "Feeding the World: Genetically Modified Crops versus Agricultural Biodiversity." *Agronomy for Sustainable Development* 33, no. 4 (2013): 651–62.

Jasper, James M. "Emotions and Social Movements: Twenty Years of Theory and Research." *Annual Review of Sociology* 37 (2011): 285–303.

Jorgenson, Andrew K. "Global Warming and the Neglected Greenhouse Gas: A Cross-National Study of the Social Causes of Methane Emissions Intensity, 1995." *Social Forces* 84, no. 3 (2006): 1779–98.

Kay, Cristóbal. *Latin American Theories of Development and Underdevelopment.* New York: Routledge, 1989.

Kay, Cristóbal. "Latin America's Agrarian Reform: Lights and Shadows." *Land Reform* 2 (1998): 8–31.

Kim, Ki-Hyun, Ehsanul Kabir, and Shamin Ara Jahan. "Exposure to Pesticides and the Associated Human Health Effects." *Science of the Total Environment* 575 (2017): 525–35.

Kimmel, Michael. *The Gendered Society.* New York: Oxford University Press, 2013.

Kinchy, Abby J. *Seeds, Science, and Struggle: The Global Politics of Transgenic Crops.* Cambridge, MA: MIT Press, 2012.

Kloppenburg, Jack. *First the Seed: The Political Economy of Plant Biotechnology.* 2nd ed. Madison: University of Wisconsin Press, 2005.

Konefal, Jason. "Forces of Social Change." In *Ten Lessons in Introductory Sociology*, edited by Kenneth A. Gould and Tammy L. Lewis, 251–86. Oxford: Oxford University Press, 2018.

Krauss, Celene. "Women and Toxic Waste Protests: Race, Class, and Gender as Resources of Resistance." *Qualitative Sociology* 16, no. 3 (1993): 247–62.

Lane, Kris. *Potosí: The Silver City That Changed the World*. Berkeley: University of California Press, 2019.

Lapegna, Pablo. "The Expansion of Transgenic Soybeans and the Killing of Indigenous Peasants in Argentina." *Societies without Borders* 8, no. 2 (2013): 291–308.

Lapegna, Pablo. *Soybeans and Power: Genetically Modified Crops, Environmental Politics, and Social Movements in Argentina*. New York: Oxford University Press, 2016.

Larraín, Jorge. *Identity and Modernity in Latin America*. Malden, MA: Blackwell, 2000.

Larraín, Jorge. "Modernity and Identity: Cultural Change in Latin America." In *Latin America Transformed: Globalization and Modernity*, edited by R. N. Gwynne and C. Kay, 22–38. New York: Arnold, 2004.

Leguizamón, Amalia. "Disappearing Nature? Agribusiness, Biotechnology and Distance in Argentine Soybean Production." *Journal of Peasant Studies* 43, no. 2 (2016): 313–30.

Leguizamón, Amalia. "Environmental Injustice in Argentina: Struggles against Genetically Modified Soy." *Journal of Agrarian Change* 16, no. 4 (2016): 684–92.

Leguizamón, Amalia. "The Gendered Dimensions of Resource Extractivism in Argentina's Soy Boom." *Latin American Perspectives* 46, no. 2 (2019): 199–216.

Leguizamón, Amalia. "Modifying Argentina: GM Soy and Socio-Environmental Change." *Geoforum* 53 (2014): 149–60.

Levine, Adeline. *Love Canal: Science, Politics, and People*. Lexington, MA: Lexington Books, 1982.

Lewis, Tammy L. *Ecuador's Environmental Revolutions: Ecoimperialists, Ecodependents, and Ecoresisters*. Cambridge, MA: MIT Press, 2016.

Livingston, Mike, Jorge Fernandez-Cornejo, Jesse Unger, Craig Osteen, David Schimmelpfennig, Timothy Park, and Dayton M. Lambert. *The Economics of Glyphosate Resistance Management in Corn and Soybean Production*. Economic Research Report no. ERR-184. Rochester, NY: US Department of Agriculture, 2015.

Lódola, Agustín. *Contratistas, cambios tecnológicos y organizacionales en el agro argentino*. Buenos Aires: Comisión Económica para América Latina y el Caribe, 2008.

Ludmer, Josefina. "The Gaucho Genre." In *The Cambridge History of Latin American Literature*, vol. 1, edited by R. González Echevarría and E. Pupo-Walker, 608–31. Cambridge: Cambridge University Press, 1996.

Lukes, Steven. *Power: A Radical View*. 2nd ed. New York: Palgrave Macmillan, 2005.

Luna, Félix. *Breve historia de los argentinos*. Buenos Aires: Planeta, 2005.

Lustig, Nora, Luis F. Lopez-Calva, Eduardo Ortiz-Juarez, and Célestin Monga. "Deconstructing the Decline in Inequality in Latin America." In *Inequality and Growth: Patterns and Policy*, 212–47. London: Palgrave Macmillan, 2016.

Lustig, Nora, and Carola Pessino. "Social Spending and Income Redistribution in Argentina during the 2000s: The Increasing Role of Noncontributory Pensions." *Public Finance Review* 42, no. 3 (2014): 304–25.

Magdoff, Fred, John Bellamy Foster, and Frederick H. Buttel, eds. *Hungry for Profit: The Agribusiness Threat to Farmers, Food, and the Environment*. New York: Monthly Review Press, 2000.

Magdoff, Fred, and Brian Tokar. *Agriculture and Food in Crisis: Conflict, Resistance, and Renewal*. New York: New York University Press, 2010.

Mangonnet, Jorge, and M. Victoria Murillo. "El *boom* sojero y la protesta fiscal de los productores rurales." *Desarrollo económico* 57, no. 221 (2017): 165–79.

Markowitz, Gerald, and David Rosner. *Deceit and Denial: The Deadly Politics of Industrial Pollution*. Berkeley: University of California Press, 2013.

Marx, Karl. *Capital*. Vol. 1, *A Critique of Political Economy*. 1867. London: Penguin Classics, 1990.

Marx, Karl, and Friedrich Engels. *Manifesto of the Communist Party*. 1848. Moscow: Progress Publishers, 1969. Marx/Engels Internet Archive. Accessed June 15, 2019. https://www.marxists.org/archive/marx/works/1848/communist-manifesto/index.htm.

Mascarenhas, Michael. *Where the Waters Divide: Neoliberalism, White Privilege, and Environmental Racism in Canada*. Lanham, MD: Rowman and Littlefield, 2012.

Mason-Deese, Liz. "Unemployed Workers' Movements and the Territory of Social Reproduction." *Journal of Resistance Studies* 2, no. 2 (2016): 65–99.

May, Rachel. "Theories and Experiences of Guerrilla Warfare across the Americas." *Oxford Research Encyclopedia of Latin American History*. March 2019. doi:10.1093/acrefore/9780199366439.013.688.

McAdam, Doug. *Political Process and the Development of Black Insurgency, 1930–1970*. Chicago: University of Chicago Press, 1982.

McCarthy, John D., and Mayer N. Zald. "Resource Mobilization and Social Movements: A Partial Theory." *American Journal of Sociology* 82, no. 6 (1977): 1212–41.

McChesney, Robert Waterman. *Rich Media, Poor Democracy: Communication Politics in Dubious Times*. New York: New Press, 2000.

McMichael, Philip. *Development and Social Change: A Global Perspective*. Newbury Park, CA: Pine Forge, 2012.

McMichael, Philip. "A Food Regime Genealogy." *Journal of Peasant Studies* 36, no. 1 (2009): 139–69.

McMichael, Philip. *Food Regimes and Agrarian Questions*. Black Point, NS: Fernwood, 2013.

Meyer, David S. *The Politics of Protest: Social Movements in America*. 2nd ed. New York: Oxford University Press, 2014.

Mills, C. Wright. *The Sociological Imagination*. New York: Oxford University Press, 1959.

Mohai, Paul, David Pellow, and J. Timmons Roberts. "Environmental Justice." *Annual Review of Environment and Resources* 34, no. 1 (2009): 405–30.

Motta, Renata. "Social Disputes over GMOs: An Overview." *Sociology Compass* 8, no. 12 (2014): 1360–76.

Motta, Renata. *Social Mobilization, Global Capitalism and Struggles over Food: A Comparative Study of Social Movements*. New York: Routledge, 2016.

Motta, Sara C. "'We Are the Ones We Have Been Waiting For': The Feminization of Resistance in Venezuela." *Latin American Perspectives* 40, no. 4 (2013): 35–54.

Motta, Sara C., and Tiina Seppälä. "Feminized Resistances." *Journal of Resistance Studies* 2, no. 2 (2016): 5–32.

Movimiento Campesino de Santiago del Estero—Via Campesina. *Recorriendo caminos polvorientos: Cuadernillo sobre trabajo de base en el MOCASE-VC.* Santiago del Estero, Argentina: MOCASE-VC, 2017.

Mumford, Lewis. *Technics and Civilization.* 1934. New York: Harcourt, Brace, 1963.

Murmis, Miguel, and Maria R. Murmis. "Land Concentration and Foreign Land Ownership in Argentina in the Context of Global Land Grabbing." *Canadian Journal of Development Studies* 33, no. 4 (2012): 490–508.

National Academies of Sciences, Engineering, and Medicine (NAS). *Genetically Engineered Crops: Experiences and Prospects.* Washington, DC: National Academies Press, 2016. doi:10.17226/23395.

Navarro, Marysa. "The Personal Is Political: Las Madres de Plaza de Mayo." In *Power and Popular Protest: Latin American Social Movements*, edited by Susan Eckstein, 241–58. Berkeley: University of California Press, 2001.

Neffa, Julio César. *Modos de regulación, regímenes de acumulación y sus crisis en Argentina (1880–1996): Una contribución a su estudio desde la teoría de la regulación.* Buenos Aires: Eudeba, PIETTE-CONICET, 1998.

Newell, Peter. "Bio-Hegemony: The Political Economy of Agricultural Biotechnology in Argentina." *Journal of Latin American Studies* 41, no. 1 (2009): 27–57.

Norgaard, Kari M. *Living in Denial: Climate Change, Emotions, and Everyday Life.* Cambridge, MA: MIT Press, 2011.

Novaro, Marcos. *Historia de la Argentina, 1955–2010.* Buenos Aires: Siglo Veintiuno, 2010.

O'Connor, James R. *Natural Causes: Essays in Ecological Marxism.* New York: Guilford, 1998.

Oliveira, Gustavo, and Susanna Hecht. "Sacred Groves, Sacrifice Zones, and Soy Production: Globalization, Intensification, and Neo-Nature in South America." *Journal of Peasant Studies* 43, no. 2 (2016): 251–85.

Oreskes, Naomi, and Erik M. Conway. *Merchants of Doubt: How a Handful of Scientists Obscured the Truth on Issues from Tobacco Smoke to Global Warming.* New York: Bloomsbury, 2011.

Ortner, Sherry B. "Gender Hegemonies." *Cultural Critique* 14 (1989): 35–80.

Otero, Gerardo. "The Neoliberal Food Regime in Latin America: State, Agribusiness Transnational Corporations and Biotechnology." *Canadian Journal of Development Studies* 33, no. 3 (2012): 282–94.

Paganelli, Alejandra, Victoria Gnazzo, Helena Acosta, Silvia L. López, and Andrés E. Carrasco. "Glyphosate-Based Herbicides Produce Teratogenic Effects on Vertebrates by Impairing Retinoic Acid Signaling." *Chemical Research in Toxicology* 23, no. 10 (2010): 1586–95.

Paige, Jeffery. *Agrarian Revolution: Social Movements and Export Agriculture in the Underdeveloped World.* New York: Free Press, 1978.

Palacio, Juan Manuel. *Chacareros pampeanos: Una historia social y productiva.* Buenos Aires: Capital Intelectual, 2006.

Paolasso, Pablo, Julieta Krapovickas, and Néstor I. Gasparri. "Deforestación, expansión agropecuaria y dinámica demográfica en el Chaco Seco Argentino durante la década de los noventa." *Latin American Research Review* 47, no. 1 (2012): 35–63.

Park, Lisa Sun-Hee, and David N. Pellow. *The Slums of Aspen: Immigrants vs. the Environment in America's Eden*. New York: New York University Press, 2013.

Parsons, Talcott. *The Evolution of Societies*. Englewood Cliffs, NJ: Prentice-Hall, 1977.

Patel, Raj. "The Long Green Revolution." *Journal of Peasant Studies* 40, no. 1 (2013): 1–63.

Patel, Raj. *Stuffed and Starved: The Hidden Battle for the World Food System*. Brooklyn, NY: Melville House, 2008.

Peet, Richard, and Elaine Hartwick. *Theories of Development: Contentions, Arguments, Alternatives*. New York: Guilford, 2015.

Pellow, David. *What Is Critical Environmental Justice?* Cambridge: Polity Press, 2018.

Pellow, David, and Hollie Nyseth Brehm. "An Environmental Sociology for the Twenty-First Century." *Annual Review of Sociology* 39, no. 1 (2013): 229–50.

Pellow, David, and Robert Brulle, eds. *Power, Justice, and the Environment: A Critical Appraisal of the Environmental Justice Movement*. Cambridge, MA: MIT Press, 2005.

Pengue, Walter A. "Transgenic Crops in Argentina: The Ecological and Social Debt." *Bulletin of Science, Technology and Society* 25, no. 4 (2005): 314–22.

Pierri, J., and M. Abramovsky. "Legislaciones de patentes de semilla y uso de insumos en la producción de soja en la Argentina y en Estados Unidos, 1990–2006." *Realidad económica* 244 (2009): 88–117.

Pigna, Felipe. *Los mitos de la historia argentina*. Vol. 2, *De San Martín a "El granero del mundo."* 2nd ed. Buenos Aires: Booket, 2009.

Pinker, Steven. *Enlightenment Now: The Case for Reason, Science, Humanism, and Progress*. New York: Viking, 2018.

Pinto, Fábio, Marcos Mattos, Farley Silva, Silma L. Rocha, and Simon Elliot. "The Spread of *Helicoverpa armigera* (Lepidoptera: Noctuidae) and Coexistence with *Helicoverpa zea* in Southeastern Brazil." *Insects* 8, no. 3 (2017): 87. doi:10.3390/insects8030087.

Polletta, Francesca, and M. Kai Ho. "Frames and Their Consequences." In *The Oxford Handbook of Contextual Political Analysis*, 187–209. Oxford: Oxford University Press, 2006.

Prévôt-Schapira, Marie-France, and Sébastien Velut. "El sistema urbano y la metropolización." In *La sociedad argentina hoy: Radiografía de una nueva estructura*, edited by Gabriel Kessler, 61–84. Buenos Aires: Siglo Veintiuno, 2016.

Pulido, Laura. "Rethinking Environmental Racism: White Privilege and Urban Development in Southern California." *Annals of the Association of American Geographers* 90, no. 1 (2000): 12–40.

Qaim, Matin. "GM Crop Regulation." In *Genetically Modified Crops and Agricultural Development*, 109–34. Palgrave Studies in Agricultural Economics and Food Policy. New York: Palgrave Macmillan, 2016. doi:10.1057/9781137405722_6.

Qaim, Matin, and Greg Traxler. "Roundup Ready Soybeans in Argentina: Farm Level and Aggregate Welfare Effects." *Agricultural Economics* 32, no. 1 (2005): 73–86.

Rauchecker, Markus. "La estructura territorial y funcional del orden político como filtro simplificador de problemas políticos: El caso de los agroquímicos en la Argentina." In *Estatalidades y soberanías disputadas: La reorganización contemporánea de lo político en América Latina*, edited by Alejandro Agudo Sanchíz, Marco Estrada Saavedra, and Marianne Braig, 171–203. Ciudad de México: El Colegio de México, 2017.

Rauchecker, Markus. "¿Sustentabilidad de qué? Las dimensiones de género en los debates argentinos por la agricultura biotecnológica." In *Sustentabilidad desde abajo: Luchas desde el género y la etnicidad*, edited by Markus Rauchecker and Jennifer Chan, 65–90. Berlin: Lateinamerika-Institut der Freien Universität Berlin; Buenos Aires: Consejo Latinoamericano de Ciencias Sociales (CLACSO), 2016.

Recchini de Lattes, Zulma. "El proceso de urbanización en la Argentina: Distribución, crecimiento y algunas características de la población urbana." *Desarrollo Económico* 12, no. 48 (1973): 867–86.

Red Agroforestal Chaco Argentina (REDAF). *Conflictos sobre la tenencia de la tierra y ambientales en la región chaqueña Argentina—Red Agroforestal Chaco Argentina*. Informes Conflictos. Reconquista, Argentina: REDAF, 2013.

Red Universitaria de Ambiente y Salud (REDUAS). *Informe del primer encuentro nacional de médicos de pueblos fumigados*. Córdoba: REDUAS, 2010. http://www.reduas.com.ar /informe-encuentro-medicos-pueblos-fumigados/.

Red Universitaria de Ambiente y Salud (REDUAS). "Plantas de bioetanol a partir de maíz transgénico. Como funcionan, como contaminan y sus efectos en la salud." Córdoba: REDUAS, 2013. http://reduas.com.ar/wp-content/uploads/downloads/2013 /08/Plantas-de-Bioetanol-a-partir-de-ma%C3%ADz-transg%C3%A9nico.pdf.

Restall, Matthew, and Kris Lane. *Latin America in Colonial Times*. Cambridge: Cambridge University Press, 2018.

Risman, Barbara. "Gender as a Social Structure: Theory Wrestling with Activism." *Gender and Society* 18, no. 4 (2004): 429–50.

Roberts, J. Timmons, and Nikki Demetria Thanos. *Trouble in Paradise: Globalization and Environmental Crises in Latin America*. New York: Routledge, 2003.

Rock, David. *Argentina, 1516–1987: From Spanish Colonization to Alfonsín*. Berkeley: University of California Press, 1987.

Rosa, Eugene A., Thomas K. Rudel, Richard York, Andrew K. Jorgenson, and Thomas Dietz. "The Human (Anthropogenic) Driving Forces of Global Climate Change." In *Climate Change and Society: Sociological Perspectives*, edited by Riley E. Dunlap and Robert J. Brulle, 32–60. Oxford: Oxford University Press, 2015.

Rosal, Miguel Ángel. "La exportación de cueros, lana y tasajo a través del puerto de Buenos Aires entre 1835 y 1854." *Anuario de estudios americanos* 55, no. 2 (1998): 565–88.

Rosati, Germán. "Patrones espaciales de expansión de la frontera agrícola: La soja en la Argentina (1987–1988/2009–2010)." In *El agro como negocio*, edited by Carla Gras and Valeria Hernández, 97–122. Buenos Aires: Editorial Biblos, 2013.

Roscigno, Vincent J. "Power, Revisited." *Social Forces* 90, no. 2 (2011): 349–74.

Rudel, Thomas K., J. Timmons Roberts, and JoAnn Carmin. "Political Economy of the Environment." *Annual Review of Sociology* 37, no. 1 (2011): 221–38.

Ruderman, L., B. Cabrera Fasolis, G. Dozzo, C. Nota, and M. Avila Vazquez. "Análisis de la salud colectiva ambiental de Malvinas Argentinas-Córdoba." Córdoba: Red

Universitaria de Ambiente y Salud, 2013. http://www.reduas.com.ar/wp-content /uploads/downloads/2013/02/Informe-Malvinas-corregido1.pdf.

Sabato, Hilda. *Historia de la Argentina, 1852–1890*. Buenos Aires: Siglo Veintiuno, 2012.

Sachs, Jeffrey D. *The Age of Sustainable Development*. New York: Columbia University Press, 2015.

Sández, Fernanda. *La Argentina fumigada: Agroquímicos, enfermedad y alimentos en un país envenenado*. Buenos Aires: Planeta, 2016.

Sanz-Villarroya, Isabel. "The Convergence Process of Argentina with Australia and Canada: 1875–2000." *Explorations in Economic History* 42, no. 3 (2005): 439–58.

Sarlo, Beatriz. *Una modernidad periférica: Buenos Aires 1920 y 1930*. Buenos Aires: Ediciones Nueva Visión, 1988.

Sarmiento, Domingo F. *Facundo: Civilization and Barbarism: The First Complete English Translation*. Translated by Kathleen Ross. Berkeley: University of California Press, 2003.

Sautu, Ruth. "La formación y la actualidad de la clase media argentina." In *La sociedad argentina hoy: Radiografía de una nueva estructura*, edited by Gabriel Kessler, 163–83. Buenos Aires: Siglo Veintiuno, 2016.

Schippers, Mimi. "Recovering the Feminine Other: Masculinity, Femininity, and Gender Hegemony." *Theory and Society* 36, no. 1 (2007): 85–102.

Schnaiberg, Allan. *The Environment, from Surplus to Scarcity*. New York: Oxford University Press, 1980.

Schnaiberg, Allan, and Kenneth Gould. *Environment and Society: The Enduring Conflict*. New York: St. Martin's, 1994.

Schnurr, Matthew A. "Can Genetically Modified Crops Help the Poor? Incomplete Answers to a Flawed Question." *Canadian Journal of Development Studies* 38, no. 1 (2017): 125–28.

Schurman, Rachel. "Micro (Soft) Managing a 'Green Revolution' for Africa: The New Donor Culture and International Agricultural Development." *World Development* 112 (2018): 180–92.

Schurman, Rachel, and William Munro. *Fighting for the Future of Food: Activists versus Agribusiness in the Struggle over Biotechnology*. Minneapolis: University of Minnesota Press, 2010.

Schurman, Rachel, and William Munro. "Targeting Capital: A Cultural Economy Approach to Understanding the Efficacy of Two Anti-genetic Engineering Movements." *American Journal of Sociology* 115, no. 1 (2009): 155–202.

Schweblin, Samanta. *Fever Dream: A Novel*. Translated by Megan McDowell. New York: Riverhead, 2017.

Scoones, Ian. "Mobilizing against GM Crops in India, South Africa and Brazil." *Journal of Agrarian Change* 8, nos. 2–3 (2008): 315–44.

Scott, James C. *Weapons of the Weak: Everyday Forms of Peasant Resistance*. New Haven, CT: Yale University Press, 1985.

Secretaría de Agricultura, Pesca y Alimentos (SAGPyA). *Plan estratégico 2005–2015 para el desarrollo de la biotecnología agropecuaria*. Buenos Aires: Secretaría de Agricultura, Pesca y Alimentos de la Nación, 2004.

Séralini, Gilles-Éric, Emilie Clair, Robin Mesnage, Steeve Gress, Nicolas Defarge, Manuela Malatesta, Didier Hennequin, and Joël Spiroux de Vendômois. "Republished Study: Long-Term Toxicity of a Roundup Herbicide and a Roundup-Tolerant Genetically Modified Maize." *Environmental Sciences Europe* 26, no. 1 (2014): 1–17.

Shiva, Vandana. *Stolen Harvest: The Hijacking of the Global Food Supply.* Cambridge, MA: South End Press, 2000.

Shiva, Vandana. *The Violence of the Green Revolution.* London: Zed, 1991.

Shriver, Thomas E., Alison E. Adams, and Chris M. Messer. "Power, Quiescence, and Pollution: The Suppression of Environmental Grievances." *Social Currents* 1, no. 3 (2014): 275–92.

Shriver, Thomas E., Sherry Cable, and Dennis Kennedy. "Mining for Conflict and Staking Claims: Contested Illness at the Tar Creek Superfund Site." *Sociological Inquiry* 78, no. 4 (2008): 558–79.

Shumway, Nicolas. *The Invention of Argentina.* Berkeley: University of California Press, 1991.

Skidmore, Thomas, and Peter H. Smith. *Modern Latin America.* 6th ed. Oxford: Oxford University Press, 2005.

Skill, Karin, and Ezequiel Grinberg. "Controversias socio-técnicas en torno a las fumigaciones con glifosato en Argentina: Una mirada desde la construcción social del riesgo." In *Cartografías del conflicto ambiental en Argentina*, edited by Gabriela Merlinsky, 91–117. Buenos Aires: Fundación CICCUS, 2013.

Skocpol, Theda. "What Makes Peasants Revolutionary?" *Comparative Politics* 14, no. 3 (1982): 351–75.

Smith, Adam M., Martyn T. Smith, Michele A. La Merrill, Jane Liaw, and Craig Steinmaus. "2,4-Dichlorophenoxyacetic Acid (2,4-D) and Risk of Non-Hodgkin Lymphoma: A Meta-Analysis Accounting for Exposure Levels." *Annals of Epidemiology* 27, no. 4 (2017): 281–89.

Sorensen, Diana. *"Facundo" and the Construction of Argentine Culture.* Austin: University of Texas Press, 1996.

Stauber, John C., and Sheldon Rampton. *Toxic Sludge Is Good for You! Lies, Damn Lies and the Public Relations Industry.* Monroe, ME: Common Courage, 1995.

Stokes, Susan. *Mandates and Democracy: Neoliberalism by Surprise in Latin America.* Cambridge: Cambridge University Press, 2001.

Stølen, Kristi Anne. "Agricultural Change in Argentina: Impacts of the Gene Modified Soybean Revolution." In *Emerging Economies and Challenges to Sustainability*, edited by Arve Hansen and Ulrikke Wethal, 149–61. New York: Routledge, 2015.

Stølen, Kristi Anne. *La decencia de la desigualdad: Género y poder en el campo argentino.* Buenos Aires: EPICa, 2004.

Stone, Glenn Davis. "The Anthropology of Genetically Modified Crops." *Annual Review of Anthropology* 39 (2010): 381–400.

Stone, Glenn Davis, and Dominic Glover. "Disembedding Grain: Golden Rice, the Green Revolution, and Heirloom Seeds in the Philippines." *Agriculture and Human Values* 34, no. 1 (2017): 87–102.

Sundberg, Juanita. "Tracing Race: Mapping Environmental Formations in Environmental Justice Research in Latin America." In *Environmental Justice in Latin America*, edited by David Carruthers, 25–47. Cambridge, MA: MIT Press, 2008.

Svampa, Maristella. "The End of Kirchnerism." *New Left Review*, no. 53 (2008): 79–95.

Szasz, Andrew. *Shopping Our Way to Safety: How We Changed from Protecting the Environment to Protecting Ourselves.* Minneapolis: University of Minnesota Press, 2007.

Taylor, Carl C. *Rural Life in Argentina.* Baton Rouge: Louisiana State University Press, 1948.

Taylor, Diana. *Disappearing Acts: Spectacles of Gender and Nationalism in Argentina's "Dirty War."* Durham, NC: Duke University Press, 1997.

Taylor, Dorceta. *The Environment and the People in American Cities, 1600s–1900s: Disorder, Inequality, and Social Change.* Durham, NC: Duke University Press, 2009.

Teubal, Miguel. "Agrarian Reform and Social Movements in the Age of Globalization: Latin America at the Dawn of the Twenty-First Century." *Latin American Perspectives* 36, no. 4 (2009): 9–20.

Teubal, Miguel. "Expansión del modelo sojero en la Argentina: De la producción de alimentos a los commodities." *Realidad económica* 220 (2006): 71–96.

Teubal, Miguel. "Genetically Engineered Soybeans and the Crisis of Argentina's Agriculture Model." In *Food for the Few: Neoliberal Globalism and Biotechnology in Latin America*, edited by Gerardo Otero, 189–216. Austin: University of Texas Press, 2008.

Tokar, Brian, ed. *Redesigning Life? The Worldwide Challenge to Genetic Engineering.* London: Zed, 2001.

Toledo, Víctor M., David Garrido, and Narciso Barrera-Bassols. "The Struggle for Life: Socio-Environmental Conflicts in Mexico." *Latin American Perspectives* 42, no. 5 (2015): 133–47.

Tönnies, Ferdinand. *Community and Society (Gemeinschaft und Gesellschaft).* Translated and edited by Charles P. Loomis. 1887. New York: Harper and Row, 1963.

Torrado, Marla. "Madres en contra de la soja: Planeamiento, salud y resistencia en Córdoba, Argentina." In *Sustentabilidad desde abajo: Luchas desde el género y la etnicidad*, edited by Markus Rauchecker and Jennifer Chan, 169–90. Berlin: Lateinamerika-Institut der Freien Universität Berlin; Buenos Aires: Consejo Latinoamericano de Ciencias Sociales (CLACSO), 2016.

Trigo, Eduardo J. "Fifteen Years of Genetically Modified Crops in Argentine Agriculture." Buenos Aires: Consejo Argentino para la Información y el Desarrollo de la Biotecnología (ArgenBio), 2011. https://www.argenbio.org/adc/uploads/15_years_Executive_summary_of_GM_crops_in_Argentina.pdf.

Trigo, Eduardo J., and Eugenio J. Cap. "The Impact of the Introduction of Transgenic Crops in Argentinean Agriculture." *AgBioForum* 6, no. 3 (2003): 87–94.

Turzi, Mariano. *The Political Economy of Agricultural Booms: Managing Soybean Production in Argentina, Brazil, and Paraguay.* Cham, Switzerland: Palgrave Macmillan, 2017.

Unidad de Manejo del Sistema de Evaluación Forestal (USDEF). *Informe sobre deforestación en Argentina.* Buenos Aires: Dirección de Bosques, Secretaría de Ambiente y Desarrollo Sustentable, 2004.

Unidad de Manejo del Sistema de Evaluación Forestal (USDEF). *Pérdida de bosque nativo en el norte de Argentina: Diciembre 2007–Octubre 2008.* Buenos Aires: Dirección de Bosques, Secretaría de Ambiente y Desarrollo Sustentable, 2008.

Vanden, Harry E., and Gary Prevost. *Politics of Latin America: The Power Game.* Oxford: Oxford University Press, 2014.

Vommaro, Gabriel, and Mariana Gené. "Argentina: El año de Cambiemos." *Revista de Ciencia Política* 37, no. 2 (2017): 231–54.

Walsh, Edward, Rex Warland, and D. Clayton Smith. "Backyards, NIMBYs, and Incinerator Sitings: Implications for Social Movement Theory." *Social Problems* 40, no. 1 (1993): 25–38.

Walter, Mariana, and Leire Urkidi. "Community Consultations: Local Responses to Large-Scale Mining in Latin America." In *Environmental Governance in Latin America*, edited by Fábio de Castro, Barbara Hogenboom, and Michiel Baud, 287–325. London: Palgrave Macmillan, 2016.

Walton, John. "Making the Theoretical Case." In *What Is a Case? Exploring the Foundations of Social Inquiry*, edited by Charles C. Ragin and Howard Saul Becker, 121–38. Cambridge: Cambridge University Press, 1992.

Weber, Max. *The Protestant Ethic and the Spirit of Capitalism.* 1904. Los Angeles: Roxbury, 2001.

Wedeen, Lisa. *Ambiguities of Domination: Politics, Rhetoric, and Symbols in Contemporary Syria.* Chicago: University of Chicago Press, 2015.

Wickham-Crowley, Timothy. *Guerrillas and Revolution in Latin America: A Comparative Study of Insurgents and Regimes since 1956.* Princeton, NJ: Princeton University Press, 1992.

Wilpert, Gregory. *Changing Venezuela by Taking Power: The History and Policies of the Chávez Government.* London: Verso, 2007.

Wilson Becerril, Michael. "How Gold Mining Companies Stifle Opposition in Peru." New York: NACLA, 2018. Accessed October 15, 2018. https://nacla.org/news/2018/08/14/how-gold-mining-companies-stifle-opposition-peruc%C3%B3mo-las-compa%C3%B1%C3%ADas-de-miner%C3%ADa-de-oro.

Wolf, Eric R. *Peasant Wars of the Twentieth Century.* 1969. Norman: University of Oklahoma Press, 1999.

York, Richard, and Marcia Hill Gossard. "Cross-National Meat and Fish Consumption: Exploring the Effects of Modernization and Ecological Context." *Ecological Economics* 48, no. 3 (2004): 293–302.

Zerubavel, Eviatar. *The Elephant in the Room: Silence and Denial in Everyday Life.* Oxford: Oxford University Press, 2006.

INDEX

AAPRESID. *See* Argentine Association of Direct Sowing Producers

ABCDS (ADM, Bunge, Cargill, and Louis Dreyfuss), 13

accumulation by dispossession, 42, 130

acquiescence/consent, 151–52n13; corporate lobbying as tool for, 73–74; creation of, 4–6; due to impoverished conditions, 86,132–33; due to mobilization of bias, 18, 64, 156n83; economic redistribution encourages, 18, 55, 64, 85–86, 92–96, 109; impeding factors to resistance, 21–22; media role in, 64, 70–71; national identity myths used to promote, 17–18, 33–34, 140; silencing, self-policing, and denial, 96, 101, 108, 144, 146; status quo, reproduction of, 6, 21, 64, 85, 91, 107, 141; scientific expertise used as a strategy for, 84–85, 106, 135–36; in everyday life, 95–102; "We don't talk about that," 96, 98–102; "We all live off the countryside," 74–86. *See also* latent grievances

activism, 22–23; consciousness transformation, 20, 118, 122, 131–32; corporate and state responses to, 113, 131–37; popular epidemiology, 118–19; scientific and professional experts as allies, 114–18, 123; citizen assemblies, 22, 113, 127. *See also* Asamblea Malvinas Lucha por la Vida (Assembly of Malvinas, AMLV); Mothers of Barrio Ituzaingó Anexo (Grupo de Madres de Barrio Ituzaingó Anexo); peasant and indigenous activism; social movements

Adamovsky, Ezequiel, 108–9

ADM, 13

affective emotions, 102

Africa, 9

Agent Orange, 153n28. *See* 2,4-D

agrarian reform, 50, 51, 131

agribusinesses, 2–10, 13–14; farms as factories, 61; financialization of land and food crops, 68; junior employees, 59–60; male-dominated, 4–5, 26, 103, 106, 143; "new agricultural paradigm," 63, 64–69, 77, 105; regional integration, 67. *See also specific businesses*

agricultural exports, 15–17, 23, 154–55n50; agro-export boom of 1870 to 1914, 33, 40, 47, 60, 61, 142; livestock-derived commodities, 38, 160n28; natural resource extraction, 1, 10, 19, 33, 35, 39, 41, 52, 55; in the nineteenth century, 44; Resolution 125 (soy export taxes), 56–57; specialization, 52. *See also* agro-export model

agricultural fairs, 68–69

Agricultural Strategic Plan for 2010–16 (PEA2), 56

agriculturización (agriculturization), 49

agrochemical exposure/pesticide drift, 2–5, 19–21, 85, 89–91, 143–44; negative health impacts of, 2, 21, 73, 84, 93–95, 101, 117, 122, 174n3; as "invisible" problem, 20, 124. *See also* glyphosate-based herbicides

agro-export model, 15, 22–23, 39, 43–44; liberal modernizing discourse of, 56. *See also* agricultural exports

contractors (*contratistas*), 30, 60, 66, 78–79, 93
Convertibility Plan, 51, 53
Coordinadora Latinoamericana de Organizaciones del Campo, 129
Córdoba city, 34, 57, 114, 144. *See also* Ituzaingó Anexo (Córdoba city neighborhood); Mothers of Barrio Ituzaingó Anexo (Grupo de Madres de Barrio Ituzaingó Anexo)
Córdoba province, 77, *88*, 114
corn, 7, 8, 14, 44, 45, 46, 48, 49, 53, 59, 71, 76, 80, 88, 114, 121, 152n19, 152n21
Coronil, Fernando, 3
corporate and state actors, 4, 141, 145; bureaucratic delays by, 133–35; responses to activism, 113, 131–37
corporate discourse, 56, 63
"corporate food regime," 14
corporate social responsibility (CSR), 132
Correa, Rafael, 54
Corrientes province, 79
Corteva Agriscience, 13
cotton, 7, 8, 23, 33, 152n19, 152n21
CREA (Regional Consortiums of Agricultural Experimentation), 67, 69
Cresud (agribusiness), 66, 166n16
criollos, 34, 40
crop/farm managers (*encargado de la chacra*), 31, 45–56, 60–61, 74–75
crop substitution, 49
Cuba, 50, 160n28
cultural economy, 23, 131, 146

decision-making power, 3, 5, 18, 25–26, 32, 49–50, 66, 107, 141, 143
deforestation, 2, 128–31, 144; acceleration of due to GM soy, 128–29
de la Cadena, Marisol, 18
de la Rúa, Fernando, 54
demobilization strategies: bureaucratic delays, 133–35; scientific establishment and, 135–37; violence, 137
democracy: "paradoxical insight" of, 133; return to, 129, 170n12
demonization, as strategy, 136, 145
denial, 97–98; construction of, 22, 91; silencing, self-policing, and denial, 96, 101, 108, 144, 146

dependency theory, 16–17
Deregulation Decree of 1991, 50, 51, 142
"desert," Pampas as, 17, 35, 36; "conquest of the desert," 41–42, 130
development: Argentina's national strategy, 1–4; discourse of, 19–20, 55–56, 113, 168n51; inward-looking model, 1940s and 1950s, 47; as linear evolution toward progress, 10; reverse, 31; sustainable, 9–10, 14, 19, 56, 62, 121, 129, 140, 147; ten-year plan (2005–15), 55–56. *See also* discourse
Diario Clarín (newspaper), 57, *57*, 69, 70, 129
Dirty War, 101–2, 108
disappeared persons, Argentina, 101–2, 163n99, 170n12
discourse: abstract, 14–15; "civilization or barbarism" dichotomy, 17, 35–39, 109; corporate, 56, 63; of development, 19–20, 55–56, 113, 168n51; directed at public, 69–74; "feeding the world," 9–10, 19, 147; "granary of the world," 2, 4, 17–18, 31–33, 40, 43–47, 49, 62, 71–72, 121, 141–42; insults and demonization, 136, 145; macro-level, 14–15, 25, 141; "new agricultural paradigm," 63, 64–69, 77; no-risk, 5; one-size-fits-all, 15; population growth, 9–10, 48–49, 70; of promise, 4–5; "pro-poor," 9, 15; public as audience for, 69–74; of sustainability, 7–10, 17–19, 62, 65–66, 69, 80, 84; "trickle down," 18, 64, 78, 83, 85, 143; "we all live off the countryside," 2, 18, 21, 64, 74–88, 92, 95, 99, 143; "we do the best agriculture in the world," 1, 26, 71, 143
displacement and dispossession, 3, 17, 19, 42, 47, 51, 63, 75, 113, 137, 141–42; indigenous activism against, 130–31
Distancia de rescate (*Rescue Distance*) (Schweblin), 139–40, 145–46, 174–75n3, 175n7
"Does the World's Top Weed Killer Cause Cancer?" (Waldman et al.), 148
Dow, 13
Duhalde, Eduardo, 54
DuPont, 13
Durkheim, Émile, 159n20, 159n22

Echeverría, Esteban, 35
ecological footprint, 109

ecological modernization theory, 10, 18–19, 62, 121, 140

economic crises, 31, 51, 54–58, 163n101

economic liberal theory, 39

Ecotierra (real-estate development), 115

Ecuador, 54

education, middle-class value of, 109–10

efficiency, 38–39, 60–61, 67, 71, 142

electric-power transformers, 115, 117

"elephant in the field," 92–111; doubt, 96–98; "we don't talk about that," 96, 98–102

elites: control of Pampas gained through military conquest, 42; criollo, 34; efforts to quell dissent, 16, ; Generation of 1837, 17

encargado de la chacra (farm manager), 31, 45, 60, 74–75

entrepreneurs, 29, 32, 45, 62, 66, 136–37, 140–41, 147; resistance to, 129–31; violence and murders by, 129–31. See also producers

Entre Ríos province, 119

environmental challenges, 9–11, 115; climate change, 10–11, 13, 20, 129; gendered component, 22; legitimation of social and environmental injustice, 3, 15, 17

environmental impact assessment, 124

environmental justice (EJ) scholarship, 4–5, 86, 112–13, 156n75; limitations of, 15–16

Environmental Protection Agency (US), 8, 148

epidemiology, popular, 118–19

Esquivel, Adolfo Pérez, 127

estancias (ranches, manors), 31, 40, 44–45

European colonists, 23, 25, 141; chacareros, gringos, and colonos, 17, 41, 44–46; emigration, 17, 39–41; tenants (colonos), 45–47; urban preference of, 46–47

European Union, 2, 9, 11, 148

evictions, forced, 22, 113, 129–31, 134–35, 137, 144

Expoagro agricultural fair, 68–69

exports. See agricultural exports

extractivism, 3–4; history of, 16–17, 32–33, 47–50, 141–42; Kirchner administrations (2003–15), 54–58; natural resources for export, 1, 10, 19, 33, 35, 39, 41, 52, 55; "new," 54–58; structuralist views, 16;

treadmill of production theory, 19, 62, 109; at the turn of the twenty-first century, 50–58. See agricultural exports; agroexport model

Facundo: Civilization and Barbarism (Sarmiento), 17, 35–39, 158–59n18

Fairbairn, Madeleine, 68

Federación Agraria Argentina, 56

"feeding the world" discourse, 9–10, 19, 147

feedlots, 11, 76, 89, 100

fencing, 130

Ferreyra, Cristian, 130, 135

fertilizer plants, 93

Fever Dream (Distancia de rescate, Schweblin), 139–40, 145–146174–175n3, 175n7

financialization of land and food crops, 68

financial market, global, 13

"flex crops," 14, 67

Flores (rural town [pseudonym]), 1

Fome Zero (Zero Hunger, Brazil), 54

Food and Agriculture Organization (United Nations), 128

food insecurity, 2, 9, 19, 48, 50, 71, 147; hunger riots of 2008, 56

Ford Foundation, 48

foreign direct investment, 39, 40, 50

Forest Law (2007), 129

Formosa province, 128, 131, 163n99

fossil fuels, 10; coal-based energy, 38; coal mining, 20

framing of grievances, 19–20, 101, 112–13, 122, 128

France, 2, 9, 34

Friedman, Thomas, 9, 10, 166n2

Friedmann, Harriet, 43

fumigation. See agrochemical/pesticide drift

fumigation workers, 73, 168n46. See also contractors

functionalism, 36, 159n20

Galeano, Eduardo, 33, 158n5

Galván, Miguel, 130, 135

Gates Foundation, 9

Gatica, Sofía, 121, 138, 171n10

gaucho judío (Jewish colono), 47

gauchos (ethnically mixed rural men), 36, 40

Gelman, Jorge, 49

gender: "emphasized femininity," 108; gendered insults, 136, 145, 146; gendered perceptions of health hazards, 21–22, 102–6, 146; "hegemonic masculinity," 103, 108; "on-the-ground female power," 110–11; "protective instinct" of mothers, 26, 107–8, 113; traditional European gendered roles, 18, 46–47, 103, 106–7; social construction of, 103; status expectations, 102; "triple burden" of women activists, 134; women excluded from decision-making, 18, 32, 49–50, 143–44; women in agribusiness as masculinized subjects, 106, 143; women-led citizen assemblies, 22. *See also* Asamblea Malvinas Lucha por la Vida (AMLV; Assembly of Malvinas); "in-between" actors; motherhood; mothers; Mothers of Barrio Ituzaingó Anexo (Grupo de Madres de Barrio Ituzaingó Anexo); race/class/gender spectrum

Gené, Mariana, 58

General Artigas (rural town [pseudonym]), 75

Generation of 1837, 17, 34–37, 141–42, 159nn19, 22. *See also* Alberdi, Juan Bautista; Echeverría, Esteban; Sarmiento, Domingo F.

Generation of 1880, 39–40

genetically modified organisms (GMOs), 152nn19, 21; Borlaug and, 48–49; common transgenic traits, 7–8; definition of, 6–11; Golden Rice, 6–7, 152n20; hectares planted, 8–9, 11, 14, 30, 45, 59, 84, 153n31, 166–67n16; as inputs/tools, 65; as a "pro-poor" technology, 9; top producing countries, 8–9, 11. *See also* glyphosate-based herbicides; Roundup Ready; technological package

Germany, 2, 9, 30

Giarracca, Norma, 50, 51

global soybean chain, 13

glyphosate-based herbicides, 1; endocrine-disrupting effects, 84; as health risk, 52–53, 72–73, 84, 93–95; increased use of, 84, 153n26; insect and weed resistance to, 7–8; invisibilization of risks of, 74, 113; media investigations, 148; Resolution 167, 52; "scientific expertise" minimizes risks, 84–85, 135–36; scientific research on, 52–53, 73, 120, 136; toxicity classifica-

tion, 8, 52, 84, 120, 134, 148, 164n112. *See also* agrochemical/pesticide drift; Roundup; Roundup Ready seeds; soybeans, herbicide-resistant GM; technological package

Golden Rice, 6–7, 152n20

Goldman Environmental Prize, 121

Goodwin, Jeff, 123

Gordillo, Gastón, 41

Gossard, Marcia Hill, 13

Gould, Kenneth, 19. *See* treadmill of production theory

"granary of the world" discourse, 2, 4, 17–18, 31–33, 40, 43–47, 49, 62, 71–72, 121, 141–42

"Granary of the World, The" (article), 71

Gras, Carla, 66

Great Britain, 43–44, 160n28

Great Depression, 47

greenhouse gases, 13

Green Revolution, 10, 47, 48–50, 64, 66, 75, 162n85

grievances, 106; children's health, framing around, 113, 122, 128; conflicts of interest indicated by latent, 95; framing, 19–20, 101, 112–13, 122, 128; latent, 21–22, 26–27, 55, 85–86, 95–102, 139–40, 149. *See also* visibility

Grobocopatel, Abraham, 47

Grobocopatel, Adolfo, 47

Grobocopatel, Bernardo, 47

Grobocopatel, Gustavo, 47, 66, 136, 162n76

Grobocopatel, Jorge, 47

Grupo Clarín, 70, 74, 168n51

Grupo de Madres de Barrio Ituzaingó Anexo. *See* Mothers of Barrio Ituzaingó Anexo

Grupo de Reflexión Rural (GRR), 119

Gudynas, Eduardo, 55

guiding fictions/myths, 34, 38, 44, 62, 140

hacendados (landowners), 34, 40

Harvey, David, 42

health issues: cancer, miscarriages, and malformations, 2, 21, 73, 84, 93–95, 101, 117, 122, 174n3; citizen assemblies for health and life, 22, 113, 144; invisibilized, 74, 113; in Malvinas Argentinas, 121–22; not directly visible, 20; gendered perceptions

lawsuits, 115, 121, 122–23, 135
"lease-operate" investment strategy, 68
leasing of land, 13, 46, 66–67, 79–80, 166n16
legislation: extensions (*prórrogas*), 135; land
    rights, 130; Law of Monetary Unification
    (1881), 160n37; local ordinances for buffer
    zones, 113, 115, 120, 144–45; need for, 133–34
Lewis, Tammy, 55
Ley Cristian Ferreyra (Law 26160), 134–35
Ley General de Ambiente (National Environ-
    ment Law), 124
Ley Veinteañal (property rights law), 130
Ligas Agrarias (Formosa), 163n99
lived experience, 15, 107, 146
lobbying, corporate, 73–74
Los Cardones (agribusiness [pseudonym]),
    59–66, 77, 78, 96–97
Los Grobo (agribusiness), 47, 66, 77, 136,
    166–67n16
Louis Dreyfus Company, 13, 77, 96
Love Canal, New York (United States), 119
Lukes, Steven, 16, 95
Lula da Silva, Luiz, 54
Lustig, Nora, 165n131

machinery, 19, 38, 44, 60–61, 98, 166n2.
    See also technological package
Macri, Mauricio, 168n51, 174n88
Madres de Plaza de Mayo, 108
male-dominated spheres, 4–5, 18, 26, 32,
    103–8, 141, 143
Malthus, Thomas, 10, 154n40
Malthusian narrative, 10, 13, 48–49, 121
Malvinas Argentinas (commuter suburb of
    Córdoba city), 107, 121–28, 138, 144; "el
    acampe de Malvinas," 124–27; Monsanto
    campaign, 121–28, 132. *See also* Asamblea
    Malvinas Lucha por la Vida (AMLV; As-
    sembly of Malvinas)
management: crop/farm managers (*encargado
    de la chacra*), 31, 45–56, 60–61, 74–75;
    remote, 25–26, 29
Manu Chao, 127
"map of death" (*mapa de la muerte*), 117–18
Marx, Karl, 16
McMichael, Philip, 14, 43
measles outbreak, Pacific Northwest, 147–48
media, 19, 58, 64, 70–73, 168n51

Menem, Carlos, 51, 142, 163n102
Mesa de Enlace, 56
Messerschmidt, James, 103
methane emissions, 13
Mexico, 2, 36, 47
Meyer, David, 133
middle classes, 13, 26, 92, 102, 108–9,
    143, 171n27
military campaigns, nineteenth century,
    41–42, 130
military dictatorship, 1976–83, 50. *See also*
    Dirty War
Ministry of Agriculture, Livestock, and
    Fisheries, 52
Misiones (Venezuelan program), 54
mobilization: absence of, 16; children's health
    as reason for, 112, 122, 128; of cultural val-
    ues by elites, 19; economic redistribution
    stifles, 18; against forced evictions and
    habitat devastation, 113, 129–31, 134–35,
    137, 144; health and environmental risks as
    focus, 112–13; local ordinances for buffer
    zones, 113, 115, 120, 144–45; single indus-
    try as deterrent to, 86; by those at bottom,
    112–13. *See also* activism
MOCAFOR (peasant movement, Formosa), 131
MOCAJU (peasant movement, Jujuy), 131
MOCASE (peasant movement, Santiago del
    Estero), 129–31, 136
modernization discourse, 55–56, 98–99, 121;
    Generation of 1837 viewpoints, 35–43
modernization theory, 10, 14, 17–19; liberat-
    ing potential of machines, 61, 166n2
Molecular Embryology Lab (University of
    Buenos Aires), 73
monocultures: costs of, 44–45, 63–64, 80–81,
    128
Monsanto (Bayer), 1, 7, 13, 105, 120; contracts
    for farmers, 53; corporate-state alliance
    and, 69–70; GM-corn-seed plant plans,
    121; lawsuits against, 2, 148; Malvinas
    Argentinas campaign against, 121–28, 132,
    138, 144; media investigations, 148. *See also*
    genetically modified organisms (GMOs);
    glyphosate-based herbicides; Intacta
    Roundup Ready 2 Pro; Roundup; Roundup
    Ready seeds
Montenegro, Raúl, 117, 123

Morales, Evo, 54
Moratoria Previsional (Pension Moratorium), 54–55. *See* non-contributory pensions
motherhood: politicization of, 107–8; as a mobilization strategy, 146, 170n21
mothers, 102–11; as "in between," 106–11
"mother's intuition," 26, 107–8, 113, 145–46
Mothers of Barrio Ituzaingó Anexo (Grupo de Madres de Barrio Ituzaingó Anexo), 107–8, 112–19, *118*, 138, 144, 171n10; health clinic, demand for, 115, 135; lawsuit, 2012, 115, 121, 122–23, 135; "map of death" (*mapa de la muerte*), 117–18. *See also* Ituzaingó Anexo (Córdoba city neighborhood)
Movimento dos Trabalhadores Rurais Sem Terra (Brazil), 66
Movimiento Nacional Campesino Indígena (MNCI), 129, 131
Munro, William, 19, 23

national identity, 4–5, 17–19, 21, 33–35, 47–48, 109, 140–41. *See also* la argentinidad (Argentineness); guiding fictions/myths
nation-building, 4, 17–18, 33–36, 41
natural resource extraction, 1, 10, 19, 33, 35, 39, 41, 52, 55. *See* extractivism
nature: Alberdi's view, 39–40; Sarmiento's view, 17, 35–39; as unruly, 35–39, 43, 61
neo-extractivism ("new extractivism"), 54–58
neoliberal restructuring, 3, 50–58, 129, 163n90; collapse of, 54–58; Deregulation Decree of 1991, 50, 51, 142; pro-GM legislation, 49
"new agricultural paradigm," 63, 64–69, 77, 105
Nidera, 164n120
noncontributory pensions, 54–55, 165nn 131, 133. *See* Moratoria Previsional (Pension Moratorium)
nongovernmental organizations (NGOs), 132
Norgaard, Kari, 20
no-till/direct-seeding methods, 7, 30, 53, 62, 65, 67, 80, 142

Oliveira, Gustavo, 13
"Only Biotechnology Can Save the World" (Huergo), 70

Ortner, Sherry, 110–11
Ospina, Mariano, 36
Otero, Gerardo, 52

Página/12 (newspaper), 72, 120, 168n42
Pampas, 1–2, 15; as core of agro-export model, 23; as unproductive "desert," 17, 35–38, 41; history of soybeans in, 31–33, 47–50, 141–42; mixed model agriculture, 44, 49; national parks, 160n32; native flora and fauna, 37. *See also* Argentina; European colonists; rural/soy towns
Paraguay, 9, 67
paraquat, 8, 153n28
Paren de Fumigar (Stop Spraying) campaign, 119–20, 127, 131–32, 144
Patagonia region, 41–42
Patel, Raj, 50
patented seeds, 53, 147, 164n120
patronage and clientelism networks, 22, 133
peasant and indigenous activism, 42, 50, 144; land conflicts, 129, 131, 135; criminalization of, 129; against forced evictions, 129–31; land titles, 130; La Vía Campesina, 129; MOCASE, 129–31; Movimento dos Trabalhadores Rurais Sem Terra (Brazil), 66
peasant and indigenous peoples: Constitution of 1994, rights given to, 130; during early twentieth century, 40; excluded from decision-making, 18, 32, 49–50; invisibilized, 18, 43, 47, 129–30, 141–42; numbers of, 161n53; under Spanish rule, 160n45; Third World revolutions and, 50; violence against, 2, 17, 41–43, 51, 130–31, 135, 160–61n45
Pellow, David, 15
Perón, Juan Domingo, 47–48
Peronista party, 48, 54, 58, 163n102
Peru, 43, 47
peso pegged to dollar, 51, 53
Pessino, Carola, 165n131
pesticide drift. *See* agrochemical exposure/ pesticide drift
philanthropic organizations, 9
Philippines, 7
Pigna, Felipe, 42
Pinker, Steven, 9, 10, 166n2
"pink tide," 54–55

plow, 38

political economy of soybeans, 3–4, 14–19, 32–33, 62, 107, 119, 137, 151n12; meso- and micro-levels, 15, 25, 58, 141; social hierarchy of, 18, 32, 143; swift adoption of herbicide-resistant soybeans explained by, 32–33

pools de siembra (sowing pools), 79–80

popular epidemiology, 118–19

population growth discourse, 9–10, 48–49, 70, 154n40. *See also* Malthusian narrative

positivism, 36, 63, 159n20

post-neoliberal governments, 54. *See* "pink tide"

Potosí, Bolivia, 33, 38, 158n5

poverty, 9, 55, 86, 115, 163n101, 165n132

power: decision-making, 3, 5, 18, 25–26, 32, 49–50, 66, 107, 141, 143; dynamic and rela- tional features, 22; legitimation of, 133–34; material interests of, 4; micro-level of social interactions and emotions, 95–96; most invasive form of, 16; roots of, 16–18; subjects of, 5. *See also* acquiescence/ consent; latent grievances; synergies of power

principle of precaution, 2, 134, 144,148

producers, 5–7, 25–26, 29–32, 39, 60–67; associations of, 56; contractors and, 30, 60, 66, 78–79, 93; Kirchner administrations and, 58, 73; land leasing by, 67; remote, 26, 29, 87

profitability, 7, 11, 30–32, 66, 102; as reason for agriculture, 61–63

Programa de Jefas y Jefes de Hogar Desem- pleados, 55

"pro-poor" discourse, 9, 15

protests: el conflicto del campo, 2008, 56–58, 57, 72, 74, 167n57; gendered differences, 107–8; 2001, 54

race/class/gender spectrum, 5–6, 18, 107–9, 112–13, 141, 144; gendered and racialized insults and demonization, 136, 145; struc- tural and symbolic barriers as limits to activism, 113–19. *See* synergies of power

racism, 15, 18, 36, 43

la raza (the race), 36

Regional Consortiums of Agricultural Experimentation (Consorcios Regionales de Experimentación Agrícola; CREA), 67, 69

"rescue distance," 145, 175n7

Resolution 125 (soy export taxes), 56–57

Resolution 167, 52, 164n111

"revolution" in farming, 7, 63, 71. *See* "new agricultural paradigm"

Ricardo, David, 39

Rich Hill (Potosí, Bolivia), 33

Río Carlo (soy town [pseudonym]), 119–20, 132, 171n15

Río Negro, 41

Risman, Barbara, 102

Robin, Marie-Monique, 127

Roca, Julio, 39–40, 160n37

Rockefeller Foundation, 48

Rosas, Juan Manuel de, 159n19

Roscigno, Vincent, 22

Roundup, 65; advertised as safe, 8, 52; cancer trial, 148; studies on, 73, 84, 120, 136, 164n115. *See also* glyphosate-based herbi- cides; Monsanto (Bayer)

Roundup Ready seeds, 1, 7–8, 52–53, 142; black market (*bolsa blanca*), 53, 164n121; Intacta Roundup Ready2 Pro, 69–70. *See also* Monsanto (Bayer); technological package

rural/soy towns, 2, 18, 63–64; dependent on large-scale industrial agriculture, 18–20, 64, 86, 91, 102, 108, 119, 127–28, 131–32, 143–45; depopulation, 75–76, 82, 162n81, 168n53, 169n54; economic dependence and cultural identity, 19–20; hierarchies within, 22. *See also* Álvarez (soy town [pseudonym]); Colonia Schoos (rural town [pseudonym]); General Artigas (rural town [pseudonym]); Flores (rural town [pseudonym]); Río Carlo (soy town [pseudonym]); Santa María (soy town [pseudonym])

Russian Jews, 40–41, 47. *See also gaucho judío* (Jewish colono)

Sachs, Jeffrey, 9–10

Samper, José María, 36

Santa Fe province, 77, 119

Santa María (soy town [pseudonym]), 21, 59, 85, 92–95, 94, 143

Santiago del Estero, 129

Sarmiento, Domingo F., 17, 35–40, 44, 158–59n18, 159n22. *See also* "civilization or barbarism" dichotomy; *Facundo: Civilization and Barbarism*; Generation of 1837

Schnaiberg, Allan, 19. *See* treadmill of production theory

Schurman, Rachel, 19, 23

Schweblin, Samanta, 139–40, 145–46, 174–75n3, 175n7

scientific research, 63, 147–48; establishment's minimization of health hazards, 84–85, 135–37, 142; on glyphosate, 52–53, 73, 120, 136

Scott, James, 111

"Second Revolution of the Pampas," 71. *See also* "new agricultural paradigm"

"seeing" negative consequences, 5, 20–22, 86

Self-Organized Neighbors for a Healthy Environment (Vecinxs Autocovocadxs por un Ambiente Sano), 119–20, 127. *See also citizen assemblies for health and life*

SENASA (Servicio Nacional de Sanidad y Calidad Agroalimentaria), 8, 52–53, 73, 134, 136, 164n112

Séralini, Gilles-Éric, 164n115

settler colonialism, 16

"Shame and Controversy in Argentina over the Deaths of Four Malnourished Children" (*El País*), 71

Shiva, Vandana, 50, 127

Shumway, Nicolas, 34, 48

Sierra, Justo, 36

Sierra de la Ventana, 30

silence: conspiracy of, 96–101; women's role in, 97, 101

silencing, self-policing, and denial, 96, 101, 108, 144, 146

Silent Spring (Carson), 148

silobolsas (silo bags), 76–77, 77

Sitrin, Marina, 123

6, 7, 8 (television show), 74

Smith, Adam, 39

social interactions and emotions: acquiescence enacted by, 96–102; conspiracy

of silence, 96–101; framing of injustice through, 101

social movements, 4, 23, 74, 122–24, 143, 145; community consultations, 124; grievance required for mobilization, 20; subjective component, 102; violent repression of, 50. *See also* activism

Sociedad Rural Argentina, 56

sociologists, 16, 159n20

soil erosion, 65, 80–82, *81*

sojización (soyification), 49

Solá, Felipe, 52, 164n111

South Africa, 2

South America, 9

"sowing pools" (*pools de siembra*), 79–80

soybean chain, 13–14, 67

soybean infant formula, 154n48

soybeans: herbicide-resistant GM, 1–6, 90; as backyard landscape, 87–91, 144; as "flex crop," 14, 67; history of in Pampas, 31–33, 47–50, 141–42; importance and uses of, 11–15; as "miracle" food, 71; as "nature," 20; no-till method, 7, 30, 53, 62, 65, 67, 80, 142; photographs of, *12, 88, 90, 94*. *See also* glyphosate-based herbicides; political economy of soybeans; Roundup Ready seeds; technological package

"Soybeans, 21st-Century Manna" (Huergo), 71

"soy boom," 1–2, 14, 56–58, 76, 131, 142

soy towns. *See* rural/soy towns

Spanish Empire, 37, 41, 158n8, 160–61n45; Viceroyalty of the Río de la Plata, 33

State of the World's Forests (Food and Agriculture Organization of the United Nations), 128

status quo, reproduction of, 6, 21, 64, 85, 91, 107, 141

Stølen, Kristi, 46

Stop Spraying (Paren de Fumigar) campaign, 119–20, 127, 131–32, 144

structural inequalities, 4, 22, 33, 140–41

structuralist theory, 16–17, 62

subjects, feminized and racialized, 32, 49–50, 102–3, 141, 145

"subjects of power," 5

sunflowers, 62, 90

"superweeds," 8

Supreme Court, Argentina, 135

sustainability, 7–10, 55–56, 121; climate change as counter to, 129; discourse of, 7–10, 17–19, 62, 65–66, 69, 80, 84; economic, 66, 80, 142; erosion problems, 82; long-term, 146.
sustainable development, 9–10, 14, 19, 56, 62, 121, 129, 140, 147
Swistun, Débora, 86
symbolic inequalities, 4, 33, 113
synergies of power, 3–4, 15–23, 25, 85, 140–43, 149, 156n67; "in-between" actors and, 106–11; temporality as key to, 15, 16, 32, 141. *See also* power
Syngenta, 105

tapera (poor, abandoned rural homes), 83
taxes for agricultural exports, 169n56; protests sparked by, 2008, 56–58, 57, 72; Resolution 125, 56–57
Taylor, Carl C., 45, 161–62n67
Taylor, Diana, 108
technological package, 7, 14, 23, 25, 38–39, 49, 75, 129, 142; as continuity with Pampas' agrarian history, 65; "new agricultural paradigm," 63, 64–69, 105; profit increase and price of, 53. *See also* glyphosate-based herbicides; no-till/direct-seeding methods; Roundup Ready seeds; soybeans, herbicide-resistant GM
TeleSur, 123
terror, state, 101–2
Teubal, Miguel, 50, 51
think tanks, 9, 69
third-party contracting, 66
Third World revolutions, 50
tierra, la (the land), 36
Toda esta sangre en el monte (documentary), 130
Todo Noticias (TN) news channel, 70, 74
Tomasi, Fabián, 73, 168n46
Tönnies, Ferdinand, 159n22
transgenic crops. *See* genetically modified organisms (GMOs)
transnational corporations, 13, 96–97
treadmill of production theory, 19, 62, 109
"trickle-down" discourse, 18, 64, 78, 83, 85, 143
Tucumán province, 71
2,4-D, 8, 84, 115, 153n28

Uganda, 9
"Una Primavera sin Monsanto" (Springtime without Monsanto), 124
unions, 137
United Kingdom, 2
United Nations, 9, 128, 147
United Nations 2030 Agenda for Sustainable Development, 10
United States, 73; climate-change deniers, 136; environmental justice struggles, 119; environmental justice studies focus on, 15; GM crops, 8–9, 11; "manifest destiny," 41; myths of, 34; Office of Pesticide Programs, 164n112; price of technological package, 53; shift to larger farms, 30
Universidad Nacional de Córdoba, 79, 123
University of Buenos Aires (UBA), 50, 73
UOCRA (construction workers' union), 137
UPOV 78 (saved seeds agreement), 53
urban areas, 3, 46, 51, 141, 162n72. *See also specific cities*
urbanization trends, 46, 142, 162nn 72, 81
US Department of Agriculture, 73
US Embassy in Buenos Aires, 73

vaccines, 147–48
Vecinxs Autoconvocadxs por un Ambiente Sano (Self-Organized Neighbors for a Healthy Environment), 119–20, 127. *See also* citizen assemblies for health and life
Venezuela, 3, 54
Viceroyalty of the Río de la Plata, 33
victims of toxic contamination (*afectados por los agrotóxicos*), 116
Vietnam, 50
violence: against activists, 125, 133, 135, 137; as demobilization strategy, 137; Dirty War, 101–2, 163n99; against indigenous peoples and ecologies, 2, 17, 41–43, 51, 130–31, 135, 160–61n45; nineteenth-century military campaigns to "conquer" indigenous peoples, 41–42; of Spanish Empire, 41
visibility, 64, 72, 124, 127, 129–30, 132; "map of death" (*mapa de la muerte*), 117–18; "seeing" negative consequences, 5, 20–22, 86; social construction of, 20
Vommaro, Gabriel, 58

Warren County, North Carolina, 137
water pollution, 115, 117
"we all live off the countryside" (todos
    vivimos del campo) discourse, 2, 18, 21, 64,
    74–88, 92, 95, 99, 143
"weapons of the weak," 111
Weber, Max, 62, 159n22
Wedeen, Lisa, 62
"we don't talk about that," 96, 98–102
"we do the best agriculture in the world"
    discourse, 1, 26, 71, 143

"whitening" of Argentina, 42–43
Wikileaks, 73
Woburn, Massachusetts, 119
Wood, Grant, 126
World against Monsanto, The (film), 127
World Bank, 48, 52
World Health Organization (who), 8, 84
World War II, 47

Yauhar, Norberto, 69–70, 136
York, Richard, 13

www.ingramcontent.com/pod-product-compliance
Lightning Source LLC
Chambersburg PA
CBHW070711280326
41926CB00089B/3778